Frommer's®

PORTABLE

London

1st Edition

**by Darwin Porter
& Danforth Prince**

D1402213

Macmillan • USA

ABOUT THE AUTHORS

Authors **Darwin Porter** and **Danforth Prince** share their love of their favorite European city with this guide. Porter, a bureau chief for the *Miami Herald* at 21 who later worked in television advertising, wrote the first-ever book to London for Frommer's. He's joined by Prince, formerly of the Paris bureau of the *New York Times*. Together, they're the authors of several bestselling Frommer's guides, notably to England, France, the Caribbean, Italy, and Germany.

MACMILLAN TRAVEL

A Simon & Schuster Macmillan Company
1633 Broadway
New York, NY 10019

Find us online at **http://www.frommers.com**
or on America Online at Keyword: **Frommers**.

ISBN 0-02-862232-4
ISSN 1094-7663

Editor: Bob O'Sullivan
Thanks to Cheryl Farr
Production Editor: Lori Cates
Design by Michele Laseau
Digital Cartography by Peter Bogaty, Roberta Stockwell, and Ortelius Design
Production Team: Eric Brinkman, David Faust, Heather Pope, and Karen Teo

SPECIAL SALES

Bulk purchases (10+ copies) of Frommer's and selected Macmillan travel guides are available to corporations, organizations, mail-order catalogs, institutions, and charities at special discounts, and can be customized to suit individual needs. For more information write to Special Sales, Macmillan General Reference, 1633 Broadway, New York, NY 10019.

Manufactured in the United States of America

Contents

List of Maps

AN INVITATION TO THE READER

In researching this book, we discovered many wonderful places—hotels, restaurants, shops, and more. We're sure you'll find others. Please tell us about them, so we can share the information with your fellow travelers in upcoming editions. If you were disappointed with a recommendation, we'd love to know that, too. Please write to:

Darwin Porter/Danforth Prince
Frommer's Portable London
Macmillan Travel
1633 Broadway
New York, NY 10019

AN ADDITIONAL NOTE

Please be advised that travel information is subject to change at any time—and this is especially true of prices. We therefore suggest that you write or call ahead for confirmation when making your travel plans. The authors, editors, and publisher cannot be held responsible for the experiences of readers while traveling. Your safety is important to us, however, so we encourage you to stay alert and be aware of your surroundings. Keep a close eye on cameras, purses, and wallets, all favorite targets of thieves and pickpockets.

WHAT THE SYMBOLS MEAN
✪ Frommer's Favorites

Our favorite places and experiences—outstanding for quality, value, or both.

The following abbreviations are used for credit cards:

AE	American Express	EU	Eurocard
CB	Carte Blanche	JCB	Japan Credit Bank
DC	Diners Club	MC	MasterCard
DISC	Discover	V	Visa
ER	enRoute		

FIND FROMMER'S ONLINE

Arthur Frommer's Outspoken Encyclopedia of Travel (http://www.frommers.com) offers more than 6,000 pages of up-to-the-minute travel information—including the latest bargains and candid personal articles updated daily by Arthur Frommer himself. No other website offers such comprehensive and timely coverage of the world of travel.

Planning a Trip to London

*L*ook out, Paris, and step aside, New York—these days, there's so much fun to be had in London that it's being called the hottest, coolest city in the world.

A BRITISH RENAISSANCE! LONDON'S GOT ITS GROOVE BACK! These headlines are part of a global media blitz heaped on a British capital that's more eclectic and electric than it's been in years. There's almost a feeding frenzy setting out to prove that London is the most pulsating, vibrant city on the planet, even rivaling New York for sheer energy, outrageous art, trendy restaurants, and a nightlife scene equal to none. *Newsweek* hailed London as a "hip compromise between the nonstop newness of Los Angeles and the aspic-preserved beauty of Paris—sharpened to New York's edge." *Wine Spectator* proclaims more modestly that "The sun is shining brighter in London these days."

The sounds of Britpop and techno pour out of Victorian pubs, experimental theater is taking over stages that were built for Shakespeare's plays, and upstart chefs are reinventing the bland dishes British mums made for generations into a new and inventive cuisine; for the first time ever, Brits are even running the couture houses of Dior and Givenchy. In food, fashion, film, pop music, the visual arts, and just about everything else, London stands at the cutting edge again, just as it did in the 1960s. But today, instead of names like Mary Quant, Twiggy, Mick Jagger, and Marianne Faithfull ruling the scene, it's such celebrities as the Spice Girls, cow-sawing artist Damien Hirst, and the couple-of-the-moment, actress Patsy Kensit and Liam Gallagher (the lead singer of Oasis, the most beloved band in England since the Beatles), whose names pop up everywhere, from fashion spreads to tabloid headlines. If there's talk of a McCartney today, it's not billionaire Paul or his wife, vegetarian-entrepreneur Linda, but their daughter Stella, whose street-smart power suits and fitted frock coats are all the rage (of course, she works for the fun of it all, not because she has to—not with all those bags of Beatle billions in her future).

But if you just don't give a hoot about the new London—if this sea change worries you more than it appeals to you—rest assured: Staid old London (as we lovingly think of it) still lives, basically intact under the veneer of hip. This ancient city has survived a thousand years of invasion, from the Normans to the Blitz, so a few scenesters moving in isn't going to change anything in the long run—London will forever be one of history's greatest cities. From high tea at Brown's to the changing of the guard at Buckingham Palace, the city still abounds with the tradition, charm, and culture of days gone by.

1 Visitor Information & Entry Requirements

VISITOR INFORMATION

Before you go, you can get information from the following **British Tourist Authority** offices: 551 5th Ave., Suite 701, New York, NY 10176-0799 (☎ **800/462-2748** or 212/986-2200); 111 Avenue Rd., Suite 450, Toronto, ON M5R 3J8, Canada (☎ **416/ 961-8124**); Level 16, Gateway, 1 Macquarie Place, Sydney, NSW 2000, Australia (☎ **02/9377-4400**); and Suite 305, Dilworth Bldg., at Customs and Queen streets, Auckland 1, New Zealand (☎ **09/ 303-1446**). The British Tourist Authority maintains a Web page at **http://www.bta.org.uk**.

For a full information pack on London, write to the **London Tourist Board,** P.O. Box 151, London E15 2HF. You can also call the recorded-message service, **Visitorcall** (☎ **0183/912-3456**), 24 hours a day. Various topics are listed; calls cost 39p (60¢) per minute cheap rate (Mon–Fri 6pm–8am and all day Sat and Sun), and 49p (80¢) per minute at all other times.

You can usually pick up a copy of *Time Out,* the most up-to-date source for what's happening in London, at any international newsstand. *Time Out* has joined the Net, so you can also log on for current information; you'll find the weekly magazine at **http:// www.timeout.co.uk**.

ENTRY REQUIREMENTS
DOCUMENTS

Citizens of the United States, Canada, Australia, New Zealand, and South Africa all require a passport to enter the United Kingdom, but no visa. The maximum stay allowed as a visitor is 6 months. Some customs officials will request proof that you have the means to eventually leave the country (usually a round-trip ticket) and visible means of support while you're in Britain. If you're planning to fly to another country from the United Kingdom, it's wise to secure the necessary visa before your arrival in Britain.

Your valid driver's license and at least 1 year's driving experience is required to drive personal or rented cars.

CUSTOMS

WHAT YOU CAN BRING INTO ENGLAND   For visitors to England, goods fall into two basic categories: goods purchased in a non-European Community (EC) country or bought tax-free within the EC; and goods purchased tax-paid in the EC. In the first category, limits on imports by individuals (17 and older) include 200 cigarettes (or 50 cigars or 250 grams of loose tobacco), 2 liters of still table wine, 1 liter of liquor (over 22% alcohol content) or 2 liters of liquor (under 22%), and 2 fluid ounces of perfume. In the second category, limits are much higher: An individual may import 800 cigarettes bought tax-paid in the EC, 200 cigars, 1 kilogram of loose tobacco, 90 liters of wine, 10 liters of alcohol (over 22%), and 110 liters of beer, plus unlimited amounts of perfume.

Sorry, but you can't bring your pet to England. Six months' quarantine is required before a pet is allowed into the country. An illegally imported animal is liable to be destroyed.

WHAT YOU CAN BRING HOME   Returning U.S. citizens who have been away for 48 hours or more are allowed to bring back, once every 30 days, $400 worth of merchandise duty-free. You'll be charged a flat rate of 10% duty on the next $1,000 worth of purchases. Be sure to have your receipts handy. On gifts, the duty-free limit is $50. You cannot bring fresh foodstuffs into the United States; tinned foods, however, are allowed. For more information, contact the **U.S. Customs Service,** 1301 Constitution Ave. (P.O. Box 7407), Washington, D.C. 20044 (☎ **202/ 927-6724**) and request the free pamphlet *Know Before You Go.* Also see "Taxes" under "Fast Facts: London" in chapter 2 and chapter 6, "Shopping."

2 Money

CURRENCY

POUNDS & PENCE   Britain's decimal monetary system is based on the pound sterling (£), which is made up of 100 pence (written as "p"). There are now £1 coins (called "quid" by Britons), plus coins of 50p, 20p, 10p, 5p, 2p, and 1p. The 0.5p coin has been officially discontinued, although it will be around for a while. Banknotes come in denominations of £5, £10, £20, and £50.

As a general guideline, the price conversions in this book have been computed at the rate of £1 = $1.60 (U.S.). Bear in mind, however, that exchange rates fluctuate daily.

EXCHANGING YOUR MONEY   It's always wise to exchange enough money before departure to get you from the airport to your hotel. This way, you avoid delays and the lousy rates at the airport exchange booths—and you might make it to the front of the taxi "queue" before everybody who wasn't so smart.

When exchanging money, you're likely to obtain a better rate for traveler's checks than for cash. London banks generally offer the best rates of exchange; they're usually open Monday to Friday from 9:30am to 3:30pm. Many of the "high street" branches are now open until 5pm; a handful of central London branches are open until noon on Saturday, including **Barclays,** 208 Kensington High St., W8 (☎ **0171/441-3200**). Money exchange is now also available at competitive rates at major London post offices, with a 1% service charge. Money can be exchanged during off-hours at a variety of bureaux de change throughout the city, found at small shops and in hotels, railway stations (including the international terminal at Waterloo Station), travel agencies, and airports, but their exchange rates are poorer and they charge high service fees. Examine the prices and rates carefully before handing over your dollars, as there's no consumer organization to regulate the activities of privately run bureaux de change.

In a recent *Time Out* survey of various exchange facilities, American Express came out on top, with the lowest commission charged on dollar transactions. **American Express** is at 6 Haymarket, SW1 (☎ **800/221-7282** or 0171/930-4411), and other locations throughout the city. Other reputable firms are **Thomas Cook,** 45 Berkeley St., W1A 1EB (☎ **800/223-7373** or 0171/408-4218), branches of which can also be found at Victoria Station, Marble Arch, and other city locations; and, for 24-hour foreign exchange, **Chequepoint,** at 548 Oxford St., W1N 9HJ (☎ **0171/723-1005**) and other locations throughout London (hours will vary). Try not to change money at your hotel; the rates they offer tend to be horrendous.

CREDIT CARDS   The way to get the best rate of exchange is not via money exchange, but to buy whatever you can with credit cards. They virtually always offer a rate of exchange better than any you can get by changing your money, and there's no accompanying service charge. Credit cards are widely accepted in London; American Express, Visa, and Diners Club are the most commonly recognized. A Eurocard or Access sign displayed at an establishment means that it accepts MasterCard.

ATM NETWORKS   Plus, Cirrus, and other networks connecting automated-teller machines (ATMs) are accessible throughout London. By using your bank card to withdraw money you'll debit the amount from your account. When using an ATM abroad, the money will be in local currency; the rate of exchange tends to be as good, more often better, than what you would receive at an airport money counter or a hotel. Note that international withdrawal fees will be higher than domestic—ask your bank for specifics. Always determine the frequency limits for withdrawals and cash advances of your credit card. Also, check to see if your PIN code must be reprogrammed for usage in London. Most ATMs outside the United States require a four-digit PIN number.

TRAVELER'S CHECKS   Before leaving home, you can purchase traveler's checks and arrange to carry some ready cash (usually about $250, depending on your habits and needs). In the event of theft, if the checks are properly documented, the value of your checks will be refunded. Most large banks sell traveler's checks, charging fees that average between 1% and 2% of the value of the checks you buy, although some out-of-the-way banks, in rare instances, have charged as much as 7%. If your bank wants more than a 2% commission, it sometimes pays to call the traveler's check issuers directly for the address of outlets where this commission will cost less.

For more information, contact **American Express** (☎ 800/221-7282 in the U.S. and Canada); **Citicorp** (☎ 800/645-6556 in the U.S. and Canada, or 813/623-1709 collect from other parts of the world); **Thomas Cook** (☎ 800/223-7373 in the U.S. and Canada, or 609/987-7300 collect from other parts of the world); or **Interpayment Services** (☎ 800/221-2426 in the U.S. and Canada, or 212/858-8500 collect from other parts of the world).

3 When to Go

THE CLIMATE   Charles Dudley Warner (in a remark most often attributed to Mark Twain) once said that the trouble with the weather is that everybody talks about it but nobody does anything about it. Well, Londoners talk about weather more than anyone, but they have also done something about it: air-pollution control, which has resulted in the virtual disappearance of the pea-soup fogs that once blanketed the city.

A typical London-area weather forecast for a summer day predicts "scattered clouds with sunny periods and showers, possibly heavy at times." Summer temperatures seldom rise above 78°F, nor do they drop below 35°F in winter. London, being in one of the mildest parts of the country, can be very pleasant in the spring and fall. Yes, it rains, but you'll rarely get a true downpour. It's heaviest in November (2½ inches on average).

The British consider chilliness wholesome and usually try to keep room temperatures about 10° below the American comfort level.

CURRENT WEATHER CONDITIONS   In the United States, you can dial ☎ **1/900-WEATHER,** then press the first four letters of the desired foreign city—in this case, LOND for London—for the time of day in that city, plus current temperatures, weather conditions, and forecasts. The cost is 95¢ per minute. Another good way to check conditions before you go is on the Weather Channel's Web site: **http://www.weather.com**.

HOLIDAYS   In England, public holidays include New Year's Day, Good Friday, Easter Monday, May Day (first Mon in May), spring and summer bank holidays (last Mon in May and Aug, respectively), Christmas Day, and Boxing Day (Dec 26).

LONDON CALENDAR OF EVENTS

January
- **London Parade,** from Parliament Square to Berkeley Square in Mayfair. Bands, floats, and carriages. January 1. Procession starts around 2:45pm.
- **January sales.** Most shops offer good reductions. Many sales now start as early as late December. The most voracious shoppers camp out at Harrods overnight to get in first.
- **London International Boat Show,** Earl's Court Exhibition Centre, Warwick Road. The largest boat show in Europe. Early January. Call ☎ **0178/447-3377** for details.
- **London Contemporary Art Fair** at the Business Design Center. Mid-January. Call ☎ **0171/359-3535** for exact dates and details.
- **Charles I Commemoration.** Anniversary of the execution of King Charles I "in the name of freedom and democracy." Hundreds of cavaliers march through central London in 17th-century

dress, and prayers are said at the Banqueting House in Whitehall. Free. Last Sunday in January.

February

- **Chinese New Year.** The famous Lion Dancers in Soho. Free. Either in late January or early February (based on the lunar calendar).

March

- **St. David's Day.** A member of the Royal Family usually presents the Welsh Guards with the principality's national emblem, a leek; call ☎ **0171/414-3291** for location and further information. March 1 (or nearest Sun).

- **Chelsea Antiques Fair,** a twice-yearly gathering of England's best dealers, held at Old Town Hall, King's Road, SW3 (☎ **0144/448-2514**). Mid-March (and again in mid-Sept).

- **Open House,** a 1-day event during which members of the public have access to normally closed buildings of architectural significance. Mid-March. Call ☎ **0181/341-1371** for schedule and further information.

- **Great Spitalfields Pancake Race.** Teams of four run in relays, tossing their pancakes. At noon on Shrove Tuesday (last day before Lent) at Old Spitalfields Market, Brushfield Street, E1. To join in, call ☎ **0171/375-0441.**

- **Oranges and Lemons Service,** at St. Clement Danes, Strand, WC2. Third Thursday in March. As a reminder of the nursery rhyme, children are presented with the fruits during service, and the church bells ring out the rhyme at 9am, noon, 3pm, and 6pm; call ☎ **0171/242-8282** for more information.

April

- **Boat Race, Putney to Mortlake.** Oxford and Cambridge University eights battle upstream with awesome power. Park yourself at one of the Thames-side pubs along the route to see the action. Early April; check *Time Out* for exact dates and times.

- **Abbey Choir** performs at Westminster Abbey, SW1, on Holy Week Tuesday; call ☎ **0171/222-5152** for information.

- **Easter Parade,** around Battersea Park. Brightly colored floats and marching bands; a full day of Easter Sunday activities. Free. April 3.

- **Harness Horse Parade,** a morning parade of heavy working horses in superb gleaming brass harnesses and plumes, at Battersea Park. Call ☎ **0173/323-4451.** Easter Monday.

- **London Marathon.** 30,000 competitors run from Greenwich Park to Buckingham Palace; call ☎ **0161/703-8161** for information. April 13.

- **The Queen's Birthday** is celebrated with 21-gun salutes in Hyde Park and on Tower Hill at noon by troops in parade dress. April 21.
- **National Gardens Scheme.** More than 100 private gardens in Greater London are open to the public on set days through October, and tea is sometimes served. Pick up a current copy of the NGS guidebook for £3.50 ($5.60) from most bookstores for schedule information, or contact the National Gardens Scheme Charitable Trust, Hatchlands Park, East Clandon, Guildford, Surrey GU4 7RT (☎ **0148/321-1535**). Late April to early May.

May

- **Shakespeare Under the Stars.** If you want to see *Macbeth, Hamlet,* or *Romeo and Juliet* (or any other Shakespeare play), our advice is to bring a blanket and a bottle of wine to watch the Bard's works performed at the **Open Air Theatre,** Inner Circle, Regent's Park, NW1. Take the tube to Regent's Park or Baker Street. Previews begin in late May and last throughout the summer. Performances are Monday to Saturday at 8pm; Wednesday, Thursday, and Saturday also at 2:30pm. Call ☎ **0171/486-2431** for more information.
- **May Fayre and Puppet Festival,** Covent Garden. Procession at 10am, service at St. Paul's at 11:30am, then Punch and Judy shows until 6pm at the site where Pepys watched England's first show in 1662; call ☎ **0171/375-0441.** Second Sunday in May.
- **FA Cup Final.** England's showpiece soccer match is held at Wembley Stadium in mid-May; for exact date and details, call ☎ **0181/902-8833.**
- The **Royal Windsor Horse Show** is held at Home Park, Windsor Castle (☎ **0175/386-0633**); you might even spot a royal. Mid-May.
- **Chelsea Flower Show,** Chelsea Royal Hospital. The best of British gardening, with displays of plants and flowers of all seasons. Tickets are available through **Ticketmaster** (☎ **0171/344-4343**). The show runs from 8am to 8pm on May 22; tickets are £24 ($38.40). On May 23, the show runs from 8am to 5pm, and tickets are £21 ($33.60). Call ☎ **0171/630-7422** for more information.
- **Glyndebourne Festival Opera Season,** Sussex. Exclusive performances in a beautiful setting, with champagne picnics in between performances. Since the completion of the theater, tickets are a bit easier to come by (☎ **0127/381-3813**). It runs from mid-May to late August.

June

- **Vodafone Derby Stakes.** Famous horse-racing event at Epsom Racecourse, Epsom, Surrey. It's the best-known event on the British horse-racing calendar and a chance for men to wear top hats and women, including the queen, to put on silly millinery creations. The "darby" (as it's called here) is run June 7 to 9. Grandstand tickets range from £17 to £55 ($27.20–$88). Call ☎ **0137/247-0047** for more information.

- **Grosvenor House Art and Antique Fair,** Grosvenor House. A very prestigious antiques fair. Call ☎ **0171/495-8743** for information. Second week of June.

- **Kenwood Lakeside Concerts,** annual concerts on the north side of Hampstead Heath, a British tradition of outdoor performances for nearly 50 years. Fireworks displays and laser shows help to enliven the premier musical performances staged here. Music drifts to the fans from a performance shell across the lake every Saturday in summer from mid-June to early September.

- **Royal Academy's Summer Exhibition.** This institution, founded in 1768 with Sir Joshua Reynolds as president and Gainsborough as a member, has sponsored Summer Exhibitions of living painters for some 2 centuries. Visitors can both browse and make art purchases, many of them quite reasonable in price. Exhibitions are presented daily at Burlington House, Piccadilly Circus, W1. Call ☎ **0171/439-7438** for details. From early June to mid-August.

- **Royal Ascot Week.** Ascot Racecourse is open year-round for guided tours, events, exhibitions, and conferences. There are 24 race days throughout the year with the feature race meetings being the Royal Meeting in June, Diamond Day in late July, and the Festival at Ascot in late September. For further information, contact Ascot Racecourse, Ascot, Berkshire, SL5 7JN (☎ **0134/422211**).

- ✪ **Trooping the Colour,** Horse Guards Parade, Whitehall. The official birthday of the Queen. A quintessential British event religiously watched by the populace on TV. The pageantry and pomp are exquisite. Held on a day designated in June (not necessarily the Queen's actual birthday). Tickets for the actual parade and two reviews, held on preceding Saturdays, are allocated by ballot. Those interested in attending must write to apply for tickets between January 1 and the end of February, enclosing a stamped, self-addressed envelope or International Reply

Coupon—exact dates and ticket prices will be supplied later. The ballot is held in mid-March, and successful applicants *only* are informed in April. For details, write to HQ Household Division, Horse Guards, Whitehall, London SW1X 6AA, enclosing a self-addressed envelope with an International Reply Coupon.

✪ **Lawn Tennis Championships,** Wimbledon, Southwest London. Ever since the players in flannels and bonnets took to the grass courts at Wimbledon in 1877, this tournament has drawn a socially prominent crowd. Although the courts are now crowded with all kinds of tennis fans, there's still an excited hush at the Centre Court and a certain thrill in being here. Savoring the strawberries and cream is part of the experience. Late June to early July. Tickets for Centre and Number One courts are handed out through a lottery; write to All England Lawn Tennis Club, P.O. Box 98, Church Road, Wimbledon, London SW19 5AE (☎ 0181/946-2244), between August and December. A certain number of tickets are set aside for visitors from abroad, so you may be able to purchase some in spring for this year's games; call to inquire. Outside court tickets available daily, but be prepared to wait in line.

• **City of London Festival,** annual arts festival throughout the city. Call ☎ 0171/377-0540 for information about the various programs and venues. Held in June and July.

July

• **City of London Festival.** Classical concerts at various venues throughout the city, including St. Paul's Cathedral; for details, call ☎ 0171/377-0540. Early July.

• **Hampton Court Palace Flower Show,** East Molesey, Surrey. This widely acclaimed 5-day international show is eclipsing its sister show in Chelsea; here, you can actually purchase the exhibits. Call ☎ 0171/834-4333 for exact dates and details. Early July.

• **Royal Tournament,** Earl's Court Exhibition Centre, Warwick Road. British armed forces put on dazzling displays of athletic and military skills, which have been called "military pomp, show biz, and outright jingoism." For information and details about performance times and tickets, call ☎ 0171/244-0244. Ticket prices range from £5 ($8) to £25 ($40). July 9 to 20.

• **The Proms.** "The Proms"—the annual Henry Wood Promenade Concerts at Royal Albert Hall—attract music aficionados from around the world. Staged almost daily (except for a few Sundays), these traditional concerts were launched in 1895 and are the principal summer venue for the BBC Symphony Orchestra.

Cheering, clapping, Union Jacks on parade, banners, and balloons create summer fun. Mid-July to mid-September.

August

- **Notting Hill Carnival,** Notting Hill. One of the largest street festivals in Europe, attracting more than a half-million people annually. Live reggae and soul music combine with great Caribbean food. Free. Two days in late August (usually the last Sun and Mon). Call ☎ **0181/964-0544** for information.

September

- **Chelsea Antiques Fair,** Chelsea Old Town Hall, King's Road, SW3. Mid-September (see "March," above, for details).
- **Raising of the Thames Barrier,** Unity Way, SE18. Once a year, a full test is done on this miracle of modern engineering; all 10 of the massive steel gates are raised against the high tide. Call ☎ **0181/854-1373** for exact date and time.

October

- ✪ **Opening of Parliament,** House of Lords, Westminster. Ever since the 17th century, when the English cut off the head of Charles I, the British monarch has had no right to enter the House of Commons. Instead, the monarch opens Parliament in the House of Lords, reading an official speech that is written by the government of the day. The monarch rides from Buckingham Palace to Westminster in a royal coach accompanied by the Yeoman of the Guard and the Household Cavalry. The Strangers' Gallery is open to spectators on a first-come, first-served basis. First Monday in October.
- **Judges Service,** Westminster Abbey. The judiciary attends a service in Westminster Abbey to mark the opening of the law term. Afterward, in full regalia—wigs and all—they form a procession and walk to the House of Lords for their "Annual Breakfast." You'll have a great view of the procession from behind the Abbey. First Monday in October.
- **Horse of the Year Show.** At Wembley Arena, outside London, this event is the premier equestrian highlight on the English calendar. Riders fly in from all continents to join in this festive display of horseflesh (much appreciated by the queen herself). The British press call it "an equine extravaganza." For more information, call ☎ **0181/902-8833.** Early October.
- **Quit Rents Ceremony,** Royal Courts of Justice, WC2. An official receives token rents on behalf of the queen; the ceremony includes splitting sticks and counting horseshoes. Late October. Call ☎ **0171/936-6131** for free tickets.

November

- **Guy Fawkes Night.** Commemorating the anniversary of the Gunpowder Plot, an attempt to blow up King James I and his Parliament. Huge organized bonfires are lit throughout the city, and Guy Fawkes, the plot's most famous conspirator, is burned in effigy. Free. Check *Time Out* for locations. Early November.

✪ **Lord Mayor's Procession and Show,** from the Guildhall to the Royal Courts of Justice, in the City of London. This impressive annual event marks the inauguration of the new lord mayor of the City of London. The queen must ask permission to enter the City's square mile—a right that has been jealously guarded by London merchants from the 17th century to this very day. You can watch the procession from the street; the banquet is by invitation only. Second week in November.

December

- **Caroling under the Norwegian Christmas Tree.** There's caroling most evenings beneath the tree in Trafalgar Square. Early December.
- **Harrods' After-Christmas Sale,** Knightsbridge. Late December. Call ☎ **0171/730-1234** for exact dates and hours.
- **Watch Night,** St. Paul's Cathedral, where a rather lovely New Year's Eve service takes place on December 31 at 11:30pm; call ☎ **0171/248-2705** for information.

4 Tips for Travelers with Special Needs

FOR TRAVELERS WITH DISABILITIES   Before you go, there are many agencies to check with about information for persons with disabilities.

One is the **Travel Information Service,** Moss Rehab Hospital, 1200 W. Tabor Rd., Philadelphia, PA 19141, which provides information to telephone callers only; call ☎ **215/456-9603** or 215/456-9602 (for TTY) for assistance with your travel needs.

You may also want to consider joining a tour specifically for visitors with disabilities, such as one offered by **FEDCAP Rehabilitation Services** (formerly known as the Federation of the Handicapped), 211 W. 14th St., New York, NY 10011; contact them at ☎ **212/727-4200** (fax 212/721-4374) for information about membership and summer tours. One of the best organizations serving the needs of people who use wheelchairs or walkers is **Flying Wheels Travel,** 143 West Bridge, P.O. Box 382, Owatoona, MN 55060 (☎ **800/535-6790** or 507/451-5005), which offers various escorted tours and cruises internationally. For names and addresses of other tour operators and additional relevant information, contact the **Society for the Advancement of Travel for the Handicapped,** 347 5th Ave., Suite 610, New York, NY 10016 (☎ **212/447-7284;** fax 212/725-8253; or send a stamped, self-addressed envelope). Yearly membership dues are $45, $30 for senior citizens and students.

For people who are blind or have visual impairments, the best source is the **American Foundation for the Blind,** 11 Penn Plaza, Suite 300, New York, NY 10001 (☎ **800/232-5463** or 212/502-7600), which offers information on travel and various requirements for the transport and border formalities for seeing-eye dogs. It also issues identification cards to those who are legally blind.

London's most prominent organization for information about access to theaters, cinemas, galleries, museums, and restaurants is **Artsline,** 54 Chalton St., London NW1 1HS (☎ **0171/388-2227;** fax 0171/383-2653). It offers free information about wheelchair access, theaters with hearing aids, tourist attractions, and cinemas. Artsline will mail information to North America, but it's even more helpful to contact Artsline once you arrive in London; the line is staffed Monday to Friday from 9:30am to 5:30pm.

FOR GAY & LESBIAN TRAVELERS   London has one of the most active gay and lesbian scenes in the world; we've recommended a number of the city's best gay clubs (at least as of press time) in chapter 7. For the gay and lesbian traveler to England, the best guides are *Spartacus Britain and Ireland* ($24.95) and *London Scene* ($11.95). For up-to-the-minute information on activities, we recommend the monthly *Gay Times* (London) for $6.95. These books and others are available from **Giovanni's Room,** 1145 Pine St., Philadelphia, PA 19107 (☎ **215/923-2960;** fax 215/923-0813).

Our World magazine, 1104 North Nova Rd., Suite 251, Daytona Beach, FL 32117 (☎ **904/441-5367;** fax 904/441-5604; $35 for 10 issues), covers worldwide travel options and bargains for gay and lesbian travelers. *Out and About,* 8 W. 19th St., Suite 401, New York, NY 10011 (☎ **800/929-2268** or 212/645-6922; fax 800/ 929-2215; $49 for 10 information-packed issues), is another great publication on gay travel that profiles the best gay or gay-friendly hotels, gyms, clubs, and other places worldwide.

With some 1,200 member agencies, the **International Gay Travel Association** (IGTA), P.O. Box 4974, Key West, FL 33041 (☎ **305/292-0217,** or 800/448-8550 for voice mail), specializes in networking travelers with the appropriate gay-friendly service organization or tour specialist. It offers quarterly newsletters, marketing mailings, and a membership directory.

FOR SENIORS   Many discounts are available for seniors. Be advised, however, that in England you often have to be a member of an association to obtain discounts. Public transportation reductions, for example, are available only to holders of British Pension books. However, many attractions do offer discounts for senior citizens (women 60 or over and men 65 or over). Even if discounts aren't posted, you might ask if they're available.

If you're over 60, you're eligible for special 10% discounts on **British Airways** through its Privileged Traveler program. You also qualify for reduced restrictions on APEX cancellations. Discounts are also granted for British Airways tours and for intra-Britain air tickets that are booked in North America.

British Rail offers seniors discounted rates on first-class rail passes for travel around Britain. For details, see "Getting There by Train," below.

If you're a member of the **American Association of Retired Persons (AARP),** 601 E. St. NW, Washington, D.C. 20049 (☎ 202/434-AARP), you may qualify for discounts on car rentals and hotels.

FOR FAMILIES   On airlines, you must request a special menu for children at least 24 hours in advance. Bring your own baby food, though; you can ask a flight attendant to warm it to the right temperature.

Arrange ahead of time for such necessities as a crib, bottle warmer, and car seat (in England, small children aren't allowed to ride in the front seat). If you're staying with friends, you can rent baby equipment from **Chelsea Baby Hire,** 83 Burntwood Lane, SW17 OAJ (☎ 0181/540-8830). The London Black Cab is a lifesaver for families; the roomy interior allows a stroller to be lifted right into the cab without unstrapping the baby.

If you want a night out without the kids, you're in luck: London has its own children's hotel, **Pippa Pop-ins,** 430 Fulham Rd., SW6 1DU (☎ 0171/385-2458), which accommodates children overnight in a wonderful nursery filled with lots of toys and caring minders. Other recommendable baby-sitting services are **Babysitters Unlimited** (☎ 0181/892-8888) and **Childminders** (☎ 0171/935-2049 or 0171/935-3000). Baby-sitters can also be found for you at most hotels.

To find out what's on for kids while you're in London, pick up the leaflet *Where to Take Children,* published by the London Tourist Board. If you have specific questions, ring **Kidsline** (☎ **0171/222-8070**) Monday to Friday 4 to 6pm and summer holidays 9am to 4pm, or the **London Tourist Board's** special children's information line (☎ **0183/912-3404**).

5 Getting There

BY PLANE

Most airlines charge different fares according to season. For flights to Europe, the fares are most expensive during midsummer, the peak travel time. Winter offers the least expensive fares. Travel during Christmas and Easter weeks is usually more expensive than in the weeks just before or after those holidays.

If you're concerned about costs, your best strategy is to shop around and, above all, to remain as flexible as you can about dates; prices tend to be higher for weekend travel, so if you want the least expensive fare, book midweek. And keep calling the airlines—if a flight isn't fully booked, an airline might discount tickets in an attempt to achieve a full load, allowing you to buy a lower-priced ticket at the last minute. (This strategy tends to work better in the off-season, when most travelers are heading to warm-weather destinations rather than Europe, and planes tend not to be full; in summer, it's riskier to wait to book a flight—in high-season the airlines often charge top dollar at the last minute.)

Even within the various seasons, most airlines also offer heavily discounted promotional fares available according to the market. But be warned: The less expensive your ticket is, the more stringent the restrictions will be.

THE MAJOR AIRLINES   The following airlines fly from North America to London:

American Airlines (☎ **800/624-6262**) offers daily routes to London's Heathrow Airport from a half-dozen U.S. gateways: New York's JFK (four times daily, six in June), Chicago's O'Hare (twice daily), and Miami International, Los Angeles International, Philadelphia International, and Boston's Logan (each once daily).

British Airways (☎ **800/AIRWAYS**) offers mostly nonstop flights from 18 U.S. cities to Heathrow and Gatwick airports. With more add-on options than any other airline, British Airways can make a visit to Britain cheaper than you might have expected. The 1993 union of some of British Airways's functions and routings with

US Airways has opened additional North American gateways to British Airways, improved services, and reduced some of its fares. Of particular interest are the "Value Plus," "London on the Town," and "Europe Escorted" packages that include both airfare and discounted accommodations throughout Britain.

Depending on day and season, **Delta Air Lines** (☎ 800/241-4141) runs either one or two daily nonstop flights between Atlanta and Gatwick, near London. Delta also offers nonstop daily service from Cincinnati and Miami to Gatwick.

Northwest Airlines (☎ 800/447-4747) flies nonstop from Minneapolis, Boston, and Detroit to Gatwick, with connections possible from other cities, such as Memphis.

TWA (☎ 800/221-2000) flies nonstop to Gatwick every day from its hub in St. Louis. Connections are possible through St. Louis from most of North America.

United Airlines (☎ 800/538-2929) flies nonstop from New York's JFK to Heathrow two or three times a day, depending on the season. United also offers nonstop service twice a day from Dulles Airport, near Washington, D.C., plus once-a-day service from Chicago, Newark, Los Angeles, and San Francisco to Heathrow.

Virgin Atlantic Airways (☎ 800/862-8621) flies daily to either Gatwick or Heathrow from Boston, Newark, New York's JFK, Los Angeles, and San Francisco. The airline also flies from Miami to Gatwick (four times a week), and five times a week from Orlando. Virgin Atlantic also offers flights to London from Chicago through interconnecting, jointly marketed service on **Kiwi Airlines.** For information, call Virgin Atlantic or Kiwi (☎ 800/JET-KIWI).

Continental Airlines (☎ 800/525-0280) flies daily to Gatwick Airport from Newark and Houston.

For travelers departing from Canada, **Air Canada** (☎ 800/776-3000) flies daily to London Heathrow nonstop from Vancouver, Montréal, and Toronto. There are also frequent direct flights from Edmonton, Calgary, Winnipeg, Ottawa, Halifax, and St. John's.

LONDON'S AIRPORTS   Located west of London in Hounslow (☎ 0181/759-4321 for flight information), **London's Heathrow Airport** is one of the world's busiest airports, with flights arriving from around the world and throughout Great Britain. It's divided into four terminals, each relatively self-contained. Terminal 4, the most modern, handles the long-haul and transatlantic operations of British Airways. Most transatlantic flights of U.S.-based airlines arrive at Terminal 3. Terminals 1 and 2 receive the intra-European flights of several European airlines.

It takes 50 minutes by **Underground** and costs £3.80 ($6.10) to make the 15-mile trip from Heathrow to center city. You can also take the **Airbus,** which gets you into central London in about an hour and costs £6 ($9.60) for adults and £4 ($6.40) for children. A **taxi** is likely to cost at least £25 to £30 ($40–$48). For more information about train or bus connections, call ☎ **0171/222-1234.**

While Heathrow still dominates, more and more scheduled flights land at relatively remote **Gatwick Airport** (☎ **0129/353-5353** for flight information), located some 25 miles south of London in West Sussex.

From Gatwick, **express trains** leave for Victoria Station in London every 15 minutes during the day and every hour at night. The charge is £9 ($14.40) for adults, half-price for children 5 to 15, free for children under 5. There's also an express bus from Gatwick to Victoria, **Flightline Bus 777,** every half hour from 6:30am to 8pm and every hour from 8 to 11pm; the fare is £7.50 ($12) per person. A **taxi** from Gatwick to central London usually costs £50 to £60 ($80–$96). However, you must negotiate a fare with the driver before you enter the cab; the meter doesn't apply because Gatwick lies outside the Metropolitan Police District. For further transportation information, call ☎ **0171/928-5100** or 0171/928-2113.

BY TRAIN

No matter which station you arrive at, each is connected to London's vast bus and Underground network, and each has phones, restaurants, pubs, luggage-storage areas, and London Regional Transport Information Centres.

If you're arriving from France, the fastest way to get to London is by taking the Hoverspeed connection between Calais and Dover, where you can pick up a BritRail train into the city. If you prefer the ease of one-stop travel, you can take the Chunnel train directly from Paris.

VIA THE CHUNNEL FROM THE CONTINENT   Queen Elizabeth and President François Mitterand officially opened the Channel Tunnel in 1994, and the **Eurostar Express** began twice-daily passenger service between London and both Paris and Brussels. The $15 billion tunnel, one of the great engineering feats of all time, is the first link between Britain and the continent since the Ice Age.

Rail Europe (☎ **800/94-CHUNNEL** for information) sells tickets on the *Eurostar* direct train service between Paris, Brussels, and London. A round-trip first-class fare between Paris and London, for example, costs $312 ($248 in second class); but you can cut costs to $152 with a second-class, 14-day advance purchase (nonrefundable) round-trip fare. In London, make reservations for *Eurostar* at ☎ **0134/530-0003;** in Paris, at ☎ **01-44-51-06-02;** and in the United States at ☎ **800/EUROSTAR.** *Eurostar* trains arrive and depart from London's Waterloo Station, Paris's Gare du Nord, and Brussels' Central Station.

Getting to Know London

*E*urope's largest city is like a great wheel, with Piccadilly Circus at the hub and dozens of communities branching out from it. Since London is such a conglomeration of sections, each having its own life and personality, first-time visitors may be intimidated until they get the hang of it. Most visitors spend all their time in the West End, where most of the attractions are located, except for the historic part of London known as the City, where the Tower of London stands.

This chapter will help you get your bearings. It provides a brief orientation and a preview of the city's most important neighborhoods and tells you what you need to know about getting around London by public transportation or on foot. In addition, the "Fast Facts" section covers everything from baby-sitters to shoe repairs.

1 Orientation

VISITOR INFORMATION

The **British Travel Centre,** Rex House, 4–12 Lower Regent St., London SW1 4PQ (tube: Piccadilly Circus), caters to walk-in visitors who need information about all parts of Britain. Telephone service has been suspended; you must show up in person and wait in an often-lengthy line. On the premises you'll find a British Rail ticket office, travel and theater-ticket agencies, a hotel-booking service, a book shop, and a souvenir shop. It's open Monday to Friday 9am to 6:30pm, Saturday and Sunday 10am to 4pm, with extended hours on Saturday from June to September.

London Tourist Board's **Tourist Information Centre,** Victoria Station Forecourt, SW1 (tube: Victoria Station), can help you with almost anything. The center deals chiefly with accommodations in all size and price categories, and can handle the whole spectrum of travelers. It also arranges tour-ticket sales and theater reservations, and offers a wide selection of books and souvenirs. From Easter to October, the center is open daily 8am to 7pm; November to Easter, it's open Monday to Saturday 8am to 6pm and Sunday 9am to 4pm.

The tourist board also has offices at **Heathrow** terminals 1, 2, and 3, and on the Underground Concourse at **Liverpool Street Railway Station.**

CITY LAYOUT
AN OVERVIEW OF THE CITY

While **central London** doesn't formally define itself, most Londoners today would probably accept the Underground's Circle Line as a fair boundary. The city center is customarily divided into two areas, the **City** and the **West End.**

The City is where London began; it's the original 1 square mile the Romans called Londinium that still exists as its own self-governing entity. Rich in historical, architectural, and social interest, the City is now one of the world's great financial centers.

The West End, on the other hand, has no precise borders, but is divided by its main thoroughfares into clearly defined neighborhoods—Mayfair, Soho, Kensington, and the like—so by simply crossing the street, it's possible to leave behind a neighborhood of one quite distinct character and enter what seems to be another world. The West End is the area that most Londoners consider the real city center—this is where you find the majority of London's shops, restaurants, and theaters.

The City and the West End are surrounded first by **Inner London** (which includes the **East End**) and then by the sprawling hinterland of **Outer London.** You'll find the greatest number of hotels in the west, in inner districts such as **Kensington, Chelsea,** and **Victoria,** and in the West End. Even though the City is jeweled with historic sights, it empties out in the evenings and on weekends.

In much the way that the City is a buffer to the east, so is the River Thames to the south. The **Barbican Centre** in the City and the **South Bank Arts Centre** across the river were both conscious attempts to extend the geographical spread of central London's nocturnal life, but central London really fades in the City and only half-heartedly crosses the Thames. Still, the new urban development of Docklands and some up-and-coming residential neighborhoods are infusing energy into the area across the river.

ORIENTING YOURSELF

There is—fortunately—an immense difference between the sprawling vastness of Greater London and the pocket-size chunk north of the River Thames that might be considered prime tourist territory. This London begins at **Chelsea,** on the north bank of the river, and stretches for roughly 5 miles north to **Hampstead.** Its western boundary runs through **Kensington,** whereas the eastern boundary lies 5 miles away at Tower Bridge. Within these 25 square miles, you'll find all the hotels and restaurants and nearly all the sights that are of primary interest to visitors.

Make no mistake: This is still a hefty portion of land to cover, and a really thorough exploration of it would take a couple of years. But it has the advantage of being flat and eminently walkable, besides boasting one of the best public transportation systems ever devised.

The logical (although not geographical) center of this area is **Trafalgar Square,** which we'll take as our orientation point. If you stand facing the steps of the imposing National Gallery, you're looking northwest. That is the direction of **Piccadilly Circus**—the real core of central London—and the maze of streets that make up **Soho.** Farther north is **Oxford Street,** London's gift to moderate shopping; still farther northwest lies **Regent's Park,** home to the London Zoo.

At your back—that is, south—is **Whitehall,** which houses or skirts nearly every British government building, from the Ministry of Defence to the official residence of the prime minister at No. 10 Downing St. In the same direction, a bit farther south, stand the Houses of Parliament and Westminster Abbey.

Flowing southwest from Trafalgar Square is the table-smooth **Mall,** flanked by magnificent parks and mansions and leading to Buckingham Palace, residence of the Queen. Farther in the same direction lie **Belgravia** and **Knightsbridge,** the city's plushest residential areas, and south of them lie the aforementioned chic **Chelsea** and **King's Road,** the famous shopping boulevard.

Due west of Trafalgar Square stretches the superb and distinctly high-priced shopping area bordered by **Regent Street** and **Piccadilly Street** (distinct from the Circus). Farther west lie the equally elegant shops and even more elegant homes of **Mayfair.** Then comes **Park Lane.** On the other side of Park Lane is **Hyde Park,** the biggest park in London and one of the largest in the world.

Charing Cross Road runs north from Trafalgar Square, past **Leicester Square,** and intersects with **Shaftesbury Avenue.** This is London's theaterland. A bit farther along, Charing Cross Road turns into a browser's paradise, lined with shops selling new and second-hand books.

Finally, Charing Cross Road funnels into **St. Giles Circus;** this is where you enter **Bloomsbury,** site of the University of London, the British Museum, and some of London's best budget hotels, as well as the erstwhile stomping ground of the famed Bloomsbury Group, led by Virginia Woolf.

Northeast of your position lies **Covent Garden,** known for its Royal Opera House and today a major—and very hip—shopping, restaurant, and cafe district.

Following the **Strand** eastward from Trafalgar Square, you'll come into **Fleet Street.** Beginning in the 19th century, this corner of London became the most concentrated newspaper district in the world (most of the papers have fled Fleet Street for the new Docklands development in the last decade or so).

Where the Strand becomes Fleet Street stands Temple Bar, and only here do you enter the actual City of London, or the **City.** Its focal point and shrine is the Bank of England on Threadneedle Street, with the Stock Exchange next door and the Royal Exchange across the street. In the midst of all the hustle and bustle rises St. Paul's Cathedral, a monument to beauty and tranquillity. At the far eastern fringe of the City looms the Tower of London, shrouded in legend, blood, and history, and permanently besieged by battalions of visitors.

And this, as far as we're concerned, concludes the London circle.

FINDING YOUR WAY AROUND

It's not easy to find an address in London, as the city's streets—both their naming and house numbering—follow no pattern whatsoever. London is checkered with innumerable squares, mews, closes, and terraces, which jut into, cross, overlap, or interrupt whatever street you're trying to follow. And house numbers run in odds and evens, clockwise and counterclockwise—when they exist at all. Many establishments, such as the Four Seasons Hotel and Langan's Brasserie, don't have numbers, even though the building right next door is numbered.

Face it—you're going to get lost. So if you plan on exploring London in any depth, you'll need a detailed street map with an index—not one of those superficial overviews given away at many hotels or tourist offices. The best ones are published by Falk, and they're available at most newsstands and nearly all bookstores, including **W. & G. Foyle Ltd.,** 113–119 Charing Cross Rd., WC2 (☎ **0171/439-8501;** tube: Leicester Square), which carries a wide range of maps and guides. And no Londoner is without the *London A to Z,* the ultimate street-by-street reference guide, available at bookstores and newsstands everywhere. Also, don't forget to check out the detailed fold-out street map included with this book; you may find that it's all you need to find your way around.

LONDON'S NEIGHBORHOODS IN BRIEF
The West End Neighborhoods

Mayfair Bounded by Piccadilly, Hyde Park, and Oxford and Regent streets, this is the most elegant, fashionable section of London, filled with luxury hotels, Georgian town houses, and swank shops. Grosvenor Square (pronounced *grov*-nor) is nicknamed "Little America," because it's home to the American embassy and a statue of Franklin D. Roosevelt; Berkeley Square (pronounced *bark*-ley) was made famous by the song, whose mythical nightingale sang here. At least once you'll want to dip into this exclusive section. One of the curiosities of Mayfair is **Shepherd Market,** a tiny village of pubs, two-story inns, book and food stalls, and restaurants, all sandwiched between Mayfair's greatness.

Marylebone All first-time visitors head to Marylebone to explore Madame Tussaud's waxworks or walk along Baker Street in the make-believe footsteps of Sherlock Holmes. The streets form a near-perfect grid, with the major ones running north-south from Regent's Park toward Oxford Street. Robert Adam laid out Portland Place, one of the most characteristic squares, from 1776 to 1780, and it was at Cavendish Square that Mrs. Horatio Nelson waited—often in vain—for the return of the admiral. Marylebone Lane and High Street still retain some of their former village atmosphere, but this is otherwise now a rather anonymous area. Dickens (who seems to have lived everywhere) wrote nearly a dozen books when he resided here. At Regent's Park, you can visit Queen Mary's Gardens or, in summer, see Shakespeare performed in an open-air theater.

St. James's Often called "Royal London," St. James's basks in its associations with everybody from the "merrie monarch" Charles II to Elizabeth II, who lives at its most famous address, Buckingham Palace. The neighborhood begins at Piccadilly Circus and moves southwest, incorporating Pall Mall, The Mall, St. James's Park, and Green Park; it's "frightfully convenient," as the English say, enclosing such addresses as American Express on Haymarket and many of London's leading department stores. In this bastion of aristocracy and royalty, a certain pomp is still evident—this is where the English gentleman seeks haven at that male-only bastion of English tradition, the gentlemen's club. Be sure to stop in at Fortnum & Mason, at 181 Piccadilly, the world's most luxurious grocery store, which was launched in 1788. The store sent hams to the Duke of Wellington's army, baskets of tinned goodies to Florence Nightingale in the Crimea, and packed a picnic basket for Stanley when he went looking for Livingstone.

Piccadilly Circus & Leicester Square   Piccadilly Circus, with its statue of Eros, is the very heart and soul of London. The circus isn't Times Square yet, but its traffic, neon, and jostling crowds don't do anything to make it fashionable. Circus might indeed be an apt word here. The thoroughfare Piccadilly was always known as "the magic mile"; traditionally the western road out of town, it was named for the "picadil," a ruffled collar created by Robert Baker, a 17th-century tailor. If you want a little more grandeur, retreat to the Regency promenade of exclusive shops, the Burlington Arcade, designed in 1819. The English gentry—tired of being mud-splashed by horses and carriages along Piccadilly—came here to do their shopping. Some 35 shops, housing a treasure trove of goodies, await you.

A bit more tawdry is **Leicester Square,** a center of theaters, restaurants, movie palaces, and nightlife. The square is no longer the chic address it was when William Hogarth or Joshua Reynolds lived here, the latter artist painting all of high society in his elegant salon. The square changed forever in the Victorian era, when four towering entertainment halls were opened (even Queen Victoria came to see a circus here on occasion). In time the old palaces changed from stage to screen; three of them are still showing films. The Café de Paris is no longer the chicest cabaret in town—now it's a disco.

Soho   Every city has its low-life area, of course, but in few are the red lights woven into a texture of such richness and variety as in London's Soho. These densely packed streets in the heart of the West End are famous for their gloriously cosmopolitan mix of people and trades. A decade ago, much was heard about the decline of Soho, when the thriving sex industry threatened to engulf it; even the pub where Dylan Thomas used to drink himself into oblivion became a sex cinema. That destruction has now largely been halted: Respectable businesses have returned, and fashionable restaurants and shops prosper; it's now the heart of London's expanding cafe society. But Soho wouldn't be Soho without a scattering of sex shops and porno theaters.

Soho starts at Piccadilly Circus and spreads out; it's basically bordered by Regent Street, Oxford Street, Charing Cross Road, and the theaters of Shaftesbury Avenue. Carnaby Street, a block from Regent Street, was the center of the universe in the Swinging '60s, but now it's just a schlocky sideshow. Across Shaftesbury Avenue, a busy street lined with theaters, is London's **Chinatown,** centered on Gerrard Street: small, authentic, and packed with excellent restaurants. But Soho's heart—with marvelous French and Italian delicatessens, fine butchers, fish stores, and wine merchants—is farther north, on Brewer, Old Compton, and Berwick streets; Berwick is also a wonderful open-air, fresh-food market. To the north of Old Compton Street, Dean, Frith, and Greek streets have fine little restaurants, pubs, and clubs, like Ronnie Scott's for jazz. The British movie industry is centered in Wardour Street.

Bloomsbury This district, a world within itself, lies northeast of Piccadilly Circus, beyond Soho. It is, among other things, the academic heart of London; here you'll find the University of London, several other colleges, and many bookstores. Despite its student population, this neighborhood is fairly staid. Its reputation has been fanned by such writers as Virginia Woolf, who lived within its bounds (it figured in her novel *Jacob's Room*). The novelist and her husband, Leonard, were once the unofficial leaders of a group of artists and writers known as "the Bloomsbury Group" (nicknamed "Bloomsberries"), which at times included Bertrand Russell.

The heart of Bloomsbury is Russell Square, and the streets jutting off from the square are lined with hotels and B&Bs. Russell Square was laid out between 1800 and 1814; in *Vanity Fair,* William Thackeray made it the stomping ground of the Osbornes and the Sedleys. Most visitors come to the neighborhood to visit the British Museum, one of the world's greatest repositories of treasures. The British Telecom Tower (1964) on Cleveland Street is a familiar landmark.

Nearby is **Fitzrovia,** bounded by Great Portland, Oxford, and Gower streets, and reached by the Goodge Street tube. Goodge Street, with its many shops and pubs, forms the heart of the "village." Once a major haunt of artists and writers—this was the stomping ground of Ezra Pound, Wyndham Lewis, and George Orwell, among others—the bottom end of Fitzrovia is a virtual extension of Soho, with a cluster of Greek restaurants.

Clerkenwell This was the site of London's first hospital and the home of several early churches, before evolving into a muck-filled 18th-century cattle yard that was also home to cheap gin distilleries. By the 1870s, London's new socialist movement centered itself here: Clerkenwell was home to John Stuart Mill's London Patriotic Club in 1872 and William Morris's socialist press of the 1890s; Lenin lived and worked here editing *Iskra.* After the socialists, the neighborhood dwindled. However, it's recently been reinvented by the moneyed and groovy—a handful of hot new restaurants and

London's Neighborhoods

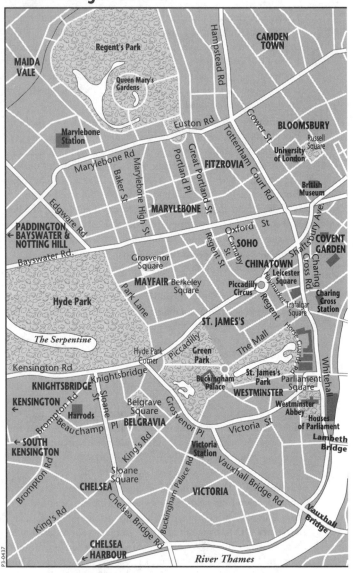

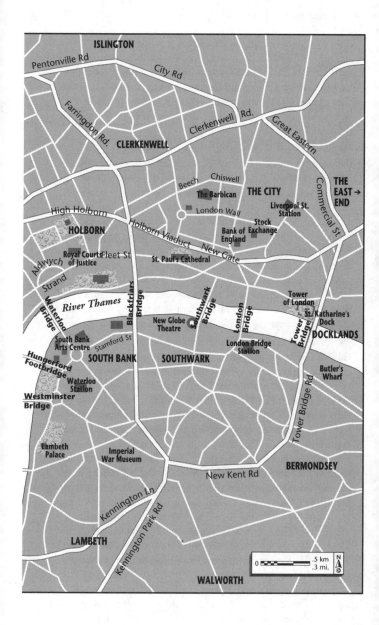

clubs have sprouted up, and art galleries now line St. John's Square and the border of Clerkenwell Green. But lorries still rumble into Smithfield Market throughout the night, unloading thousands of beef carcasses for trade, and the church of St. Bartholomew-the-Great, built in 1123, still stands as London's oldest church, and the best piece of large-scale Norman building in the city. Farringdon is the central tube stop.

Holborn　The old borough of Holborn, which abuts the City to the west, takes in the heart of legal London—the city's barristers, solicitors, and law clerks call it home. Still Dickensian in spirit, the area lets you follow in the Victorian author's footsteps, passing the two Inns of Court and arriving at Bleeding Heart Yard of *Little Dorritt* fame. A 14-year-old Dickens was once employed as a solicitor's clerk at Lincoln's Inn Fields. Old Bailey has stood for English justice down through the years (Fagin went to the gallows from this site in *Oliver Twist*). Everything here seems steeped in history. Even as you're quenching your thirst with a half-pint of bitter at the Viaduct Tavern, 126 Newgate St. (tube: St. Paul's), you learn the pub was built over the notorious Newgate Prison (which specialized in death by pressing) and was named after the Holborn Viaduct, the world's first overpass.

Covent Garden & the Strand　The flower, fruit, and "veg" market is long gone (since 1970), but memories of Professor Higgins and his "squashed cabbage leaf," Eliza Doolittle, linger on. **Covent Garden** now contains the city's liveliest group of restaurants, pubs, and cafes outside Soho, as well as some of the city's hippest shops—including the world's only Dr. Marten's Super Store. The restored marketplace with its glass-and-iron roofs has been called a "magnificent example of urban recycling." Covent Garden is traditionally London's theater area, and Inigo Jones's St. Paul's Covent Garden is known as the actors' church; it has attracted over the years everybody from Ellen Terry to Vivien Leigh, and is still attended by actors and artists. The Theatre Royal Drury Lane was where Charles II's mistress Nell Gwynne made her debut in 1665, and the Irish actress Dorothea Jordan first caught the eye of the duke of Clarence, later William IV. (She became not only his mistress, but the mother of 10 of his children.)

Beginning at Trafalgar Square, the **Strand** runs east into Fleet Street and borders Covent Garden to the south. It's flanked with theaters, shops, hotels, and restaurants. Ye Olde Cheshire Cheese pub, Dr. Johnson's House, tearooms fragrant with brewing

Twinings English tea—all these evoke memories of the rich heyday of this district. The Strand runs parallel to the River Thames, and to walk it is to follow in the footsteps of Charles Lamb, Mark Twain, Henry Fielding, James Boswell, William Thackeray, and Sir Walter Raleigh. The Savoy Theatre helped make Gilbert and Sullivan a household name.

Westminster Westminster has been the seat of the British government since the days of Edward the Confessor. Dominated by the Houses of Parliament and Westminster Abbey, the area runs along the Thames to the east of St. James's Park. **Trafalgar Square,** at the area's northern end and one of the city's major landmarks, remains a testament to England's victory over Napoléon in 1805, and the paintings in its landmark National Gallery will restore your soul. Whitehall is the main thoroughfare, linking Trafalgar Square with Parliament Square. You can visit Churchill's Cabinet War Rooms and walk down Downing Street to see No. 10, the world's most famous street address, home to Britain's prime minister. No visit is complete without a call at Westminster Abbey, one of the greatest Gothic churches in the world. It has witnessed a parade of English history, beginning when William the Conqueror was crowned here on Christmas Day, 1066.

Westminster also encompasses **Victoria,** an area that takes its unofficial name from bustling Victoria Station, known as "the gateway to the Continent."

The City & Environs
The City When the Londoners speak of "the City," they don't mean all of London; they mean the original square mile that's now the British version of Wall Street. The buildings of this district are known all over the world: the Bank of England, the London Stock Exchange, and the financially troubled Lloyd's of London. This was the origin of Londinium, as it was called by its Roman conquerors. Despite its age, the City doesn't easily reveal its past; much of it has been swept away by the Great Fire of 1666, the bombs of 1940, the IRA bombs of the early 1990s, and the zeal of modern developers. Still, it retains its medieval character, and landmarks include **St. Paul's Cathedral,** the masterpiece of Sir Christopher Wren, which stood virtually alone among the rubble after the Blitz. Some 2,000 years of history unfold at the Museum of London and the Barbican Centre, opened by Queen Elizabeth II in 1982, and hailed by her as a "wonder" of the cultural world. At the Guildhall, the first lord mayor of London was installed in 1192.

Fleet Street was London's journalistic hub since William Caxton printed the first book in English here. The *Daily Consort,* the first daily newspaper printed in England, was launched at Ludgate Circus in 1702. However, most of the London tabloids have recently abandoned Fleet Street for the Docklands development across the river.

The City of London still prefers to function on its own, separate from the rest of the city; in keeping with its independence, it maintains its own **Information Centre** at St. Paul's Churchyard, EC4 (☎ **0171/332-1456**).

The East End   Traditionally, this was one of London's poorest districts, and was nearly bombed out of existence by the Nazis. Hitler, in the words of one commentator at the time, created "instant urban renewal." The East End extends from the City Walls east encompassing Stepney, Bow, Poplar, West Ham, Canning Town, and other districts. The East End has always been filled with legend and lore. It's the home of the Cockney, London's most colorful character. To be a true Cockney, it's said that you must have been born "within the sound of Bow Bells," a reference to a church, St. Mary-le-Bow, rebuilt by Sir Christopher Wren in 1670. Many immigrants to London have found a home here.

South Bank   Although not officially a district like Mayfair, South Bank is the setting today for the **South Bank Arts Centre,** now the largest arts center in Western Europe and still growing. Reached by Waterloo Bridge, it lies across the Thames from the Victoria Embankment. Culture buffs flock to its many galleries and halls, including the National Theatre, Queen Elizabeth Hall, Royal Festival Hall, and the Hayward Gallery. It's also the setting of the National Film Theatre and the Museum of the Moving Image (MOMI). Nearby are such neighborhoods as Elephant and Castle and **Southwark,** home to grand Southwark Cathedral. To get here, take the tube to Waterloo Station.

Central London Beyond the West End

Knightsbridge   One of London's most fashionable neighborhoods, Knightsbridge is a top residential and shopping district, just south of Hyde Park. Harrods on Brompton Road is its chief attraction. Founded in 1901, it's been called "the Notre Dame of department stores"—they'll even arrange your burial. Right nearby, Beauchamp Place (pronounced *beech*-am) is one of London's most fashionable shopping streets, a Regency-era, boutique-lined little street with a scattering of restaurants such as San Lorenzo, once frequented by the late Princess Diana. Shops include Bruce Oldfield at 27 Beauchamp Place, where the likes of Joan Collins come for evening wear. And, at the end of a shopping day, if Harrods's five restaurants and five bars haven't tempted you, retreat to Bill Bentley's at 31 Beauchamp Place for a dozen oysters, washed down with a few glasses of muscadet.

Belgravia   South of Knightsbridge, this area has long been the aristocratic quarter of London, rivaling Mayfair in grandness and richness. Although it reached the pinnacle of its prestige during the reign of Queen Victoria, it's still a chic address; the duke and duchess of Westminster, one of England's richest families, still live at Eaton Square. Its centerpiece is Belgrave Square (1825–35). When the town houses were built, the aristocrats followed—the duke of Connaught, the earl of Essex, even Queen Victoria's mother, the duchess of Kent. Chopin, on holiday in 1837, was appropriately impressed: "And the English! And the houses! And the palaces! And the pomp, and the carriages! Everything from soap to the razors is extraordinary."

Chelsea   This stylish Thames-side district lies south of Belgravia. It begins at Sloane Square, with Gilbert Ledward's Venus fountain playing watery music (if the noise of the traffic doesn't drown it out). Flower sellers hustle their flamboyant blooms here year-round. The area has always been a favorite of writers and artists, including such names as Oscar Wilde (who was arrested here), George Eliot, James Whistler, J. M. W. Turner, Henry James, Augustus John, and Thomas Carlyle (whose former home can be visited). Mick Jagger and Margaret Thatcher (not together) have been more recent residents, and Princess Diana and her "Sloane Rangers" of the 1980s gave it even more fame.

Its major boulevard is **King's Road,** where Mary Quant launched the miniskirt in the 1960s and where the English punk look began. King's Road runs the entire length of Chelsea; it's at its liveliest on Saturday. The hip-hop of King's Road isn't typical of otherwise upmarket Chelsea, an elegant village filled with town houses and little mews dwellings that only successful stockbrokers and solicitors can afford to occupy.

Kensington   This Royal Borough (W8) lies west of Kensington Gardens and Hyde Park and is traversed by two of London's major shopping streets, Kensington High Street and Kensington Church Street. Since 1689, when asthmatic William III fled Whitehall Palace for Nottingham House (where the air was fresher), the district has enjoyed royal associations. In time, Nottingham House became Kensington Palace, and the royals grabbed a chunk of Hyde Park to plant their roses. Queen Victoria was born here. "KP," as the royals say, is still home to Princess Margaret (20 rooms with a view), Prince and Princess Michael of Kent, and the duke and duchess of Gloucester; it was also the residence of the late Princess Diana and her two sons. Kensington Gardens is now open to the public, ever since George II decreed that "respectably dressed" people would be permitted in on Saturday—providing that no servants, soldiers, or sailors came. In the footsteps of William III, Kensington Square developed, attracting artists and writers. Thackeray wrote *Vanity Fair* while living here.

Southeast of Kensington Gardens and Earl's Court, primarily residential **South Kensington** is often called "museumland" because it's dominated by a complex of museums and colleges—set upon land bought with the proceeds from Prince Albert's Great Exhibition, held in Hyde Park in 1851—that includes the Natural History Museum, the Victoria & Albert Museum, and the Science Museum; nearby is Royal Albert Hall. South Kensington is also home to some fashionable restaurants and town-house hotels. One of the district's chief curiosities is the Albert Memorial, completed in 1872 by Sir George Gilbert Scott; for sheer excess, the Victorian monument is unequaled in the world.

2 Getting Around

BY PUBLIC TRANSPORTATION

If you know the ropes, transportation in London can be easy and inexpensive. Both the Underground (the subway casually known as the "tube") and bus systems are operated by London Transport.

Travel Information Centres are located in the Underground stations at Hammersmith, King's Cross, Oxford Circus, St. James's Park, Liverpool Street Station, and Piccadilly Circus, as well as in the British Rail stations at Euston and Victoria and in each of the terminals at Heathrow Airport. They take reservations for London Transport's guided tours and offer free Underground and bus maps and other information leaflets. A **24-hour information service** is available (☎ **0171/222-1234**). You can get information before you go by writing **London Transport,** Travel Information Service, 55 Broadway, London SW1H 0BD.

TRAVEL PASSES London Transport offers **Travelcards** for use on bus, Underground, and British Rail services in Greater London.

Available in combinations of adjacent zones, Travelcards are available for a minimum of 7 days or for any period from a month to a year. A Travelcard allowing travel in two zones for 1 week costs adults £15.70 ($25.10), children £5.30 ($8.50). Travelcards must be used in conjunction with a Photocard (a photo ID used for identification by London Transport as well as by several other entities in London). A free Photocard is issued simultaneously with your Travelcard—bring along a passport photo of yourself—when you buy your Travelcard at main post offices in the London area, the ticket window of any tube station, or at the Travel Information Service of London Transport (see above).

For shorter stays in London, consider the **One-Day Off-Peak Travelcard.** This Travelcard can be used on most bus, Underground, and British Rail services throughout Greater London Monday to Friday after 9:30am and at any time on weekends and bank holidays. The Travelcard is available from Underground ticket offices, Travel Information Centres, and some newsstands. For two zones, the cost is £3.20 ($5.10) for adults and £1.70 ($2.70) for children 5 to 15. Children 4 and under travel free.

The **Visitor Travelcard** is worthwhile if you plan to travel a lot within Greater London. This card allows unlimited transport within all six zones of Greater London's Underground and bus network. You'll most likely travel within the first two zones of the network's boundaries, but you're able to travel as far as Heathrow during valid times. However, you must buy this pass in North America; it's not available in England. A pass good for 3 consecutive days of travel is $25 for adults, $11 for children 5 to 15; for 4 consecutive days of travel, it's $33 for adults, $13 for children; and for 7 consecutive days of travel, it's $53 for adults, $21 for children. Contact **BritRail Travel International,** 1500 Broadway, New York, NY 10036 (☎ **800/677-8585** or 212/575-2667).

Another pass is the 1-day **Family Travelcard.** It's a go-as-you-please ticket, allowing as many journeys as you wish on the tube, buses (excluding night buses) displaying the London Transport bus sign, and even the Docklands Light Railway or any rail service within the travel zones designated on your ticket. The family card is valid Monday to Friday after 9:30am and all day on weekends and public holidays. It's available for families as small as two (one adult and one child) and as large as six (two adults and four children). The cost is £2.50 ($4) per adult, 50p (80¢) per child. Yet a final discount pass is the **Weekend Travelcard,** which allows you 2 days of weekend transportation on the Underground or buses. The cost ranges from £6.40 to £8 ($10.25 to $12.80) for adults or £3.40 ($5.45) for children. These passes are available at all Underground stations.

You can now buy **Carnet** tickets, a booklet of 10 single Underground tickets valid for 12 months from the issue date. Carnet tickets are valid for travel only in zone 1 (central London), and cost £10 ($16) for adults and £4.80 ($7.70) for children up to 15. A book of Carnet tickets gives you a savings of £2 ($3.20) over the cost of 10 separate single tickets.

THE UNDERGROUND

The Underground, or tube, is the fastest and easiest way to get from place to place. All Underground stations are clearly marked with a red circle and blue crossbar. You descend by stairways, escalators, or huge elevators, depending on the depth. Some Underground stations have complete subterranean shopping arcades and several have push-button information machines.

You pick the station for which you're heading on the large diagram displayed on the wall, which includes an alphabetical index. You note the color of the line (Bakerloo is brown, Central is red, and so on). Then, by merely following the colored band, you can see at a glance whether and where you'll have to change and how many stops are between you and your destination. *Be sure to pick up a complimentary pocket-sized Underground map, available at every station.*

If you have British coins, you can get your ticket at a vending machine. Otherwise, buy it at the ticket office. You can transfer as many times as you like as long as you stay in the Underground. The flat fare for one trip within the central zone is £1.20 ($1.90). Trips from the central zone to destinations in the suburbs range from £1.20 to £4.30 ($1.90–$6.90) in most cases.

Be sure to keep your ticket, as it must be presented when you exit the station at your destination. If you're caught without a valid ticket, you'll be fined £10 ($16) on the spot. If you owe extra money, you'll be asked to pay the difference by the attendant. Also keep in mind that many trains stop running at midnight (11:30pm on Sun). For information on the London tube system, call the **London Underground** at ☎ **0171/222-1234,** but expect to stay on hold for a good while before a live person comes on the line.

BUSES

The first thing you learn about London buses is that nobody just boards them. You "queue up"—that is, form a single-file line at the bus stop.

The comparably priced bus system is almost as good as the Underground, and gives you better views of the city. To find out about current routes, pick up a free bus map at one of London Transport's Travel Information Centres, listed above. The map is available in person only, not by mail.

London still has some old-style Routemaster buses, with both driver and conductor: After you've boarded the bus, a conductor will come to your seat; you pay a fare based on your destination, and receive a ticket in return. This type of bus is being phased out and replaced with buses that have only a driver; you pay the driver as you enter, and exit via a rear door.

As with the Underground, the fares vary according to distance traveled. Generally, bus fares are 50p to £1.20 (80¢–$1.90)—less than tube fares. If you travel for two or three stops, the cost is 60p (95¢); longer runs within zone 1 cost 90p ($1.45). If you want your stop called out, simply ask the conductor.

Buses generally run between about 5am and 11:30pm. There are a few night buses on special routes, running once an hour or so; most pass through Trafalgar Square. Call the **24-hour hot line** (☎ **0171/222-1234**) for schedule and fare information.

BY TAXI

London cabs are among the most comfortable and best-designed in the world. You can pick one up either by heading for a cab rank or by hailing one in the street (the taxi is free if the yellow taxi sign on the roof is lighted); once they have stopped for you, taxis are obliged to take you anywhere you want to go within 6 miles of the pick-up point, provided it's within the metropolitan area. For a **radio cab,** call ☎ **0171/272-0272** or 0171/253-5000.

The minimum taxi fare is £1.40 ($2.25) for the first third of a mile, with increments of 20p (30¢) thereafter, based on distance or time. Each additional passenger is charged 40p (65¢). Passengers pay 10p (16¢) for each piece of luggage in the driver's compartment and any other item more than 2 feet long. Surcharges are imposed after 8pm and on weekends and public holidays. All these tariffs include value-added tax (VAT). Fares usually increase annually. It's recommended that you tip 10% to 15% of the fare.

If you call for a cab, the meter starts running when the taxi receives instructions from the dispatcher, so you could find £1.20 ($1.90) or more already on the meter when you step inside.

FAST FACTS: London

American Express   The main AmEx office is 6 Haymarket, SW1 (☎ **0171/930-4411;** tube: Piccadilly Circus). Full services are available Monday to Friday 9am to 5:30pm and Saturday 9am to 4pm. At other times—Saturday 9am to 6pm and Sunday 10am to 6pm—only the foreign-exchange bureau is open.

Climate   See "When to Go" in chapter 1.

Currency Exchange   See "Money" in chapter 1.

Doctors   In an emergency, contact **Doctor's Call** at ☎ **0181/900-1000.** Some hotels also have physicians on call. **Medical Express,** 117A Harley St., W1 (☎ **0171/499-1991;** tube: Regent's Park), is a private British clinic; it's not part of the free British medical establishment. For filling the British equivalent of a U.S. prescription, there's sometimes a surcharge of £20 ($32) on top of the cost of the medications. The clinic is open Monday to Friday 9am to 6pm and Saturday 9:30am to 2:30pm.

Documents Required   See "Visitor Information & Entry Requirements" in chapter 1.

Drugstores   In Britain they're called chemist shops. Every police station in the country has a list of emergency chemists (dial "0" and ask the operator for the local police). One of the most centrally located chemists, keeping long hours, is **Bliss the Chemist,** 5 Marble Arch, W1 (☎ **0171/723-6116;** tube: Marble Arch), open daily 9am to midnight. Every London neighborhood has a branch of **Boots,** Britain's leading pharmacist.

Electricity   British current is 240 volts, AC cycle, roughly twice the voltage of North American current, which is 115–120 volts, AC cycle. You'll probably not be able to plug the flat pins of your appliance's plugs into the holes of British wall outlets without suitable converters or adapters. Some (but not all) hotels will supply them for guests. Experienced travelers bring their own transformers. An electrical supply shop will also have what you need. Be forewarned that you'll destroy the inner workings of your appliance (and possibly start a fire as well) if you plug an American appliance directly into a European electrical outlet without a transformer.

Embassies & High Commissions   We hope you won't need such services, but in case you lose your passport or have some other emergency, here's a list of addresses and phone numbers:

• **Australia**   The high commission is at **Australia House,** Strand, WC2 (☎ **0171/379-4334;** tube: Charing Cross or Aldwych); it's open Monday to Friday from 10am to 4pm.

- **Canada**   The high commission, located at MacDonald House, 38 Grosvenor Sq., W1 (☎ **0171/258-6600;** tube: Bond Street), handles visas for Canada. Hours are Monday to Friday from 8 to 11am only.
- **Ireland**   The embassy is at 17 Grosvenor Place, SW1 (☎ **0171/235-2171;** tube: Hyde Park Corner); it's open Monday to Friday from 9:30am to 1pm and 2:15 to 5pm.
- **New Zealand**   The high commission is at New Zealand House, 80 Haymarket at Pall Mall, SW1 (☎ **0171/930-8422;** tube: Charing Cross or Piccadilly Circus); it's open Monday to Friday from 9am to 5pm.
- **The United States**   The embassy is located at 24 Grosvenor Sq., W1 (☎ **0171/499-9000;** tube: Bond Street). For passport and visa information, go to the **U.S. Passport & Citizenship Unit,** 55–56 Upper Brook St., W1 (☎ **0171/499-9000,** ext. 2563 or 2564; tube: Marble Arch or Bond Street). Hours are Monday to Friday from 8:30am to noon and from 2 to 4pm (there are no afternoon hours on Tues).

Emergencies   For police, fire, or an ambulance, dial ☎ **999.**

Holidays   See "When to Go" in chapter 1.

Hospitals   The following offer emergency care in London 24 hours a day, with the first treatment free under the National Health Service: **Royal Free Hospital,** Pond Street, NW3 (☎ **0171/794-0500;** tube: Belsize Park), and **University College Hospital,** Grafton Way, WC1 (☎ **0171/387-9300;** tube: Warren Street or Euston Square). Many other London hospitals also have accident and emergency departments.

Liquor Laws   No alcohol is served to anyone under 18. Children under 16 aren't allowed in pubs, except in certain rooms, and then only when accompanied by a parent or guardian. Restaurants are allowed to serve liquor during the same hours as pubs; however, only people who are eating a meal on the premises can be served a drink. In hotels, liquor may be served from 11am to 11pm to both residents and nonresidents; after 11pm, only residents may be served.

Money   See "Money" in chapter 1.

Newspapers/Magazines   *The Times* is tops, then the *Telegraph,* the *Daily Mail,* and the *Manchester Guardian,* all London dailies carrying the latest news. The *International Herald Tribune,* published in Paris, and an international edition of *USA Today,* beamed via satellite, are available daily. Copies of *Time* and *Newsweek* are also sold at most newsstands. Magazines such as *Time Out, City Limits,* and *Where* contain lots of useful information about the latest happenings in London.

Police In an emergency, dial ☎ **999** (no coin required). You can also go to one of the local police branches in central London, including **New Scotland Yard,** Broadway, SW1 (☎ **0171/230-1212;** tube: St. James's Park).

Taxes To encourage energy conservation, the British government levies a 25% tax on gasoline (petrol). There is also a 17.5% national value-added tax (VAT) that is added to all hotel and restaurant bills, and included in the price of many items you purchase. This can be refunded if you shop at stores that participate in the Retail Export Scheme (signs are posted in the window).

In October 1994, Britain imposed a departure tax: £5 ($8) for flights within Britain and the European Community or £10 ($16) for passengers flying elsewhere, including to the United States.

Taxis See "Getting Around," earlier in this chapter.

Telephone For **directory assistance** for London, dial 142; for the rest of Britain, 192. To call London from the United States, dial 011 (international code), 44 (Britain's country code), 171 or 181 (London's area codes), and the seven-digit local phone number.

There are three types of public pay phones: those taking only coins, those accepting only phone cards (called Cardphones), and those taking both phone cards and credit cards. At coin-operated phones, insert your coins before dialing. The minimum charge is 10p (15¢).

Phone cards are available in four values—£2 ($3.20), £4 ($6.40), £10 ($16), and £20 ($32)—and are reusable until the total value has expired. Cards can be purchased from newsstands and post offices. Finally, the credit-call pay phone operates on credit cards—Access (MasterCard), Visa, American Express, and Diners Club—and is most common at airports and large railway stations.

Time England follows Greenwich mean time (5 hours ahead of eastern standard time). Throughout most of the year, including during the summer, Britain is 5 hours ahead of the time observed on the East Coast of the United States. Because of a lead and lag factor associated with the imposition of daylight saving time within the two nations, there's a brief period (about a week) in autumn when Britain is only 4 hours ahead of New York, and a brief period in spring when it's 6 hours ahead of New York.

Tipping   In restaurants, service charges in the 15% to 20% range are usually added to the bill. Sometimes this is clearly marked; at other times it isn't. When in doubt, ask. If service isn't included, it's customary to add 15% to the bill. Sommeliers get about £1 ($1.60) per bottle of wine served. Tipping in pubs isn't common, although in cocktail bars the server usually gets about 75p ($1.20) per round of drinks.

Hotels, like restaurants, often add a service charge of 10% to 15% to most bills. In smaller B&Bs, the tip isn't likely to be included. Therefore, tip for special service, such as for the person who served you breakfast. If several persons have served you in a B&B, many guests ask that 10% or 15% be added to the bill and divided among the staff.

It's standard to tip taxi drivers 10% to 15% of the fare, although a tip for a taxi driver should never be less than 20p (30¢), even for a short run. Barbers and hairdressers expect 10% to 15%. Tour guides expect £2 ($3.20), although it's not mandatory.

Transit Information   Call ☎ **0171/222-1234,** 24 hours a day.

Weather   Call ☎ **0171/922-8844** for current weather information, but chances are the line will be busy.

3

Accommodations

*F*ace it—you're just going to pay more than you'd like for a hotel room in London. London boasts some of the most famous hotels in the world—such temples of luxury as Claridge's, the Dorchester, the Park Lane, and the Savoy, as well as recent-vintage rivals like the Four Seasons—and they're all superlative. The problem (and it's a serious one) is that there are too many upscale joints and not enough of the moderately priced options so typical of other European capitals.

Even at the luxury level, you might be surprised at what you *don't* get at a London hotel. Many are stately Victorian and Edwardian gems so steeped in tradition that they still lack most or all of the modern conveniences that come standard in the luxury hotels of, say, New York. Some have gone to no end to modernize, but others have remained at Boer War level. London does have some cutting-edge, chintz-free hotels that seem to have been shifted bodily from Los Angeles—complete with high-end sound systems and gadget-filled marble baths—but they're not necessarily superior; what the others lack in streamlining and convenience they frequently make up in personal service and spaciousness. It all depends on what you like.

If you're looking for reasonably priced options, don't despair. Although there are fewer than we'd like, London does have some good-value options; we've included the best of them here. An affordable way to go is to book a bed-and-breakfast. At their best, they're clean, comfortable, and friendly. Currently, however, good B&Bs are in short supply in London; don't reserve a room at one without a recommendation you can trust. The following services will arrange a B&B room for you: **Bed & Breakfast** (☎ **800/367-4668** or 423/690-8484), and **Worldwide Bed & Breakfast Association** (☎ **800/852-2632** in the U.S., or 0181/742-9123; fax 0181/749-7084).

You can almost always get a room at a deluxe hotel if you're willing to pay the price. But during certain peak periods, including the high season (roughly Apr–Oct), and during certain trade shows, seasonal events, and royal occasions, rooms in the most desirable and most value-oriented hotels may be snatched up early. Book ahead. If you arrive without a reservation, begin your search for a room as early in the day as possible. If you arrive late at night, you may have to take what you can get, often at a much higher price than you'd like to pay.

A NOTE ABOUT PRICES

Unless otherwise noted, prices are published rack prices for rooms with private bath, and include breakfast (often continental instead of English), 17.5% VAT, and a 10% to 15% service charge. (VAT and service charges are always included in the prices quoted in this guide, unless otherwise indicated.) Always ask for a better rate, particularly at the first-class and deluxe hotels (B&Bs generally charge a fixed rate). Be aware that you may not get it, particularly in the busy summer season or during certain trade fairs, when practically every room in the city is booked. But it never hurts to ask. You can sometimes negotiate a 20% to 30% discount in winter. The best ways to save money are to call the hotel directly rather than going through an 800 number or travel agent, by booking off-season or weekends, and by same-day booking—provided it's after 8pm. Knowing how hard it is to fill unbooked rooms at that late hour, you can sometimes negotiate a hefty discount with the reception desk. Parking rates are per night.

1 Best Bets

- **Best Historic Hotel:** Founded by the former manservant to Lord Byron, stylish **Brown's,** 29–34 Albemarle St., W1 (☎ **800/225-5843**), dates back to Victorian times. It's one of London's most genteel hotels, from its legendary afternoon tea to its centenary *Times* clock in the reception area.
- **Best for Business Travelers:** For wheeling and dealing, head to the **Langham Hilton,** 1 Portland Place, W1 (☎ **800/445-8667**), Hilton's flagship hotel in Europe. The world's business is seemingly conducted from this nerve center. At times it sounds like the Tower of Babel—and it's humming along just fine.
- **Best for a Romantic Getaway: The Gore,** 189 Queen's Gate, SW7 (☎ **800/637-7200**), has been sheltering lovers both on and off the record since 1892. The place is eccentric and a lot of fun, and the staff doesn't bother you unless you need something. For

nostalgia-accented romance, request the Venus Room—its bed was once owned by Judy Garland.

- **Best Trendy Hotel: The Lanesborough,** 1 Lanesborough Place, Hyde Park Corner, SW1 (☎ **800/999-1828**), is a sumptuous temple of luxury—$1.7 million was spent on each guest room. Not surprisingly, it attracts glitterati galore.

- **Best Lobby for Pretending That You're Rich: The Dorchester,** 53 Park Lane, W1 (☎ **800/727-9820**), has a long promenade with London's largest floral display and rows of faux-marble columns with ornate gilt capitals. Even if you can't afford to stay at this citadel of luxury, come by for traditional afternoon tea.

- **Best Newcomer: The Hempel,** 31–35 Craven Hill Gardens, W2 (☎ **0171/298-9000**), is the latest creation of designer Anouska Hempel, who also gained fame as a hotelier when she opened Blake's, a mandatory stop on the media and celeb circuit. Her newest hotel immediately became one of London's choicest addresses. Jackie O. would've loved it.

- **Best Thoroughly British Ambience:** In a gaslit courtyard in back of St. James's Palace, **Dukes Hotel,** 35 St. James's Place, SW1 (☎ **0171/491-4840**), has all the dignity of an elderly duke. From the bread-and-butter pudding served in the clubby dining room to the staff's impeccable attentions, it's the epitome of what Britain used to be.

- **Best Choice for Traditionalists: The Stafford,** 16–18 St. James's Place, SW1 (☎ **800/535-4800**), takes you back to the Edwardian era like no other hotel—you expect Edward VII and Lily Langtry to check in at any minute. The Stafford practically invented the word "gentlemanly." At first you think it might be one of those exclusive St. James's men's clubs, but women are welcomed too, and might even be called "M'Lady." Much of the interior is in the style of Robert Adam.

- **Best Re-creation of an English Country House:** Tim and Kit— the Kemps, that is—are hoteliers of charm, taste, and sophistication. They were in top form when they combined two Georgian town houses into the **Dorset Square Hotel,** 39–40 Dorset Sq., NW1 (☎ **800/543-4138**). They've created an English country house right in the heart of the city: Gilt-framed paintings, antiques, tapestry cushions, and mahogany bathrooms make you feel warm, cozy, and elegantly refined.

- **Best Service: 22 Jermyn Street,** SW1 (☎ **0171/734-2353**), does more for its guests than any other hotel in London. The owner, a technology buff, even offers information superhighway services to his guests. He also diligently informs you of the hottest and newest restaurants, along with old favorites, the best shopping buys, and even what's hot in theater. The staff doesn't deny any reasonable request—they even grant some unreasonable ones.

- **Best Location:** Creaky, quirky **Fielding Hotel,** Broad Court, Bow Street, WC2 (☎ **0171/497-0064**), is hardly London's finest hotel, but oh, the location! It's in an alleyway in the dead center of Convent Garden. You're in the heart of the real excitement of London, almost opposite the Royal Opera House and with pubs, shops, markets, and restaurants, even street entertainment, just outside your door. Stay here, and London is yours.

- **Best Health Club & Pool: The Savoy,** The Strand, WC2 (☎ **800/223-6800**), has a unique health club—called a Fitness Centre here—with a large swimming pool, built atop the historic Savoy Theatre overlooking the heart of London. For guests looking to tone up or wind down, it's the best gym in central London; the views make it extra-special. There is also a massage room, plus state-of-the-heart health and beauty treatments.

- **Best Moderately Priced Hotel:** Tucked away in the Knightsbridge/Belgravia area is **Diplomat Hotel,** 2 Chesham St., SW1 (☎ **0171/235-1544**), a 1892 town house converted into a charming and graceful small hotel that prides itself on the good value it offers. Personal service is one of its hallmarks; you'll even find a box of chocolates waiting in your room.

- **Best Inexpensive Hotel:** Kensington's **Abbey House,** 11 Vicarage Gate, W8 (☎ **0171/727-2594**), was built in the 1860s on a Victorian square. It's refurbished annually, but still manages to offer one of the best values in London.

- **Best Bed-and-Breakfast:** The **Claverley Hotel,** 13–14 Beaufort Gardens, SW3 (☎ **800/747-0398**), has won awards as the best B&B in London—and they're much deserved. It's tranquil and well located, close to Harrods for that special buy. For breakfast, try the cook's special, the fresh salmon kedgeree.

- **Best Value:** Savvy hotel shoppers seek out **Aston's Budget Studios,** 39 Rosary Gardens, SW7 (☎ **800/525-2810**). The accommodations here range widely in price, and well they should: They run the gamut from basic lodgings to designer suites.

2 The West End Hotels

MAYFAIR
VERY EXPENSIVE

✪ **Brown's Hotel.** 29–34 Albemarle St., London W1X 4BP. ☎ **800/225-5843** or 0171/493-6020. Fax 0171/493-9381. 118 rms, 10 suites. A/C MINIBAR TV TEL. £294–£364 ($470.40–$582.40) double; from £429 ($686.40) suite. AE, DC, MC, V. Tube: Green Park.

Almost every year a hotel sprouts up trying to create an English country house ambience with Chippendale and chintz; this quintessential town-house hotel watches these upstarts come and go, and always comes out on top. This fine traditional hotel was founded by James Brown, a former manservant of Lord Byron's, who wanted to create a dignified, clublike place for gentlemen. He opened the doors of Brown's in 1837, the same year Queen Victoria took the throne.

Brown's, which occupies 11 historic houses just off Berkeley Square, is still a thorough realization of its founder's vision. Old-fashioned comfort is dispensed with courtesy. A liveried doorman ushers you to an antique reception desk. The guest rooms vary considerably and are a tangible record of the history of England, showing restrained taste in decoration and appointments; even the washbasins are antiques.

Dining/Entertainment: The dining room has a quiet dignity and unmatched service. Afternoon tea is served in the Albemarle Room. In keeping with the atmosphere of the rest of the hotel, the inviting lounges pay homage to the past: They include the Roosevelt Room (Theodore Roosevelt spent his honeymoon at Brown's in 1886), the Rudyard Kipling Room (the famous author was a frequent visitor), and the paneled St. George's Bar.

Services: Room service (24 hours), dry cleaning, laundry, baby-sitting.

Facilities: Car-rental agency, men's hairdresser.

Claridge's. Brook St., London W1A 2JQ. ☎ **800/223-6800** or 0171/629-8860. Fax 0171/499-2210. 132 rms, 65 suites. A/C MINIBAR TV TEL. £255–£280 ($408–$448) double; £410 ($656) junior suite; from £550 ($880) suite. AE, DC, MC, V. Tube: Bond Street.

This is a prime choice for traditionalists. Although other upper-crust addresses, like the Connaught, conjure up images of Empire, nobody does it better than Claridge's, which has cocooned royal visitors in discreet elegance since the time of the Battle of Waterloo. This is stuffy British formality at its appealing best: As a reviewer once wrote, the "staff here will never try to be your friends"—as they might at, say, the Dorchester.

The hotel took on its present modest exterior in 1898. Inside, art-deco decor was added in the 1930s; much of it still exists agreeably alongside antiques and TVs. The guest rooms are spacious, many having generous-size baths complete with dressing rooms and other extras. The emphasis is on old-fashioned room layouts instead of modern comforts, so you may feel embarrassed if you check in without your valet, à la Prince Charles.

Dining/Entertainment: Excellent food is stylishly served in the intimacy of the Causerie, renowned for its lunchtime smörgåsbord and pretheater suppers, and the more formal Restaurant, with its English and French specialties. The strains of the Hungarian Quartet, a Claridge's institution since 1902, can be heard in the adjacent foyer during lunch and dinner.

Services: Concierge, room service (24 hours), laundry, baby-sitting, secretarial services, valet, on-call physician, currency exchange.

Facilities: Men and women have use of separate nearby health clubs. Guests of the hotel with a recognized golf handicap (30 for women, 20 for men) may play unlimited golf (complimentary) at Berkshire's Wentworth Golf Club. Tennis provided at Vanderbilt Club in West London. Travel and theater desk, salon.

✪ **The Dorchester.** 53 Park Lane, London W1A 2HJ. ☎ **800/727-9820** or 0171/629-8888. Fax 0171/409-0114. 192 rms, 52 suites. A/C MINIBAR TV TEL. £265–£295 ($424–$472) double; from £400 ($640) suite. AE, DC, MC, V. Tube: Hyde Park Corner.

This is the best hotel in London today. It has all the elegance of Claridge's or the Connaught, but without the upper-crust attitudes that can verge on snobbery. The Lanesborough is also a premier address, but it doesn't have the time-honored experience of "The Dorch," which has maintained a tradition of fine comfort and cuisine since it opened its doors in 1931.

Breaking from the neoclassical tradition, the most ambitious architects of the era designed a building of reinforced concrete clothed in terrazzo slabs. Within you'll find a 1930s take on Regency motifs: The monumental arrangements of flowers and the elegance of the gilded-cage promenade seem appropriate for a diplomatic reception, yet they convey a kind of sophisticated comfort in which guests from all over the world feel at ease.

The Dorchester boasts guest rooms outfitted with linen sheets, all the electronic gadgetry you'd expect from a world-class hotel, and

Hotels & Restaurants from Mayfair to Leicester Square

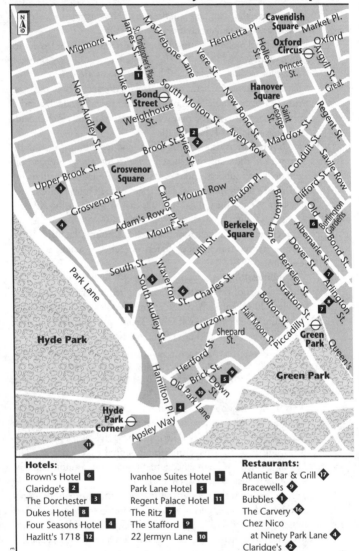

Hotels:

Brown's Hotel **6**
Claridge's **2**
The Dorchester **3**
Dukes Hotel **8**
Four Seasons Hotel **4**
Hazlitt's 1718 **12**

Ivanhoe Suites Hotel **1**
Park Lane Hotel **5**
Regent Palace Hotel **11**
The Ritz **7**
The Stafford **9**
22 Jermyn Lane **10**

Restaurants:

Atlantic Bar & Grill **17**
Bracewells **9**
Bubbles **1**
The Carvery **16**
Chez Nico
  at Ninety Park Lane **4**
Claridge's **2**
Cork & Bottle Wine Bar **19**

P3-0413

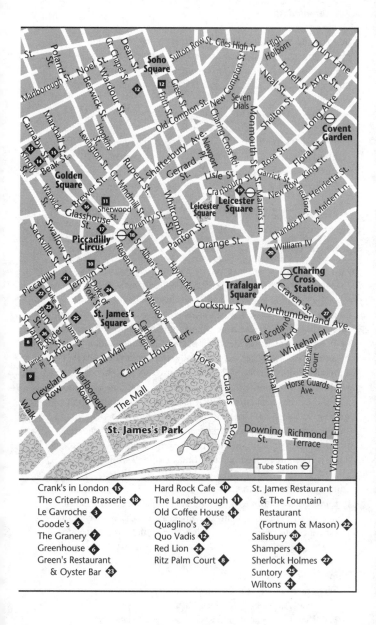

Crank's in London 🔶15	Hard Rock Cafe 🔶10	St. James Restaurant
The Criterion Brasserie 🔶18	The Lanesborough 🔶11	& The Fountain
Le Gavroche 🔶3	Old Coffee House 🔶14	Restaurant
Goode's 🔶5	Quaglino's 🔶26	(Fortnum & Mason) 🔶22
The Granery 🔶7	Quo Vadis 🔶12	Salisbury 🔶20
Greenhouse 🔶6	Red Lion 🔶24	Shampers 🔶13
Green's Restaurant	Ritz Palm Court 🔶8	Sherlock Holmes 🔶27
& Oyster Bar 🔶23		Suntory 🔶25
		Wiltons 🔶21

double- and triple-glazed windows to keep out noise, along with plump armchairs, cherry-wood furnishings, and in many cases, four-poster beds. The bathrooms are equally stylish, with mottled Italian marble and Lalique-style sconces. The best rooms open onto views of Hyde Park.

Dining/Entertainment: The hotel's restaurant, The Grill Room, is among the finest dining establishments in London, and the Dorchester Bar is a legendary meeting place. The hotel also offers Cantonese cuisine at The Oriental, London's most exclusive—and expensive—Chinese restaurant.

Services: Room service (24 hours), dry cleaning, laundry, medical service.

Facilities: One of the best-outfitted health clubs in London, the Dorchester Spa; exclusive nightclub; barbershop; hairdresser.

Four Seasons Hotel. (Formerly the Inn at the Park.) Hamilton Place, Park Lane, London W1A 1AZ. ☎ **800/332-3442** or 0171/499-0888. Fax 0171/493-1895. 227 rms, 27 suites. A/C MINIBAR TV TEL. £285–£295 ($456–$472) double; £375–£400 ($600–$640) conservatory double; from £695 ($1,112) suite. AE, DC, MC, V. Parking £15.50 ($24.80). Tube: Hyde Park Corner.

This deluxe hotel has captured the imagination of glamourmongers the world over ever since it was inaugurated by Princess Alexandra in 1970; its clientele includes heads of state, superstars, and top-brass business execs. It sits behind a tastefully modern facade, occupying a premier location in one of the most exclusive neighborhoods in the world, directly opposite its major competitors, the London Hilton and the Inter-Continental—but it has better food, better rooms, more style, and more taste and refinement than either of its rivals. Inside, acres of superbly crafted paneling and opulent but conservative decor create the impression that the hotel is far older than it is. The guest rooms are large and beautifully outfitted with well-chosen chintz, reproductions, plush upholstery, and dozens of well-concealed electronic extras.

Dining/Entertainment: Both restaurants have an alluring atmosphere, particularly the highly acclaimed Four Seasons, where the finest wines and continental specialties dazzle guests at lunch and at dinner. The less expensive Lanes Restaurant is popular with London's business community. Wellington would have felt right at home in the Cocktail Bar.

Services: Room service (24 hours), laundry, baby-sitting, business services available around the clock, valet.

Facilities: Conservatory fitness club with all the latest equipment, garden, car-rental agency, theater-reservations desk, quality shops.

⭘ **Park Lane Hotel.** Piccadilly, London W1Y 8BX. ☎ **800/325-3535** or 0171/499-6321. Fax 0171/499-1965. 308 rms, 42 suites. MINIBAR TV TEL. £230 ($368) double; from £300 ($480) suite. AE, DC, MC, V. Parking £26 ($41.60). Tube: Hyde Park Corner or Green Park.

The most traditional of the Park Lane mansions and once the lone holdout against chain management, the Park Lane Hotel was sold in 1996 (at least 95% of it, anyway) to the Sheraton Corporation, which upgraded it but has maintained its quintessential British character. Today, its Silver Entrance remains an art deco marvel that has been used as a backdrop in many films, including the classic BBC miniseries *Brideshead Revisited*.

Designed in a U shape, with a view overlooking Green Park, the hotel offers luxurious accommodations that are a surprisingly good deal—they're among the least expensive on Park Lane. Many of the suites have marble fireplaces and original marble bathrooms. The rooms have benefited from an impressive refurbishment—they're larger, and the decor is lighter in tone. All have double-glazed windows to block out noise.

Dining/Entertainment: The hotel's award-winning restaurant, Bracewells (reviewed in chapter 4), adjoins Bracewells Bar, one of London's most charming cocktail lounges, a stylish rendezvous with a talented evening pianist. Less expensive than Bracewells is the still-very-charming Brasserie, serving French cuisine. A harpist plays in The Palm Court Lounge every Sunday.

Services: Concierge, room service (24 hours), dry cleaning, laundry, baby-sitting, valet.

Facilities: Fitness center, business center, barbershop, women's salon, gift and newspaper shop, safety-deposit boxes, and Daniele Ryman Aromatherapy Shop.

INEXPENSIVE

Ivanhoe Suite Hotel. 1 St. Christopher's Place, Barrett St. Piazza, London W1M 5HB. ☎ **0171/935-1047.** Fax 0171/224-0563. 8 rms. TV. £65–£72 ($104–$115.20). Rates include continental breakfast. AE, DC, MC, V. Tube: Bond Street.

Serious shoppers flock to this little hidden discovery uniquely located in a part of town off Oxford Street that's not known for its hotels. Situated above a restaurant on a pedestrian street of boutiques and restaurants, and close to the shops of New and Old Bond streets, this town-house hotel has attractively furnished singles and doubles, each with a sitting area. Each stylish room has its own entry security video and beverage-making facilities along with a fridge/bar, plus a wide selection of video tapes. Breakfast is served in the downstairs restaurant, and you can stop off for a nightcap at the corner pub, a real neighborhood local.

MARYLEBONE
VERY EXPENSIVE

✪ **The Langham Hilton.** 1 Portland Place, London W1N 4JA. ☎ **800/445-8667** or 0171/636-1000. Fax 0171/323-2340. 462 rms, 20 suites. A/C MINIBAR TV TEL. £220–£255 ($352–$408) double; £320–£340 ($512–$544) executive room; from £550 ($880) suite. Rates include breakfast. AE, DC, MC, V. Parking £21 ($33.60). Tube: Oxford Circus.

When this extremely well-located hotel was inaugurated in 1865 by the Prince of Wales, its was a suitably fashionable address for dozens of aristocratic squires seeking respite from their country estates. After it was bombed in World War II, it languished as dusty office space for the BBC until the early 1990s, when Hilton International took it over. Its restoration was painstaking; today, it's Hilton's European flagship: The Langham's public rooms reflect the power and majesty of the British Empire at its apex. Guest rooms are somewhat less opulent, but they're still attractively furnished and comfortable, featuring French provincial furniture and red-oak trim. And the location is still terrific: within easy reach of Mayfair and Soho restaurants and theaters, and Oxford and Regent Street shopping; Regent's Park is just blocks away.

Dining/Entertainment: Vodka, caviar, and champagne flow liberally at the Tsar's Russian Bar and Restaurant. Drinks are served in the Chukka Bar, a re-creation of a private polo club. The most upscale restaurant is a high-ceilinged Victorian fantasy called Memories of the Empire, serving patriotic nostalgia and cuisine from the far corners of the British Commonwealth. Afternoon tea is served amid the potted palms of the Edwardian-style Palm Court.

Services: Concierge, room service (24 hours).

Facilities: Health club, business center, beauty salon.

EXPENSIVE

✪ **Dorset Square Hotel.** 39–40 Dorset Sq., London NW1 6QN. ☎ **800/553-6674** or 0171/723-7874. Fax 0171/724-3328. 35 rms, 2 junior suites. MINIBAR TV TEL. £120–£175 ($192–$280) double; £175 ($280) junior suite. AE, MC, V. Tube: Baker Street or Marylebone.

Situated in a lovely Regency square steps away from Regent's Park, this is one of London's best and most stylish "house hotels," overlooking Thomas Lord's first cricket pitch. Hot hoteliers Tim and Kit Kemp have designed the interior of these two Georgian town houses in a comfy mix of antiques, reproductions, and chintz that will make you feel like you're in an elegant private home. All of the impressive guest rooms come with marble baths; about half are air-conditioned. They're all decorated in a personal yet extravagantly beautiful style—the owners are interior decorators known for their taste, which is often bold and daring.

Dining/Entertainment: The menu at the Potting Shed changes seasonally and features the best of English cuisine. The restaurant occupies an old servants' hall, with a *trompe l'oeil* mural of a cricket pitch and a sisal-decked floor.

Services: Room service (24 hours), laundry, baby-sitting. You can ride in the owner's chauffeured vintage Bentley for a fee; it'll make you feel like Norma Desmond in *Sunset Boulevard.*

MODERATE

✪ **Durrants Hotel.** George St., London W1H 6BJ. ☎ **0171/935-8131.** Fax 0171/487-3510. 96 rms, 3 suites. TV TEL. £115–£125 ($184–$200) double; £165 ($264) family room for 3; from £235 ($376) suite. AE, MC, V. Tube: Bond Street.

Established in 1789 off Manchester Square, this historic hotel with its Georgian-detailed facade is snug, cozy, and traditional—almost like a poor man's Brown's. We find it one of the most quintessentially English of all London hotels, and a soothing retreat on a cold, rainy day. In the hundred years that the Miller family has owned the hotel, several neighboring houses have been incorporated into the original structure. A walk through the pine- and mahogany-paneled public rooms is like stepping back into another time: You'll even find an 18th-century letter-writing room. The rooms are rather bland except for elaborate cove moldings and very comfortable furnishings; some are air-conditioned. Alas, all of them are just too small.

The hotel restaurant serves full afternoon tea and a satisfying French or traditional English cuisine in one of the most beautiful Georgian rooms in the neighborhood. The less formal breakfast room is ringed with 19th-century political cartoons by a noted Victorian artist. The pub, a neighborhood favorite, has Windsor chairs, an open fireplace, and decor that hasn't changed much in 2 centuries. Services include 24-hour room service, laundry, and baby-sitting.

INEXPENSIVE

Edward Lear Hotel. 28–30 Seymour St., London W1H 5WD. ☎ **0171/402-5401.** Fax 0171/706-3766. 31 rms (8 with bath), 4 suites. TV TEL. £60 ($96) double without bath, £79.50 ($127.20) double with bath; from £85 ($136) suite. Rates include English breakfast. DC, MC, V. Tube: Marble Arch.

This popular hotel 1 block from Marble Arch is made all the more desirable by the bouquets of fresh flowers in the public rooms. It occupies a pair of brick town houses, both of which date from 1780. The western house was the London home of the 19th-century artist and poet Edward Lear, famous for his nonsense verse; his illustrated limericks adorn the walls of one of the sitting rooms. Steep stairs lead up to the cozy rooms, which are fairly small but comfortable. One major drawback: This is an extremely noisy part of London. Rooms in the rear are quieter.

Kenwood House Hotel. 114 Gloucester Place, London W1H 3DB. ☎ **0171/935-3473.** Fax 0171/224-0582. 16 rms (9 with bath). TV. £44 ($70.40) double without bath; £56 ($89.60) double with bath; £64 ($102.40) triple without bath; £70 ($112) family room for 4 with bath. Rates include English breakfast. AE, MC, V. Tube: Baker Street.

This 1812 Adam-style town house was a family home until 1942, when the owner's two sons died in the war. Disheartened, the owner sold it to the British army, which used it to billet officers. Now converted into a small hotel (run by English-born Arline Woutersz and her Dutch husband, Bryan), it's a historical landmark; the front balcony is said to be original. Guests gather in the mirrored lounge with its antimacassars in place, just as they were in Victoria's day. Most of the basically furnished bedrooms were upgraded and restored in 1993. Some rooms have private baths; on every floor are spick-and-span modern bathrooms with showers. Baby-sitting can be arranged.

Regency Hotel. 19 Nottingham Place, London W1M 3FF. ☎ **0171/486-5347.** Fax 0171/224-6057. 20 rms. MINIBAR TV TEL. £79 ($126.40) double; £95 ($152) family room. AE, CB, DC, MC, V. Tube: Baker Street or Regent's Park.

This centrally located hotel was originally built along with most of its neighbors in the late 1800s. Although it has functioned as some kind of hotel since the 1940s, in 1991 it was gutted and tastefully renovated into its upgraded present format.

One of the better hotels on the street, it offers simple, conservatively decorated modern bedrooms scattered over four floors, and a breakfast room set in what used to be the cellar. Each room has a radio, hair dryer, trouser press, and ironing board. Room service is available. The neighborhood is protected as a historic district, and Marble Arch, Regent's Park, and Baker Street all lie within a 12-minute walk.

ST. JAMES'S
VERY EXPENSIVE

✪ **Dukes Hotel.** 35 St. James's Place, London SW1A 1NY. ☎ **800/381-4702** or 0171/491-4840. Fax 0171/493-1264. 64 rms, 12 suites. A/C TV TEL. £175–£215 ($280–$344) double; from £225 ($360) suite. AE, DC, MC, V. Parking £35 ($56). Tube: Green Park.

Dukes provides elegance without ostentation in what was presumably someone's Upstairs-Downstairs town house. Along with its nearest competitors, the Stafford and 22 Jermyn Street, it caters to those looking for charm, style, and tradition. A hotel since 1908 (and last renovated in 1994), it stands in a quiet courtyard off St. James's Street with turn-of-the-century gas lamps that create the appropriate mood. Each well-furnished guest room is decorated in the style of a particular English period, ranging from Regency to Edwardian. All rooms are equipped with marble baths, satellite TV, and private bar. A short walk away are Buckingham Palace, St. James's Palace, and the Houses of Parliament. Shoppers will be near Bond Street and Piccadilly, and literature buffs will be interested to note that Oscar Wilde lived and wrote at St. James's Place for a time.

Dining/Entertainment: Dukes Restaurant is small, tasteful, and elegant, combining classic British and continental cuisine. The hotel also has a clublike bar, which is known for its rare collection of vintage ports, armagnacs, and cognacs.

Services: Even though it's claustrophobically small—it was once described as England's smallest castle—Dukes offers full hotel services, including room service (24 hours), car-rental and ticket services, and photocopying and typing services.

Facilities: Access to nearby health club.

The Ritz. 150 Piccadilly, London W1V 9DG. ☎ **800/525-4800** or 0171/493-8181. Fax 0171/493-2687. 116 rms, 14 suites. MINIBAR TV TEL. £225–£325 ($360–$520) double; from £525 ($840) suite. Children under 12 stay free in parents' room. AE, DC, MC, V. Parking £40 ($64). Tube: Green Park.

Built in the French Renaissance style and opened by César Ritz in 1906, this hotel overlooking Green Park is synonymous with luxury: Gold-leafed molding, marble columns, and potted palms abound, and a gold-leafed statue, *La Source,* adorns the fountain of the oval-shaped Palm Court. After a major restoration, this hotel is better than ever. New carpeting and air-conditioning have been installed in the guest rooms, and an overall polishing has returned much of the Ritz's original splendor. Still, this Ritz lags far behind the much grander one in Paris (to which this hotel is not affiliated). The *belle époque* guest rooms, each with its own character, are spacious and comfortable; most are air-conditioned. Many have marble fireplaces, elaborate gilded plasterwork, and a decor of soft pastel hues. All have radios, and in-house movies are available.

Dining/Entertainment: The Ritz is still the most fashionable place in London to meet for afternoon tea. The Ritz Restaurant, one of the loveliest dining rooms in the world, has already been faithfully restored to its original splendor. Service is efficient yet unobtrusive, and the tables are spaced to allow the most private of conversations (perhaps the reason Edward and Mrs. Simpson dined here so frequently before they married). The Palm Court serves coffee and breakfast, and the formal Louis XVI restaurant provides lunch and dinner meals.

Services: Concierge, room service (24 hours), laundry, turndown, in-room massage, twice-daily maid service, baby-sitting, express checkout, valet.

Facilities: Access to nearby St. James's Health Club.

✪ **The Stafford.** 16–18 St. James's Place, London SW1A 1NJ. ☎ **800/525-4800** or 0171/493-0111. Fax 0171/493-7121. 67 rms, 7 suites. A/C TV TEL. £205–£245 ($328–$392) double; from £310 ($496) suite. AE, DC, MC, V. Tube: Green Park.

This hotel is famous for its American Bar, its clubby St. James's address, its discretion, and the warmth of its Edwardian decor. The Stafford was built in the late 19th century on a cul-de-sac off one of London's most centrally located and busiest neighborhoods; it's reached via St. James's Place or by a cobble-covered courtyard originally designed as a mews and known today as the Blue Ball Yard. The recently refurbished hotel has retained a country-house atmosphere, with touches of antique charm and modern amenities. It's not the Ritz, but the Stafford competes well with Dukes and 22 Jermyn Street (both highly recommendable as well) for a tasteful, discerning clientele. All of the guest rooms are individually decorated, reflecting the hotel's origins as a private home. Many singles contain queen-size beds. A handful of the hotel's newest and plushest accommodations in the historically restored stable mews require a walk across the yard.

Dining/Entertainment: Classic international dishes are prepared from select fresh ingredients at the elegant Stafford Restaurant, lit with handsome chandeliers and accented with flowers, candles, and white linen. The famous American Bar, which brings to mind the memento-packed library of an English country house, is an especially cozy place serving light meals and cocktails.

Services: Concierge, room service (24 hours), laundry, baby-sitting, secretarial service.

Facilities: Privileges at a nearby health club.

✪ **22 Jermyn Street.** 22 Jermyn St., London SW1Y 6HL. ☎ **800/682-7808** or 0171/734-2353. Fax 0171/734-0750. 5 rms, 13 suites. MINIBAR TV TEL. £200 ($320) double; from £240 ($384) suite. AE, DC, MC, V. Valet parking £24 ($38.40). Tube: Piccadilly Circus.

This is London's premier town-house hotel, a gem of elegance and discretion. Set behind a facade of gray stone with neoclassical details, this structure, only 50 yards from Piccadilly, was originally built in 1870 as an apartment house for English gentlemen doing business in London. Since 1915, it has been administrated by three generations of the Togna family, whose most recent scion closed it for a radical restoration in 1990. Now a chic boutique hotel, 22 Jermyn offers an interior filled with greenery, the kind of art you might find in an elegant private home, and the best "information superhighway services" of any hotel in London. This hotel doesn't have the bar or restaurant facilities of The Stafford or Dukes, but its rooms are even more richly appointed than its main competitors. They're done in traditional English style, with masses of fresh flowers and chintz.

Services: Concierge, room service (24 hours), dry cleaning, laundry, baby-sitting, secretarial services, fax, videophones, and a weekly newsletter that keeps guests up to date with restaurants, theater, and exhibitions.

Facilities: Video library, CD-ROM library, Internet access, access to a nearby health club.

PICCADILLY CIRCUS
INEXPENSIVE

Regent Palace Hotel. 12 Sherwood St., London W1A 4BZ. ☎ **0171/734-7000**. Fax 0171/734-6435. 950 rms (none with bath). TV TEL. £85 ($136) double. For stays of 2 or more nights, £68–£88 ($108.80–$140.80) per person depending on the time of year. Rates include English breakfast. AE, DC, MC, V. Tube: Piccadilly Circus.

The Regency Palace, a major focal point since it was built in 1915 at the edge of Piccadilly Circus, is one of the largest hotels in Europe, a beacon for those who want to be near the bright lights of London's theaterland. The shared facilities in the hallways are adequate, though, and each simply furnished room has a sink with hot and cold running water and coffee- and tea-making facilities.

The hotel's Original Carvery is a good (but expensive) place to dine; The Dome bistro is open for pretheater meals. Drinks are served in the Half Sovereign and the Planters bars. Coffee, sandwiches, and snacks are available in Antonio's Coffee Bar. There are souvenir and gift shops, a bureau de change, and a theater-booking agency on the premises.

SOHO
EXPENSIVE

Hazlitt's 1718. 6 Frith St., London W1V 5TZ. ☎ **0171/434-1771.** Fax 0171/439-1524. 22 rms, 1 suite. £138 ($220.80) double, £185 ($296) suite. AE, DC, MC, V. Tube: Leicester Square or Tottenham Court Road.

This gem, housed in three historic homes on Soho Square—the most fashionable address in London 2 centuries ago—is one of London's best small hotels. Built in 1718, the hotel is named for William Hazlitt, who founded the Unitarian church in Boston and wrote four volumes on the life of his hero, Napoléon; the essayist died here in 1830.

Hazlitt's is a favorite with artists, actors, media people, and models. It's eclectic, filled with odds and ends picked up around the country at estate auctions. Some find the Georgian decor a bit Spartan, but the 2,000 original prints hanging on the walls brighten it considerably. Many bedrooms have four-poster beds, and some baths have their original claw-footed tubs (only one unit has a shower). If you can afford it, opt for the elegant Baron Willoughby suite, with its giant four-poster bed and wood-burning fireplace. Some of the floors dip and sway and there's no elevator, but it's all part of the charm. Swinging Soho is at your doorstep; the young, hip staff will be happy to direct you to the local hot spots.

BLOOMSBURY
MODERATE

Academy Hotel. 17–21 Gower St., London WC1E 6HG. ☎ **800/678-3096** or 0171/631-4115. Fax 0171/636-3442. 36 rms, 6 suites. TV TEL. £115 ($184) double; £160 ($256) suite. AE, DC, MC, V. Tube: Tottenham Court Road or Goodge Street.

Right in the heart of London's publishing district, the Academy attracts budding British John Grishams who haven't hit the really big time yet. Although tacky modern rears its ugly head here and there, many of the original architectural details were preserved when these three 1776 Georgian row houses were joined. The hotel was substantially upgraded in the 1990s, with a bath added to every bedroom (whether there was space or not). Grace notes include the glass

Hotels from Bloomsbury to the Strand

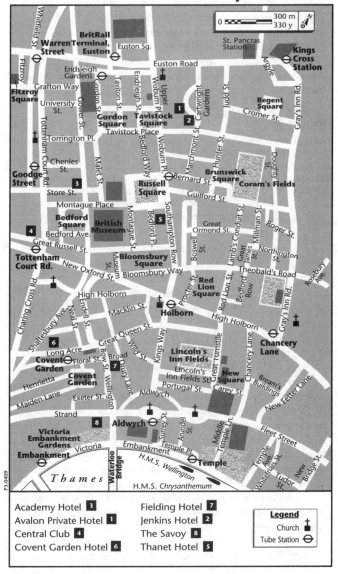

0 ‖‖‖‖‖ 300 m
330 y

Whitfield St.
BritRail Terminal, Euston
Warren Street
Euston Sq.
St. Pancras Station
Kings Cross Station
Fitzroy St.
Endsleigh Gardens
Euston Road
Argyle
Fitzroy Square
Grafton Way
Gordon St.
Taviton St.
Endsleigh St.
Upper Woburn Pl.
Cartwright Gardens
Judd St.
Regent Square
University St.
Gower St.
Gordon Square
Tavistock Square
Marchmont St.
Cromer St.
Grays Inn Rd.
Tottenham Court Rd.
Torrington Pl.
Tavistock Place
Bedford Way
Woburn Pl.
Hunter St.
Brunswick Square
Doughty St.
Chenies St.
Malet St.
Russell Square
Bernard St.
Coram's Fields
Goodge Street
Store St.
Guilford St.
Montague Place
Great Ormond St.
Roger St.
Bedford Square
British Museum
Montague St.
Bedford Pl.
Southampton Row
Boswell St.
Lamb's Conduit St.
Great James St.
Millman St.
Northington St.
Tottenham Court Rd.
Bedford Ave.
Great Russell St.
Bloomsbury Square
Museum St.
Bloomsbury Way
Theobald's Road
Rosebury Ave.
New Oxford St.
Procter St.
Red Lion Square
Red Lion St.
Bedford Row
Grays Inn Rd.
Charing Cross Rd.
High Holborn
Macklin St.
Holborn
High Holborn
Shaftesbury Ave.
Neal St.
Endell St.
Great Queen St.
Kings Way
Great Turnstile
Chancery Lane
Covent Garden
Long Acre
Floral St.
Bow St.
Broad
Wild St.
Lincoln's Inn Fields
Bream's Buildings
Covent Garden
Henrietta
Drury Lane
St. Wellington
Lincoln's Inn Fields
New Square
Carey St.
New Fetter Lane
Maiden Lane
Exeter St.
Aldwych
Portugal St.
Strand
Surrey St.
Arundel St.
Fleet Street
Victoria Embankment Gardens
Aldwych
Middle Temple Ln.
Temple Ave.
New Bridge St.
Embankment
Victoria
Embankment
Temple Pl.
H.M.S. Wellington
Temple
Whitefriars St.
Tudor St.
Waterloo Bridge
Thames
H.M.S. *Chrysanthemum*

P3-0409

Academy Hotel	**3**	Fielding Hotel	**7**
Avalon Private Hotel	**1**	Jenkins Hotel	**2**
Central Club	**4**	The Savoy	**8**
Covent Garden Hotel	**6**	Thanet Hotel	**5**

Legend
† Church
⊖ Tube Station

panels, colonnades, and intricate plaster work on the facade. Rooms are decorated in a neutral style guaranteed not to offend anybody—except maybe by their very blandness—but they're well cared for. The theater district and Covent Garden are within walking distance. Facilities include an elegant bar, a library room, a secluded patio garden, and a restaurant serving French and Swiss food that often attracts business people entertaining their clients.

INEXPENSIVE

Avalon Private Hotel. 46–47 Cartwright Gardens, London WC1H 9EL. ☎ **0171/387-2366.** Fax 0171/387-5810. 28 rms (5 with shower). TV. £51 ($81.60) double without shower, £64 ($102.40) double with shower; £69 ($110.40) triple without shower, £78 ($124.80) triple with shower; £78 ($124.80) quad without shower, £89 ($142.40) quad with shower. Rates include English breakfast. AE, MC, V. Tube: Russell Square, King's Cross, or Euston.

The Avalon was built in 1807 as two Georgian houses, in residential Cartwright Gardens. Guests feel privileged because they have use of a semiprivate garden across the street with tennis courts. Top-floor rooms, often filled with students, are reached via impossibly steep stairs, but bedrooms on the lower levels have easier access. The place obviously didn't hire a decorator; everything is wildly mismatched in the bedrooms and the droopy lounge—but the price is right.

Central Club. 16–22 Great Russell St., London WC1B 3LR. ☎ **0171/636-7512.** Fax 0171/636-5278. 100 rms (none with bath). TV TEL. £61.25 ($98) double; £21.50 ($34.40) per person triple or quad. MC, V. Tube: Tottenham Court Road.

After Sir Edwin Lutyens designed this building, Her Majesty Queen Elizabeth (the Queen Mother) appeared to dedicate it in 1932. It's gone through a lot of rough times since, including the Blitz, but it's still here. If anything, its accommodations are better than ever, having been modernized; they might not get the Laura Ashley seal of approval, but what you get isn't bad. "It's a decent sleep, and quite comfortable at that," a frequent visitor from Devon told us in the lobby. Although still vaguely affiliated with the YWCA, it now functions as a full-fledged hotel and accepts men, women, families, and groups traveling together. Even if the hotel doesn't live up to its motto, "a home away from home"—it's too impersonal for that—it offers well-furnished bedrooms, with adequate hallway showers and baths. Rooms have radios and coffeemakers. Facilities include lounges, coin-operated laundry, hair salon, gym, solarium, and a coffee shop catering to carnivores and vegetarians both.

✪ **The Jenkins Hotel.** 45 Cartwright Gardens, London WC1H 9EH. ☎ **0171/ 387-2067.** Fax 0171/383-3139. 15 rms (6 with bath). TV TEL. £52 ($83.20) double without bath, £62 ($99.20) double with bath; £76 ($121.60) triple with bath. MC, V. Rates include English breakfast. Tube: Euston Station.

Followers of the Agatha Christie TV series *Poirot* might recognize this Cartwright Gardens residence—it was featured in the series. The antiques are gone and the rooms are small, but some of the original charm of the Georgian house remains—enough so that the *London Mail on Sunday* recently proclaimed it one of the "ten best hotel values" in the city. And the location is great: near the British Museum, London University, theaters, and antiquarian book shops. There are some drawbacks—no lift and no reception or sitting room, but it's a place where you can settle in and feel at home.

Thanet Hotel. 8 Bedford Place, London WC1B 5JA. ☎ **0171/636-2869.** Fax 0171/323-6676. 12 rms. TV TEL. £54 ($86.40) single; £71 ($113.60) double; £87 ($139.20) triple; £95 ($152) quad. Rates include English breakfast. MC, V. Tube: Russell Square.

The myriad hotels around Russell Square become peas in a pod at some point, but the Thanet stands out. It no longer charges the same rates it did when it first appeared in *England on $5 a Day,* but it's still a winning choice nonetheless: still a fine address—and an affordable choice—for those who want to be close to the British Museum, theaterland, and Covent Garden. It's a landmark-status building on a quiet Georgian terrace between Russell and Bloomsbury squares; although restored many times over the years, many original features of the house remain. Third-generation hoteliers, the Orchard family offers small, comfortably furnished and decorated rooms—no glaring contrasts in decor here. Amenities include beverage maker, radio, and TV.

COVENT GARDEN
VERY EXPENSIVE

Covent Garden Hotel. 10 Monmouth St., London WC2H 9HB. ☎ **0171/ 806-1000.** Fax 0171/806-1100. 47 rms, 3 suites. A/C MINIBAR TV TEL. £175–£195 ($280–$312) double; £260–£350 ($416–$560) suite. AE, MC, V. Tube: Covent Garden or Leicester Square.

Built as a French-directed hospital around 1850, this building lay derelict for years until it was reconfigured in 1996 by hot hoteliers Tim and Kit Kemp—whose flair for interior design is now legendary—into one of London's most charming boutique hotels, situated in one of the West End's hippest shopping neighborhoods. The Kemps' latest creation epitomizes all that's fine in London town-house hotels; *Travel and Leisure* just called it one of 1997's 25 hottest places to stay in the *world.*

Across from Neal's Yard and behind a bottle-green facade reminiscent of a 19th-century storefront, the hotel has a welcoming lobby outfitted with elaborate marquetry furniture and sweeping draperies, plus two charming restaurants. Upstairs, above a dramatic stone staircase, soundproof bedrooms are lushly outfitted in English style with Asian fabrics, many elaborately adorned with hand-embroidered designs, some with crewel work. Their decorative trademark? Each room has a clothier's mannequin—a lithe female form draped in the fabric that's the predominant theme of that particular room. Each comes with VCR, CD player, two phone lines with voice mail, and marble baths with double vanities and deep soaking tubs. The young, well-mannered staff works hard to please, and succeeds—the friendly concierge even walked blocks in a downpour to hail us a cab.

Dining/Entertainment: The old-fashioned Max's Brasserie serves up very good French-English bistro fare. With high stools at the bar and crisp table linens, it's a chic place for lunch. There's also Nippon Tuk, a Japanese restaurant with a sushi bar offering beautifully presented, high-quality fish.

Services: Concierge, room service (24 hours), secretarial services, valet.

Facilities: Small video library, small gym, office facilities.

INEXPENSIVE

✪ **Fielding Hotel.** 4 Broad Court, Bow St., London WC2B 5QZ. ☎ **0171/ 836-8305.** Fax 0171/497-0064. 26 rms (24 with bath). £85–£95 ($136–$152) double with bath; £130 ($208) triple with bath; £175 ($280) suite for 4. AE, DC, MC, V. Tube: Covent Garden.

One of London's more eccentric hotels, the Fielding is cramped, quirky, and quaint, but an enduring favorite nonetheless. The hotel—named after novelist Henry Fielding of *Tom Jones* fame, who lived in Broad Court—lies on a pedestrian street still lined with 19th-century gas lamps; the Royal Opera House is across the street, and the pubs, shops, and restaurants of lively Covent Garden are just beyond the front door. Rooms are a little less than small, but they're charmingly old-fashioned and traditional. Bathrooms are minuscule, and very few rooms have anything approaching a view; floors dip and sway, and the furnishings and fabrics have known better times—so be duly warned. But with a location like this, in the very heart of London, the Fielding keeps guests coming back; many love the hotel's rickety charm. There's no room service or restaurant, but breakfast is served. Be sure to introduce yourself to Smokey the African Grey parrot in the bar; he's the hotel's oldest resident.

ALONG THE STRAND
VERY EXPENSIVE

✪ **The Savoy.** The Strand, London WC2R 0EU. ☎ **800/223-6800** or 0171/836-4343. Fax 0171/240-6040. 154 rms, 48 suites. A/C MINIBAR TV TEL. £255–£330 ($408–$528) double; from £360 ($576) suite. AE, CB, DC, MC, V. Parking £22 ($35.20). Tube: Charing Cross.

Although not as swank as the Dorchester, this London landmark is the premier address if you want to be in the Strand and Covent Garden area. Impresario Richard D'Oyly Carte built the hotel in 1889 as an annex to his nearby Savoy Theatre, where many Gilbert and Sullivan operettas were originally staged. Eight stories of glazed tiles rising in ponderous dignity between the Strand and the Thames, it dwarfs all of its nearby competition, including the Waldorf at Aldwych and the Howard on Temple Place. Each guest room is uniquely decorated with color-coordinated accessories, solid and comfortable furniture, large closets, and an eclectic blend of antiques, such as gilt mirrors, Queen Anne chairs, and Victorian sofas; 48 have their own sitting rooms. The expensive river-view suites are the most sought after, and for good reason—the views are the best in London.

Dining/Entertainment: The world-famous Savoy Grill has long been popular with the theater crowd; Sarah Bernhardt was a regular. The even more elegant River Restaurant has tables overlooking the Thames; there's dancing to a live band in the evening. The room known as Upstairs specializes in champagne, Chablis, and seafood.

Services: Room service (24 hours), same-day laundry and dry cleaning, nightly turndown, baby-sitting, limousine service.

Facilities: The city's best health club (the pool has fabulous views), hairdresser, news kiosk. Guests also have temporary membership in the exclusive Wentworth Club, a golf and country club on the outskirts of London (proof of handicap required).

WESTMINSTER/VICTORIA
VERY EXPENSIVE

✪ **Goring Hotel.** 15 Beeston Place, Grosvenor Gardens, London SW1W 0JW. ☎ **0171/396-9000.** Fax 0171/834-4393. 73 rms, 3 suites. TV TEL. £170–£215 ($272–$344) double; from £260 ($416) suite. AE, DC, MC, V. Parking £17.50 ($28). Tube: Victoria.

For tradition and location, the Goring is our top pick in the Westminster area. Located just behind Buckingham Palace, it also lies within easy reach of the royal parks, Victoria Station, Westminster Abbey, and the Houses of Parliament. It also happens to offer the finest personal service of all its nearby competitors.

Built in 1910 by O. R. Goring, this was the first hotel in the world to have central heating and a private bath in every room. While no longer on the cutting edge, today's well-furnished guest rooms still offer all the comforts, including refurbished marble baths; many have air-conditioning. The charm of a traditional English country hotel is evoked in the paneled drawing room, where fires crackle in the ornate fireplaces on nippy evenings. The adjoining bar overlooks the rear gardens.

Dining/Entertainment: At the restaurant, the chef uses only the freshest ingredients in his classic English recipes; specialties include medallions of venison with chestnuts, roast boned quail, braised lamb in a rich red-wine sauce, and grilled Dover sole. Afternoon tea is served in the lounge.

Services: Room service (24 hours), valet service.

Facilities: Free use of local health club, laundry, salon.

MODERATE

Tophams Belgravia. 28 Ebury St., London SW1W 0LU. ☎ **0171/730-8147.** Fax 0171/823-5966. 42 rms (23 with bath), 1 suite. TV TEL. £95 ($152) double without bath, £115–£135($184–$216) double with bath; £230 ($368) suite. AE, DC, MC, V. Tube: Victoria.

Tophams came into being in 1937, when five small row houses were interconnected; with its flower-filled window boxes, the place still has a country-house flavor. It was completely renovated in 1997. The petite, informal reception rooms are done in flowery chintzes and nice antiques. All rooms have coffeemakers, hair dryers, and satellite TVs; the best of the bunch are comfortably appointed with private baths and four-poster beds. The restaurant offers both traditional and modern English cooking for lunch and dinner. And the location is great, especially if you're planning to cover a lot of ground by tube or train: It's only a 3-minute walk to Victoria Station.

INEXPENSIVE

Astors Hotel. 110–112 Ebury St., London SW1W 9QD. ☎ **0171/730-3811.** Fax 0171/823-6728. 22 rms (12 with bath). TV. £55 ($88) double without bath, £64 ($102.40) double with bath; £84 ($134.40) triple with bath. Rates include English breakfast. MC, V. Tube: Victoria.

This well-located choice is a stone's throw from Buckingham Palace, and just a 5-minute walk from Victoria's main-line and tube stations.

The brick-fronted Victorian is a good bet for frugal travelers looking for a decent, affordable, and respectable address in pricey London. Although more functional than glamorous, the rooms are satisfactory in every way. Space and furnishings vary greatly, so, if possible, ask to take a little peek before committing yourself to a room (since the hotel is often full, that won't always be possible).

Caswell Hotel. 25 Gloucester St., London SW1V 2DB. ☎ **0171/834-6345.** 18 rms (7 with bath). TV. £50 ($80) double without bath; £70 ($112) double with bath. Rates include English breakfast. MC, V. Tube: Victoria.

The Caswell, run with consideration and thoughtfulness by Mr. and Mrs. Hare, lies on a cul-de-sac that's a calm oasis in an otherwise busy area. The fancy neighbors are all gone—Mozart lived nearby while he completed his first symphony, and that "notorious couple," Harold Nicolson and Vita Sackville-West, are long departed—but this is still a choice address. Beyond the chintz-filled lobby, the decor is understated: There are four floors of well-furnished but not spectacular bedrooms, each with such amenities as hair dryer and beverage maker. How do they explain the success of the place? One staff member said, "This year's guest is next year's business."

✪ **James House/Cartref House.** 108 and 129 Ebury St., London, SW1W 9QD. James House ☎ **0171/730-7338;** Cartref House ☎ **0171/730-6176.** Fax 0171/730-7338. 21 rms (9 with bath). £55 ($88) double without bath, £65 ($104) double with bath; £80 ($128) quad without bath, £90 ($144) quad with bath. MC, V. Tube: Victoria.

Hailed by many publications, including the *Los Angeles Times,* as one of the top 10 B&B choices in London, James House and Cartref House (across the street), deserve their accolades. Derek and Sharon James seem to have real dedication in their work. They're the finest hosts in the area, and they're constantly refurbishing, so everything looks up to date. Each room is individually designed; some of the large ones have bunk beds that make them suitable for families. The English breakfast is so generous that you might end up skipping lunch. There's no elevator, but the happy guests don't seem to mind. Don't worry about which house you're assigned; each one's a winner.

3 In & Around Knightsbridge

VERY EXPENSIVE

✪ **The Beaufort.** 33 Beaufort Gardens, London SW3 1PP. ☎ **800/888-1199** or 0171/584-5252. Fax 0171/589-2834. 21 rms, 7 junior suites. TV TEL. £150–£215 ($240–$344) double; £240 ($384) junior suite. AE, DC, MC, V. Tube: Knightsbridge.

If you'd like to stay in one of London's finest boutique hotels, offering personal service in an elegant, tranquil town-house atmosphere, head to the Beaufort. It's the market leader. Only 200 yards from Harrods, the Beaufort sits on a cul-de-sac behind two Victorian porticoes and an iron fence. Owner Diana Wallis, a TV producer, combined a pair of adjacent houses from the 1870s, ripped out the old decor, and created a stylish hotel of merit and grace; it has the feeling of a private house in the heart of London. You register at a small desk extending off a bay-windowed parlor, then climb the stairway used by the queen of Sweden during her stay. Each guest room is thoughtfully done in a modern color scheme and adorned with several well-chosen paintings by London artists; they come with earphone radios, hair dryers, flowers, and a selection of books. The all-female staff is exceedingly helpful—a definite plus.

Dining/Entertainment: Light meals are available from room service. There's a 24-hour honor bar.

Services: Concierge, baby-sitting, secretarial services, fax machines.

Facilities: Access to nearby health club for a small fee, car rental, theater-ticket service, sightseeing.

The Capital. 22–24 Basil St., London SW3 1AT. ☎ **800/926-3199** in the U.S., or 0171/589-5171. Fax 0171/225-0011. 40 rms, 8 suites. A/C MINIBAR TV TEL. £207–£260 ($331.20–$416) double; from £310 ($496) suite. AE, DC, MC, V. Parking £20 ($32). Tube: Knightsbridge.

One of the most personalized hotels in the West End, this small, modern place is a stone's throw from Harrods. It doesn't have the five-star quality of the nearby Hyatt, but the cuisine is far better than at many of London's more highly rated hotels. With extensive refurbishment, the owner, David Levin, has created a warm town-house ambience; the elegant *fin-de-siècle* decor is matched by the courtesy and professionalism of the staff. The corridors and staircase, lined with original oils, literally function as an art gallery. The guest rooms are tastefully decorated, often with Ralph Lauren furnishings.

Dining/Entertainment: The Capital Restaurant was refurbished in the early 1990s in a vaguely French style, with David Linley panels for the windows (Linley is Princess Margaret's son). Under the direction of chef Phillip Britton, it's among the finest restaurants in London, specializing in seafood and offering exquisitely prepared French cuisine.

Services: Room service (24 hours), laundry.

EXPENSIVE

Basil Street Hotel. 8 Basil St., London SW3 1AH. ☎ **0171/581-3311.** Fax 0171/581-3693. 90 rms (80 with bath). TV TEL. £120–£180 ($192–$288) double. Children under 16 stay free in parents' room. AE, DC, MC, V. Parking £27 ($43.20) at 24-hour lot nearby. Tube: Knightsbridge.

The Basil, an Edwardian charmer totally unmarred by moderniza-tion, has long been a favorite for those who make an annual pilgrim-age to Harrods—"just 191 steps away"—and the Chelsea Flower Show (Harvey Nichols is also nearby). Several spacious, comfortable lounges are furnished in a fitting style and accented with 18th- and 19th-century accessories; off the many rambling corridors are smaller sitting rooms. Bedrooms are well maintained, but furnished in a rather standard way; some are air-conditioned (a few singles are without baths).

In the restaurant, candlelight and piano music re-create the atmosphere of a bygone era. The Parrot Club, a rendezvous reserved only for women, is ideal for afternoon tea. There's 24-hour room service.

Dining/Entertainment: Their restaurant ("The Dining Room") has a live pianist, and is open for lunch and dinner daily. There's an adjacent lounge and bar, and the ladies' tearoom, the Parrot Club.

Services: 24-hour room service, baby-sitting, concierge, laundry.

Facilities: Small-scale conference rooms, access to a neighbor-hood health club.

✪ **Claverley Hotel.** 13–14 Beaufort Gardens, London SW3 1PS. ☎ **800/747-0398** or 0171/589-8541. Fax 0171/584-3410. 25 rms (23 with bath), 7 suites. TV TEL £110–£190 ($176–$304) double with bath; from £190 ($304) suite. Rates include English breakfast. AE, MC, V. Tube: Knightsbridge.

Set on a quiet cul-de-sac in Knightsbridge a few blocks from Harrods, this small, cozy place has been called the best B&B in Lon-don. Awarded the British Tourist Authority's Certificate of Distinc-tion for Bed-and-Breakfast Hotels in 1988, the Claverley continues to maintain the high standards that garnered it such praise. Reno-vated in 1995 and 1996, it's tastefully accented with Georgian-era accessories; the appealing lounge has 19th-century oil portraits, a Regency fireplace, and a collection of elegant antiques and leather-covered sofas—much like what you'd find in a private country house. Most guest rooms have Victorian-inspired wallpaper, wall-to-wall carpeting, and upholstered armchairs, plus marble bathrooms with power showers and hair dryers (some singles don't have ensuite facilities). The full English breakfast—with bacon, tomato, eggs, and

Hotels from Knightsbridge to Earl's Court

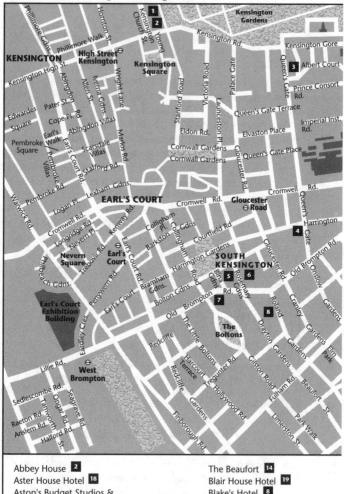

Abbey House **2**

Aster House Hotel **18**

Aston's Budget Studios &
  Aston's Designer Studios & Suites **6**

Basil Street Hotel **9**

The Beaufort **14**

Blair House Hotel **19**

Blake's Hotel **8**

The Capital **11**

Claverley Hotel **13**

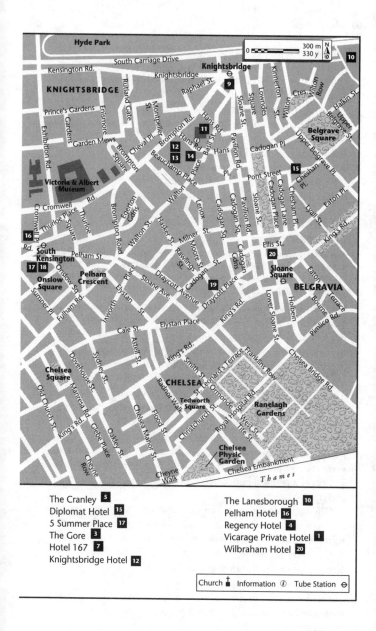

The Cranley 5		The Lanesborough 10
Diplomat Hotel 15		Pelham Hotel 16
5 Summer Place 17		Regency Hotel 4
The Gore 3		Vicarage Private Hotel 1
Hotel 167 7		Wilbraham Hotel 20
Knightsbridge Hotel 12		

Church ⛪ Information ⓘ Tube Station ⊖

Cumberland sausage, as well as homemade waffles with maple syrup and the cook's specialty, fresh salmon kedgeree—is outstanding. Complimentary tea, coffee, hot chocolate, and cookies are available around the clock in the lounge. Laundry service is available.

Dining/Entertainment: None, other than breakfast, and a lounge where nonalcoholic drinks, including tea, coffee, and cocoa, are available 24 hours a day.

Services: The reception staff provides limited concierge services: laundry, acquisition of theater tickets, etc.

Facilities: Residents receive temporary membership at a nearby health club, l'Aquila, a former favorite of the late Princess Diana.

IN NEARBY BELGRAVIA
VERY EXPENSIVE

✪ **The Lanesborough.** 1 Lanesborough Place, London SW1X 7TA. ☎ **800/ 999-1828** or 0171/259-5599. Fax 0171/259-5606. 49 rms, 46 suites. A/C MINIBAR TV TEL. £285–£375 ($456–$600) double; from £420 ($672) suite. AE, DC, MC, V. Parking £20 ($32). Tube: Hyde Park Corner.

One of London's grandest hotels was created from the dreary hospital wards that Florence Nightingale made famous. This Regency-style four-story hotel vies with the Dorchester for sophistication (although it falls short of the Dorch's time-honored experience). When Rosewood Hotels and Resorts (known for managing top hotels like the Bel-Air in Los Angeles and Dallas's Mansion on Turtle Creek) upgraded the building into a luxury hotel, most of the Georgian details were retained. The guest rooms are as opulent and antique-stuffed as the public spaces; each has electronic sensors to alert the staff as to when a resident is in or out, a CD player, VCR, personal safe, fax machine, 24-channel satellite TV, a bathroom with every conceivable amenity, triple glazing on the windows, and the services of a personal butler. Security is tight—there are at least 35 surveillance cameras.

Dining/Entertainment: The Conservatory is an elegant restaurant with decor inspired by the Chinese, Indian, and Gothic motifs of the Brighton Pavilion. The Library Bar—which opens into a Regency-era hideaway, charmingly named "The Withdrawing Room"—re-creates the atmosphere of an elegant private club.

Services: Personal butlers, concierges.

Facilities: Small fitness studio, exercise equipment (Stairmasters, stationary bicycles) can be delivered directly to your room; business center, car rental.

MODERATE

✪ **Diplomat Hotel.** 2 Chesham St., London SW1X 3DT. ☎ **0171/235-1544.** Fax 0171/259-6153. 27 rms. TV TEL. £115–£145 ($184–$232) double. Rates include English buffet breakfast. AE, CB, DC, MC, V. Tube: Sloane Square or Knightsbridge.

This is a small, reasonably priced hotel in an otherwise prohibitively expensive neighborhood. Only minutes from Harrods, it was originally built in 1882 as a private residence by the noted architect Thomas Cubbitt, and it's very well appointed: The registration desk is framed by the sweep of a partially gilded circular staircase; above it, cherubs gaze down from a Regency-era chandelier. The staff is helpful, well-mannered, and discreet. The high-ceilinged guest rooms are tastefully done in a Victorian style; many were renovated in 1996. Amenities include a massage service, business center, afternoon tea, and a snack menu available daily 1 to 8:30pm.

4 Chelsea

MODERATE

Blair House Hotel. 34 Draycott Place, London SW3 2SA. ☎ **0171/581-2323.** Fax 0171/823-7752. 11 rms. TV TEL. £105–£115 ($168–$184) double. Extra bed £18 ($28.80). Rates include continental breakfast. AE, DC, MC, V. Tube: Sloane Square.

If you can't afford a luxury hotel, this comfortable B&B–style hotel in the heart of Chelsea near Sloane Square is a good alternative. An older building of some architectural interest, it's been completely refurbished inside. The rooms are individually decorated, but may have too many flowery prints for most tastes. They all come with such amenities as coffeemakers, TV, hair dryer, and trouser press. Although most singles are small, some rooms are spacious enough to accommodate four. Baby-sitting and laundry can be arranged. Only breakfast is served. If you're bothered by noise, ask for a quieter room in the back.

INEXPENSIVE

Wilbraham Hotel. 1–5 Wilbraham Place (off Sloane St.), London SW1X 9AE. ☎ **0171/730-8296.** Fax 0171/730-6815. 53 rms, 6 suites. TV TEL. £86–£88 ($137.60–$140.80) double; from £89 ($142.40) suite. Rates include English breakfast. No credit cards. Parking £12 ($19.20). Tube: Sloane Square.

This dyed-in-the-wool British hotel is set on a quiet residential street, just a few hundred yards from Sloane Square. Occupying three Victorian town houses, it's the kind of place you'd expect Margaret Rutherford to stay, were she alive today. Sure, it's faded a bit, but the traditionally furnished, wood-paneled bedrooms are well maintained and have fireplaces and leaded-glass windows. There are even heated towel racks in the bathroom—a lovely comfort on a cold, gray London morning. The best double—certainly the most spacious—is no. 1. There's an attractive old-fashioned lounge where you can order drinks, simple lunches, and traditional English dinners.

5 Kensington

VERY EXPENSIVE

✪ **Blake's Hotel.** 33 Roland Gardens, London SW7 3PF. ☎ **800/926-3173** or 0171/370-6701. Fax 0171/373-0442. 41 rms, 9 suites. MINIBAR TV TEL. £180–£340 ($288–$544) double; from £540 ($864) suite. AE, DC, MC, V. Parking £18 ($28.80). Tube: South Kensington or Gloucester Road.

This opulent and highly individual creation of actress Anouska Hempel Weinberg is one of London's best small hotels. No expense was spared in converting this former row of Victorian town houses into one of the city's most original hotels. It's now Oriental nights down in old Kensington: The individually decorated, elaborately appointed rooms boast such treasures and touches as Venetian glassware, cloth-covered walls, swagged draperies, even the Empress Josephine's daybed; the richly appointed lobby boasts British Raj–era furniture from India. Although a formidable rival, the Pelham (see below) doesn't match Blake's in sophistication and style. Go for a deluxe room if you can manage it; the standard singles and doubles are tiny.

Dining/Entertainment: The stylish restaurant is one of the best in town; Neville Campbell's cuisine blends the best of East and West, ranging from baked sea bass with a crispy fennel skin to chicken and crab shaped like a large delectable egg of the Fabergé variety. With cuisine this fabulous, it's no wonder that reservations are strictly observed.

Services: An arrange-anything concierge, room service (24 hours), laundry, baby-sitting, secretarial services.

Facilities: Access to a nearby health club for a fee.

INEXPENSIVE

✪ **Abbey House.** 11 Vicarage Gate, London W8 4AG. ☎ **0171/727-2594.** 16 rms (none with bath). TV. £60 ($96) double; £74 ($118.40) triple; £86 ($137.60) quad. Rates include English breakfast. No credit cards. Tube: Kensington High Street.

Some hotel critics have rated this among the best B&Bs in London, and it's recommended by more travel guides than any of its peers.

So it must be doing something right—and it is, offering peace, tranquillity, and affordability in a very good location, next to Kensington Gardens and the Royal Palace. This is a family-run business, and you can tell: A keen sense of dedication and hospitality abounds. Built about 1860 on a typical Victorian square, Abbey House has been completely modernized, and rooms are refurbished annually, but many original features have been retained. All the spacious rooms have central heating and washbasins; two units share a bath. Rooms may be too frilly for some, but if you're looking for a small London hotel offering charm, cheery service, and a touch of class, look no further. Complimentary tea and coffee are available around the clock in the tearoom.

Vicarage Private Hotel. 10 Vicarage Gate, London W8 4AG. ☎ **0171/229-4030.** Fax 0171/792-5989. 18 rms (none with bath). £60 ($96) double; £75 ($120) triple; £84 ($134.40) family room for 4. No credit cards. Tube: Kensington High Street or Notting Hill Gate.

Eileen and Martin Diviney have a host of admirers on all continents. Their hotel is tops for old-fashioned English charm, affordable prices, and hospitality. This Victorian town house—on a residential garden square close to High Street, Kensington, and Knightsbridge shopping as well as Portobello Market—retains many original features. Furnished individually in a homey country-house style, bedrooms can accommodate up to four. If you want a little nest to hide away in, opt for the top floor eyrie (no. 19), a private retreat like Noël Coward used to occupy before "I got rich enough to move downstairs." Guests meet in a cozy sitting room for conversation and to watch the telly. As a thoughtful extra, hot drinks are available 24 hours a day. In the morning, a hearty English breakfast awaits.

SOUTH KENSINGTON
VERY EXPENSIVE

✪ **The Gore.** 189 Queen's Gate, London SW7 5EX. ☎ **800/637-7200** or 0171/584-6601. Fax 0171/589-8127. 54 rms. MINIBAR TV TEL. £156–£220 ($249.60–$352) double; £249 ($398.40) the Tudor Room. AE, DC, MC, V. Tube: Gloucester Road.

Once owned by the Marquess of Queensberry's family, the Gore has been a hotel since 1892—and it's always been one of our favorites. Victorians would still feel at home here, surrounded by walnut and mahogany, walls covered in antique photos, and Oriental carpets on the floors; throughout the hotel is a collection of some 4,000 English prints. The Gore has always been cited for its eccentricity—the Venus Room, for example, has a bed once owned by Judy Garland.

Every room is different, so try to find one that suits your personality. The dark-paneled Tudor Room is the most fascinating, with its gallery and fireplace. Rooms no longer go for 50p, but they're still a good value.

Dining/Entertainment: It's worth a trip across town to dine at renowned chef Antony Worrall Thompson's Bistro 190, especially for marinated squid, the roast cod with twice-baked endive, and the steamed mussels with green curry.

Services: Concierge, room service daily from 7am to 12:20am, laundry and dry cleaning. Newspaper delivery, in-room massage, baby-sitting, secretarial services, and express checkout may be arranged.

Facilities: Access to health club next door.

EXPENSIVE

The Cranley. 10–12 Bina Gardens, London SW5 OLA. ☎ **800/553-2582** or 0171/373-0123. Fax 0171/373-9497. 32 rms, 5 suites. A/C TV TEL. £120–£140 ($192–$224) double; £150–£200 ($240–$320) suite. Rates include continental breakfast. AE, DC, MC, V. Tube: Gloucester Road.

A trio of adjacent 1875 town houses became the Cranley Hotel when its Michigan-based owners upgraded the buildings into one of the most charming hotels in South Kensington. All of the high-ceilinged guest rooms have enormous windows, much of their original plasterwork, a scattering of antiques, and plush upholstery, and the public rooms are like a stage set for an English country house. It all adds up to a vivid 19th-century ambience that makes this feel more like a private residence than a hotel. All but one of the guest rooms—which also come with such extras as hair dryers and bathrobes—have tiny kitchenettes. Ground-floor suites open onto a private terrace and have Jacuzzis.

Dining/Entertainment: There's no restaurant, but light meals are served in a small cafe.

Services: Room service (daily 7am–11pm), laundry and dry cleaning, secretarial services (available during office hours).

Facilities: Access to a nearby health club.

✪ **Pelham Hotel.** 15 Cromwell Place, London SW7 2LA. ☎ **0171/589-8288.** Fax 0171/584-8444. 40 rms, 4 suites. A/C MINIBAR TV TEL. £155–£195 ($248–$312) double; from £240 ($384) suite. AE, MC, V. Tube: South Kensington.

This small hotel is sure to please discerning travelers from all walks of life. Hoteliers extraordinaire Kit and Tim Kemp preside over one of the most stunningly decorated establishments in London, formed from a row of early 19th-century terrace houses with a white portico facade. In the drawing room, 18th-century paneling, high ceilings, and fine moldings create a suitable backdrop for a collection of antiques and Victorian art; needlepoint rugs and cushions evoke a homelike warmth; and an honor bar completes the clublike atmosphere. The sumptuously decorated rooms are outfitted with eiderdown duvets, Oriental carpets, and unique oils; even the smallest room will have a handsome desk. The location is ideal, close to the Victoria and Albert, Hyde Park, and Harrods, and returning guests are welcomed here like part of an extended family. Kemps is one of the finest restaurants in South Kensington. Services include 24-hour room service and concierge.

Dining/Entertainment: The renowned Kemps Restaurant, with its adjacent bar, is open to the public.

Services: 24-hour room service, with limited snack menu available from 11pm to 7am. A concierge arranges virtually anything.

Facilities: Limited meeting and convention facilities for small groups. Also, residents can use the facilities at a nearby health club.

Regency Hotel. 100 Queen's Gate, London SW7 5AG. ☎ **800/328-9898** or 0171/370-4595. Fax 0171/370-5555. 198 rms, 11 suites. A/C MINIBAR TV TEL. £123 ($196.80) double; from £189 ($302.40) suite. AE, DC, MC, V. Tube: South Kensington.

On a street lined with Doric porticoes close to museums, Kensington, and Knightsbridge, six Victorian terrace houses were converted into one stylish, seamless whole by an army of construction engineers and decorators. A Chippendale fireplace, flanked by wing chairs, greets you in the polished reception area. One of the building's main stairwells has what could be London's most unusual lighting fixture: five Empire chandeliers suspended vertically, one on top of the other. The modernized guest rooms are tasteful and elegant.

Dining/Entertainment: The Pavilion is a glamorous but reasonably priced restaurant specializing in international cuisine.

Services: Room service (24 hours), laundry, baby-sitting.

Facilities: Health club with steam rooms, saunas, and a sensory-deprivation tank; a mini gym, and a business center.

MODERATE

♻ **Aster House Hotel.** 3 Sumner Place, London SW7 3EE. ☎ **0171/581-5888.** Fax 0171/584-4925. 12 rms. MINIBAR TV TEL. £98–£110 ($156.80–$176) double. Rates include buffet breakfast. MC, V. Tube: South Kensington.

At the end of an early Victorian terrace built in 1848, there's not even a sign outside to indicate this is a hotel. Ring the bell and traverse a pink marble floor, where you'll be greeted by a welcoming staff; the owners, Rachel and Peter Carapiet, will even give you your own front door key. By now they've won so many awards they've lost count; prizes range from The Spencer Trophy for the best B&B in London to the "London in Bloom" award for their back garden (the only place you're allowed to smoke). Each bedroom is individually decorated in English country–house style, many with four-poster, half-canopied beds and silk wallpaper; although many other hotels do this better, the effect is warm, cozy, and inviting (the minuscule showers are a bit too cozy, however). Breakfasts, served in the glassed-in garden conservatory, are more health-conscious than what you expect from an English B&B. The place is a charmer, especially for the price—some hotels this good are getting £250 ($400) for these allures.

✪ **5 Sumner Place.** 5 Sumner Place, London SW7 3EE. ☎ **0171/584-7586.** Fax 0171/823-9962. 14 rms. MINIBAR TV TEL. £116–£130 ($185.60–$208) double. Rates include English breakfast. AE, MC, V. Tube: South Kensington.

This little charmer is frequently cited as one of the best B&Bs in the greater Kensington area, and we agree. Completely restored in an elegant, classically English style that captures the flavor of its bygone era, this Victorian terrace house (ca. 1848) now enjoys landmark status. You'll feel the ambience as soon as you enter the reception hall and are welcomed by the graceful staff. After you register, you're given your own front door key—and London is yours. An elevator will take you up to the guest floors, where the well-maintained rooms are tastefully done in traditional period furnishings; all have TV, radio, and phones, and a few have refrigerators. Breakfast is served in a Victorian-style conservatory.

INEXPENSIVE

✪ **Aston's Budget Studios & Aston's Designer Studios and Suites.** 39 Rosary Gardens, London SW7 4NQ. ☎ **800/525-2810** in the U.S., or 0171/370-0737. Fax 0171/835-1419. 60 studios and apts (38 with bath). A/C TV TEL. Budget Studios £62 ($99.20) double; £93 ($148.80) triple; £109 ($174.40) quad. Designer Studios £105 ($168) double. Weekly rentals are preferred, but daily rentals are accepted. MC, V. Tube: Gloucester Road.

This carefully restored row of Victorian town houses offers comfortably furnished studios and suites that are London's best values. Heavy oak doors and 18th-century hunting pictures give the foyer a rich, traditional atmosphere. Accommodations range in size and style, from budget to designer, depending on price; every one has a compact but complete kitchenette concealed behind doors. If you go for a budget studio, you'll share a fully serviced bathroom with only a handful of other guests. The air-conditioned designer studios and two-room designer suites are decorated with rich fabrics and furnishings, and have their own marble baths. Amenities include laundry service, secretarial services, guests' message line, fax machines, private catering on request, car and limousine service, and daily maid service in the Designer Studios and Suites.

Hotel 167. 167 Old Brompton Rd., London SW5 OAN. ☎ **0171/373-0672.** Fax 0171/373-3360. 19 rms. MINIBAR TV TEL. £75–£82 ($120–$131.20) double. Rates include continental breakfast. AE, DC, MC, V. Tube: South Kensington or Gloucester Road.

Hotel 167 is one of the more fashionable guest houses in the area, attracting a mix of Generation-Xers and young thirty-somethings as well as business people and journalists who like its central location; the Manic Street Preachers even wrote a song about it. Occupying a three-story Victorian town house, it's quite stylishly decorated, with Scandinavian modern and Japanese accents: Each room is a comfortable medley of contemporary, antique, and art deco, with big, modern paintings decorating the walls. The basement rooms have big windows; being assigned a room in the basement doesn't sound very appealing, but returning guests often end up requesting them because of their cozy feeling. *Tattler* magazine has compared Hotel 167 with Blake's (above) for its amenities, but we wouldn't get that carried away. Owner-manager Frank Cheevers is helpful and friendly, and a font of information about London.

Swiss House Hotel. 171 Old Brompton Rd., London SW5 OAN. ☎ **0171/373-2769.** Fax 0171/373-4983. 16 rms (14 with bath). TV TEL. £72 ($115.20) double with bath; £84 ($134.40) triple with bath; £96 ($153.60) quad with bath. Rates include continental breakfast. AE, CB, DC, MC, V. Tube: Gloucester Road.

This appealing B&B, in a Victorian row house with a portico festooned with flowers and vines in the heart of South Kensington, is close to Harrods, Oxford Street, Hyde Park, and the main exhibition centers of Earl's Court and Olympia. Its guest rooms are individually designed in country style; some have fireplaces, and there's enough chintz to please the most avid Anglophile. Try to avoid the rooms along the street, as traffic is heavy; even with double-glazing, they get noisy. Instead, try to book one of the rear bedrooms, which overlook a communal garden and have a view of the London skyline. A luxury that you won't get in most B&Bs: Room service—nothing elaborate, just soups and sandwiches—is available from noon to 9pm. Baby-sitting services are also available.

6 Notting Hill

EXPENSIVE

The Abbey Court. 20 Pembridge Gardens, London W2 4DU. ☎ **0171/221-7518.** Fax 0171/792-0858. 22 rms, 3 suites. TV TEL. £130–£145 ($208–$232) double; £175 ($280) suite with 4-poster bed. AE, CB, DC, MC, V. Tube: Notting Hill Gate.

This is a small, first-rate hotel. The white-fronted mid-Victorian town house has a patio with lots of flowers in front and a conservatory in back where breakfast is served. The recently renovated lobby is graciously decorated and has a sunny bay window, floral draperies, and a comfortable sofa and chairs. You'll always find fresh flowers in the reception area and the hallways. Each room has carefully coordinated fabrics and fine furnishings, mostly 18th- and 19th-century country antiques. Done in Italian marble, bathrooms are equipped with a Jacuzzi bath, shower, and heated towel racks. Kensington Gardens is a short walk away, as are the antiques stores along Portobello Road and Kensington Church Street.

Dining/Entertainment: In lieu of a restaurant, the hotel serves breakfast, and then throughout the day, a very limited array of simple platters (club sandwiches, scones, etc.) in a glass-ringed conservatory. Within the conservatory is an "honor bar" where clients pour their own drinks, make a note of what they consumed, and pay for it upon departure from the hotel.

Services: 24-hour room service (with a limited menu between 11pm and 7am), laundry. The reception staff fulfills some of the functions of a bona fide concierge.

Facilities: None that are noteworthy, except that clients receive slight reductions (and entrance) to a nearby health club that contains sauna, steam rooms, massage, exercise equipment, and racquetball facilities.

Pembridge Court Hotel. 34 Pembridge Gardens, London W2 4DX. ☎ **0171/229-9977.** Fax 0171/727-4982. 20 rms, 1 junior suite. TV TEL. £135–£170 ($216–$272) double. Rates include English breakfast. AE, DC, MC, V. Tube: Notting Hill Gate.

In an 1852 private Victorian home, this hotel presents an elegant, cream-colored neoclassical facade to a residential Notting Hill Gate neighborhood that grows increasingly fashionable. Avid antique hunters like its proximity to Portobello Road. Most guest rooms contain at least one antique, as well as 19th-century engravings and plenty of warm-toned floral fabrics. Some of the largest and most stylish rooms are on the top floor, with baths tiled in Italian marble. Three air-conditioned deluxe rooms, all with VCRs, overlook Portobello Road: The Spencer and Churchill rooms are decorated in blues and yellows, whereas the Windsor Room has a contrasting array of tartans. Also called Spencer and Churchill are a pair of ginger cats, two of the most adorable in London. Churchill likes the pop stars who stay at the hotel; Spencer tries to avoid them.

Dining/Entertainment: Good French, Thai, and English food is served at Caps, the hotel restaurant, which also boasts a well-chosen wine list; it's open to guests only from 4 to 11pm.

Services: Room service (24 hours), same-day dry cleaning, laundry, baby-sitting.

Facilities: Membership in a nearby health club is available, car-rental agency on the premises.

INEXPENSIVE

The Gate Hotel. 6 Portobello Rd., London W11 3DG. ☎ **0171/221-2403.** Fax 0171/221-9128. 6 rms (5 with bath). MINIBAR TV. £55 ($88) double without bath; £65–£72 ($104–$115.20) double with bath. Rates include continental breakfast. AE, DC, MC, V. Tube: Notting Hill Gate.

This antique-hunters' favorite is the only hotel along the entire length of Portobello Road—and because of rigid zoning restrictions, it will probably remain the only one for many years to come. It was originally built in the 1820s as housing for the farmhands working the orchards and vegetable plots at the now-defunct Portobello Farms, and has functioned as a hotel since 1932. It has two cramped but cozy bedrooms on each of its three floors, plus a renovated breakfast room in the cellar. Rooms are color coordinated, with a bit of style, and have such amenities as a full-length mirror and built-in wardrobe. Especially intriguing are the wall paintings that show what the Portobello Market was in its early days: Every character looked straight from a Dickens novel. Be prepared for some *very* steep English stairs. The on-site manager can direct you to the nearby antiques markets and the attractions of Notting Hill Gate and nearby Kensington Gardens, both of which lie within a 5-minute walk.

Marylebone, Paddington, Bayswater & Notting Hill Gate Hotels

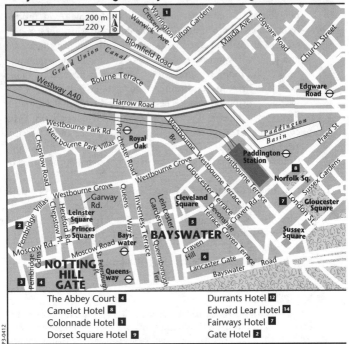

The Abbey Court **4**
Camelot Hotel **8**
Colonnade Hotel **1**
Dorset Square Hotel **9**
Durrants Hotel **12**
Edward Lear Hotel **14**
Fairways Hotel **7**
Gate Hotel **2**

P3-0412

7 Paddington & Bayswater

VERY EXPENSIVE

✪ **The Hempel.** 31–35 Craven Hill Gardens, London W2 3EA. ☎ **0171/298-9000.** Fax 0171/402-4666. 36 rms, 6 suites. A/C MINIBAR TV TEL. £240–£299 ($384–$478.40) double; from £430 ($688) suite. AE, DC, MC, V. Tube: Lancaster Gate.

Set in a trio of nearly identical 19th-century row houses, this hotel is the newest statement of flamboyant interior designer Anouska Hempel. Don't expect the swags, tassels, and labyrinthine elegance she brought to Blake's (see above)—the feeling here is radically different. The Hempel manages to combine a grand Italian sense of proportion with Asian simplicity, all meant for capitalists rich enough to afford it. Its artful simplicity is like that of a Zen temple. Soothing monochromatic tones prevail. The deliberately underfurnished lobby is flanked by symmetrical fireplaces; throughout the hotel are carefully positioned mementos from Asia, including Thai bullock carts that double as coffee tables. Bedrooms

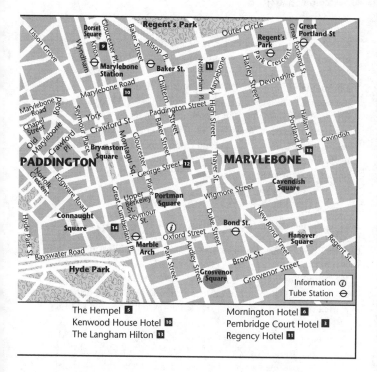

The Hempel **5**
Kenwood House Hotel **10**
The Langham Hilton **13**

Mornington Hotel **6**
Pembridge Court Hotel **3**
Regency Hotel **11**

Information ⓘ
Tube Station ⊖

continue the minimalist theme, except for their carefully concealed battery of electronic accessories, which includes a VCR, satellite TV control, CD player, twin phone lines, and modem hookup. Most of the vision here involves catering to business travelers from around the world, most of whom appreciate the tactful service and undeniably snobbish overtones of the place.

Dining/Entertainment: In the cellar is an innovative restaurant and bar, I-Thai (see review in chapter 4).

Services: Concierge, room service (24 hours), dry-cleaning, laundry, turndown, twice-daily maid service, baby-sitting can be arranged, express checkout.

Facilities: Access to nearby health club, limited business services, car-rental and tour desk.

MODERATE

Mornington Hotel. 12 Lancaster Gate, London W2 3LG. ☎ **800/528-1234** or 0171/262-7361. Fax 0171/706-1028. 68 rms. TV TEL. £98–£150 ($156.80–$240) double. Rates include Scandinavian buffet breakfast. AE, DC, MC, V. Tube: Lancaster Gate.

Affiliated with Best Western, the Mornington brings a touch of northern European hospitality to the center of London. Just north of Hyde Park and Kensington Gardens, the hotel has a Victorian exterior—it was built at the height of Victoria's reign, in 1860—and a Scandinavian-inspired decor. The area isn't London's most fashionable, but the location is still very good: close to Marble Arch, Oxford Street shopping, and the ethnic restaurants of Queensway; it's also convenient to Hyde Park. The recently renovated guest rooms are tastefully conceived and comfortable; all include coffee/tea facilities and pay movies. You can wind down in the library, and order snacks or afternoon tea from the well-stocked bar. The hotel staff is a very helpful crew.

INEXPENSIVE

Fairways Hotel. 186 Sussex Gardens, London W2 1TU. ☎ **0171/723-4871.** Fax 0171/723-4871. 17 rms (10 with bath). TV. £56 ($89.60) double without bath; £62 ($99.20) double with bath. Rates include English breakfast. MC, V. Tube: Paddington.

Jenny and Steve Adams welcome you into one of the finest B&Bs along Sussex Gardens. Even though it doesn't enjoy the pedigree it used to, this little place near Hyde Park is still a favorite address of bargain-hunting travelers. The black-and-white town house is easily recognizable: Just look for its colonnaded front entrance with a wrought-iron balustrade stretching across the front second-floor windows. Scorning modern, the Adams family prefers the traditional touch, opting for charm and character whenever possible. They call their breakfast room "homely," which Americans might call home-like instead; it's decorated with photographs of the family and a collection of china. Bedrooms are attractively decorated and comfortably furnished, each with hot and cold running water, intercom, TV, and beverage-makers. The breakfast is hearty and home cooked—fit fortification for a day of sightseeing.

4

Dining

*G*eorge Mikes, Britain's famous Hungarian-born humorist, once wrote about the culinary prowess of his adopted country: "The Continentals have good food. The English have good table manners."

Quite a lot has happened since.

London has emerged as one of the great food capitals of the world. In the last few years, its chefs—both the veterans and young upstarts of the scene—have fanned out around the globe seeking culinary inspiration, and they've returned with innovative dishes, flavors, and ideas that London diners have never seen before—or at least not at such unprecedented rates. These chefs are pioneering the new style of cooking called "Modern British," which is forever changing, forever innovative, yet comfortingly familiar in many ways. The chefs operating under this rubric center their dishes around local ingredients from field, stream, and air, and have become daringly innovative with traditional recipes—too much so in the view of some critics, who don't like fresh mango over their blood pudding.

Traditional British cooking has made a comeback, too. The dishes that British mums the nation over have been feeding their reluctant families for what seems like forever have become fashionable again. Yes, we're talking British soul food: faggots, bangers and mash, Norfolk dumplings, nursery puddings, cottage pie—the works. This may be a rebellion against the excessive minimalism of the nouvelle cuisine that ran rampant over London in the 1980s, but who knows? Maybe it's just plain old nostalgia. Pig's nose with parsley and onion sauce may not be your idea of cutting-edge cuisine, but Simpson's-in-the-Strand is serving it for breakfast.

The revolution of the London dining scene in this decade caused quite a stir. A number of megastar chefs emerged on the scene, and London gushed over its crowned culinary heads. But the cult of the personality chef is on the wane. These days, many of the personality chefs spend a lot more time writing cookbooks and performing on TV than they do cooking in their own kitchens. As is so often the case, that chef you've read about in *Condé Nast Traveler* or

Travel & Leisure may not be in the kitchen when you get here. But never fear: The cuisine isn't suffering for it. Many an up-and-comer who's even better—and whose primary concern is cooking for you and your fellow restaurant patrons—has taken over. And since the dinner-as-theater concept has kicked in, with many London restaurants becoming so mammoth—with 200-plus seats—the identity of the chef presiding over the kitchen is irrelevant—as long as he or she can cook.

SOME DINING NOTES

Hours   Restaurants in London keep varied hours, but in general, lunch is offered from noon to 2pm and dinner is served from 7:30 to 9:30pm—but more and more restaurants are staying open later these days. Sunday is the typical closing day for London restaurants, but there are many exceptions to that rule (many restaurants also close for a few days or a week around Christmas, so call ahead if you're dining during the holiday season). We've listed each restaurant's serving hours in the listings below.

Reservations   Nearly all places, except pubs, cafeterias, and fast-food joints, prefer or require reservations. Almost invariably, you get a better table if you book in advance. For a few of the really famous places, you might need to reserve weeks in advance, even before leaving home (such reservations should always be confirmed when you land in London).

Taxes & Tipping   All restaurants and cafes in Britain are required to display the prices of the food and drink they offer in a place visible from outside the establishment. Charges for service, as well as any minimum charge or cover charge, must also be made clear. The prices shown must include 17.5% VAT. Most of the restaurants add a 10% to 15% service charge to your bill, but you'll have to check to make sure of that. If nothing has been added to your bill, leave a 12% to 15% tip.

1 Best Bets

- **Best Restaurant for Romance:** The atmosphere is about as romantic as it can get at **Bracewells,** in the Park Lane Hotel, Piccadilly, W1 (☎ **0171/499-6321**). You can enjoy some of the finest hotel dining in London today in an intimate, elegant setting of gilded torchères, comfortable armchairs, and candlelight.
- **Best Place for a Business Lunch:** Instead of some noisy city tavern serving up bangers and mash, impress your clients by taking

them to **Poons in the City,** 2 Minster Pavement, Minster Court, Mincing Lane, EC3 (☎ **0171/626-0126**). This fabled Chinese restaurant is elegantly outfitted with furniture and accessories from China, and the menu is wide ranging enough to please most clients. After a taste of the finely chopped, wind-dried meats or the crispy aromatic duck, it'll be a snap to seal the deal.

- **Best Spot for a Celebration:** There's no spot in all of London that's more fun than **Quaglino's,** 16 Bury St., SW1 (☎ **0171/ 930-6767**). On some nights, as many as 800 diners show up at Sir Terence Conran's gargantuan Mayfair eatery to dine, laugh, and gossip. It's the best place in London to celebrate almost any occasion—and the food's good, too. There's live jazz on Friday and Saturday nights.

- **Best Wine List:** The renowned wine list at the **Tate Gallery Restaurant,** in the Tate Gallery, Millbank, SW1 (☎ **0171/887-8877**) reads like a who's who of famous French châteaux. So does the one at Le Gavroche—but this one is affordable. The Tate offers the city's best bargains on fine wines; the management keeps the markups between 40% and 65%, as opposed to the 100% to 200% that most restaurants add to the price of a bottle.

- **Best Newcomer:** Cleverly combining two of the world's greatest cuisines—Thai and Italian—**I-Thai,** in the Hempel Hotel, Hempel Square, W2 (☎ **0171/298-9000**), is all the rage. Like the postmodern decor, the menu is sparse but innovative. Chic London shows up nightly to dine on some of most delectable dishes in town, such as the to-die-for breadcrumb-encrusted halibut with Thai eggplant and shiitakes in a pineapple and tamarind sauce, accompanied by lime-flavored rice.

- **Best Value:** Cheap and cheerful **Simply Nico,** 48A Rochester Row, SW1 (☎ **0171/630-8061**), grand Chef Nico Ladenis' "moment of whimsy," offers some of the best value, fixed-price meals in London. This isn't the fabled haute cuisine Nico serves on Park Lane, but quality ingredients are beautifully prepared into some of the best French food in central London. Breast of guinea fowl with lentils and other specialties will keep you coming back for more.

- **Best Traditional British Cuisine:** No restaurant, not even Simpson's-in-the-Strand, is quite as British as **Wiltons,** 55 Jermyn St., SW1 (☎ **0171/629-9955**). As other British restaurants loosen up in the rigidity, Wiltons remains fiercely entrenched in tradition—or, as one London diner put it, "Wiltons refuses to unclench its upper-class buttocks." It serves the same menu it did to the 18th-century nobs of St. James's. We're talking grilled plaice, steaks, chops, kidneys, whitebait (a Victorian favorite), and game dishes such as roast widgeon (a wild, fish-eating river duck).

- **Best Pub Grub:** Tom Conran, son of über-restaurateur Sir Terence Conran, is attracting all of London to **The Cow,** 89 Westbourne Park Rd., W2 (☎ 0171/221-0021)—even people who haven't been in a pub for years. Leading the revolution in upgrading pub cuisine, The Cow somehow manages to secure the biggest and juiciest oysters in town. Ox tongue poached in milk? Don't knock it 'til you've tried it. Proof that the London pub scene has changed radically: The hip young staff even serves finger bowls to its even hipper clientele.

- **Best Desserts: Nico Central,** 35 Great Portland St., W1 (☎ 0171/436-8846), is the place to satisfy your sweet tooth. The "puddings" menu is extremely limited, but is it ever choice: The caramelized lemon tart is the best we've ever been served in London. The nougat ice cream with a strongly flavored blackberry coulis was also worth a return visit, as was the walnut and armagnac parfait. Other unforgettable desserts accompanying memorable meals here have included a velvety smooth, warm chocolate mousse with pear sorbet, and a poached pear sable made even more delectable with a caramel-ginger sauce.

- **Best People-Watching:** In Karl Marx's former apartment house, **Quo Vadis,** 26–29 Dean St., W1 (☎ 0171/437-9585), is a joint venture of London's *enfant terrible* chef, Marco Pierre White, and Damien Hirst, the artist who wowed the London art world with his cow carcasses in formaldehyde. With a pedigree like this, it's no wonder this is the hottest see-and-be-seen circuit in town. If Goldie Hawn should come to London, this is where you'd find her. And the food's not bad, either.

- **Best Afternoon Tea:** While everyone else is donning their fancy hats and heading for the Ritz (where, chances are, they won't be able to get a table), you should retreat to the **Palm Court at the Waldorf Meridien,** Aldwych, WC2 (☎ 0171/836-2400), in the grand 1908 Waldorf Hotel. The Sunday tea dances here are legendary: Originating with the famous "Tango Teas" of the 1920s and 1930s, they've been going strong ever since, interrupted only by war and a few other inconveniences.

- **Best Pretheater Menu:** Opposite the Ambassador Theatre, **The Ivy,** 1–5 West St., WC2 (☎ 0171/836-4751), is popular for both pre- and *après*-theater dining. The brasserie-style food reflects both traditional English and modern continental influences. You can try longtime favorites such as potted shrimp or tripe and onions, or more imaginative dishes such as butternut pumpkin salad or a wild-mushroom risotto.

- **Best for Kids:** After you and the kids have visited the Tower of London, take them to **Dickens Inn by the Tower,** St. Katharine's Way, E1 (☎ **0171/488-2208**), an old spice warehouse turned three-floor restaurant with sweeping views of the Thames and Tower Bridge. Dickens Inn serves tasty well-stuffed sandwiches, platters of lasagna, and steaming bowls of chili. One whole floor is devoted to serving pizza.

- **Best Fish 'n' Chips:** The best place to introduce yourself to this trad British dish is **North Sea Fish Restaurant,** 7–8 Leigh St., WC1 (☎ **0171/387-5892**). Unlike the overcooked frozen fish served at those joints around Leicester Square, North Sea's fresh cod comes perfectly prepared: crisp batter on the outside, moist and tender fish inside. The haddock is equally delectable—and what a big platter it is.

2 In the West End

Note to Reader: For the locations of the following West End restaurants, please refer to the map on page 46.

MAYFAIR
VERY EXPENSIVE

✪ **Chez Nico at Ninety Park Lane.** In Grosvenor House, 90 Park Lane, W1. ☎ **0171/409-1290.** Reservations required (at least 2 days in advance for lunch, 10 days for dinner). Fixed-price lunch £31 ($49.60) for 3 courses; à la carte dinner £51 ($81.60) for 2 courses, £63 ($100.80) for 3 courses. AE, DC, MC, V. Mon–Fri noon–2pm, Mon–Sat 7–11pm. Tube: Marble Arch. FRENCH.

The setting is as opulent as the cuisine, but nothing takes precedence over the food here. It's the work of one of London's supreme culinary artists, the temperamental but always amusing Nico Ladenis. This former oil company executive, self-taught cook, and economist remains one of Britain's most talked-about chefs; his food is always impressive, always stylish, and he's constantly reinventing dishes we thought he had already perfected.

As starters go, who can top his quail salad with sweet breads, flavored with an almond vinaigrette? The main courses are a tour de force of culinary skill in the best post-nouvelle tradition, in which the tenets of classical cuisine are creatively and flexibly adapted to local fresh ingredients. With great mastery of technique, Nico's chefs dazzle with ever-changing entrees, including a ravioli of langoustine that's a virtual signature dish. The char-grilled sea bass with basil purée or the Bresse pigeon are rivaled only by the work of Le Gavroche (see below).

✪ **Le Gavroche.** 43 Upper Brook St., W1. ☎ **0171/408-0881.** Reservations required as far in advance as possible. Main courses £28–£38 ($44.80–$60.80); fixed-price lunch £39 ($62.40); fixed-price dinner £60 ($96). AE, DC, MC, V. Mon–Fri noon–2pm and 7–11pm. Tube: Marble Arch. FRENCH.

Le Gavroche has long stood for quality French cuisine, perhaps England's finest, although Michelin gives it only two stars. Though it may have fallen off briefly in the early 1990s, it's fighting its way back to the stellar ranks. There's always something special coming out of the kitchen of Burgundy-born brothers Michel and Albert Roux; service is faultless, and the ambience is formally chic without being stuffy.

The menu changes constantly, depending on the fresh produce that's available and the current inspiration of the Roux brothers— but it always remains classically French, although not of the "essentially old-fashioned bourgeois repertoire" that some critics suggest. There are signature dishes that have been honed over years of unswerving practice: Try, if featured, the soufflé Suissesse, *papillote* of smoked salmon, or *tournedos gratinés aux poivres*. Desserts, including the *sablé* of pears and chocolate, are sublime. The wine cellar is among the most interesting in London, with many quality Burgundies and Bordeaux.

MODERATE

✪ **Bracewells.** In the Park Lane Hotel, Piccadilly, W1. ☎ **0171/499-6321.** Reservations required. Main courses £9.50–£19 ($15.20–$30.40); 2-course set lunch menu £19.50 ($31.20); 3-course set lunch menu £26 ($41.60). AE, DC, MC, V. Mon–Fri 12:30–2:30pm; Mon–Sat 7–10:30pm. Tube: Hyde Park Corner or Green Park. BRITISH.

Award-winning Bracewells is one of London's most popular restaurants for truly classic British fare. The cuisine, prepared by ex-Ritz chef Alain Allard, is among the best in the city, and the decor and five-star service are worthy of the distinguished clientele. Amid the gilded torchères and comfortable armchairs of Bracewells' bar, you might begin with a drink and canapés of lobster, foie gras, and caviar. Later, you'll be ushered into an intimately lit room, whose Louis XVI paneling was long ago removed from the London home of the American banker and philanthropist Pierpont Morgan.

The specialties are prepared with the freshest ingredients. The main courses include a luscious loin of venison with apples, prunes, and celeriac; some dishes have a modern twist, such as rabbit with prunes and pâté, or perfectly seared sea scallops with pan-fried artichokes, asparagus, and cane mushrooms. The set lunch menu offers outstanding value.

Greenhouse. 27A Hays Mews, W1. ☎ **0771/499-3331.** Reservations essential. Main courses £9.50–£17.50 ($15.20–$28). AE, DC, MC, V. Mon–Fri noon–2:45pm and 7–10:45pm, Sat 7–11pm, Sun 12:30–3pm and 7–10:30pm. Closed Christmas, bank holidays. Tube: Green Park. BRITISH.

Celebrated TV chef Gary Rhodes may have departed for a lower-profile career in corporate catering, but don't strike the Greenhouse from your list just yet. New head chef Graham Grafton is quite inspired, and seems to spend more time here perfecting dishes than Gary ever did. The modern British cookery, served in a comfortable room accented with prints and dried flowers, is prepared using only the finest fresh ingredients. Grafton has a winning way with fish, if his poached skate is any example—and his deep-fried cod-and-chips are galaxies beyond what you'd get at the local chippie. But you may prefer the lip-smacking fare from the heart of England, which includes a roast breast of pheasant that Henry VIII would've loved, and grilled farmhouse pork; we're also fond of the wilted greens wrapped in bacon. The menu is backed up by a well-chosen wine list of some 20 selections. Some of the delightfully sticky desserts, including a moist bread-and-butter pudding and a ginger pudding with orange marmalade, would've pleased your Midlands grandmum.

✪ **Quaglino's.** 16 Bury St., SW1. ☎ **0171/930-6767.** Reservations recommended. Main courses £10.50–£19.50 ($16.80–$31.20); set-price 3-course menu (available only at lunch and for pretheater dinner between 5:30–6:30pm) £14.50–£19.50 ($23.20–$31.20). AE, DC, MC, V. Daily noon–3pm and 5:30pm–midnight (till 1am Fri–Sat). Tube: Green Park. CONTINENTAL.

It's vast, it's convivial, it's fun, and it was voted the restaurant of 1994 by *Time Out* magazine. It occupies the premises of a restaurant originally established in 1929 by Giovanni Quaglino, from Italy's Piedmont district; personalities who paraded through these premises in ermine and pearls could fill a between-the-wars roster of *Who's Who* for virtually every country of Europe. In 1993, noted restaurateur and designer Sir Terence Conran brought the place into the postmodern age with a vital new decor that's been likened to a stylishly decorated ocean liner. Eight artists were commissioned to decorate the octet of massive columns supporting the soaring ceiling. A mezzanine with a bar features live jazz every Friday and Saturday night and live piano music the rest of the week, and an "altar" in the back is devoted to what must be the most impressive display of crustaceans and shellfish in Britain.

Everything seems to be served in bowls. Menu items have been criticized for their quick preparation and standardized format—not as marvelously subtle as what you might expect in more manageably sized eateries. But considering that on some nights up to 800 people might show up here for food, laughter, and gossip, the marvel is that the place functions as well as it does. That's not to say there isn't an occasional delay. Come for fun, not for culinary finesse. The menu changes often, but your choices might include goat cheese and caramelized-onion tart; seared salmon with potato pancakes; crab tartlet with saffron; and roasted cod and ox cheek with char-grilled vegetables.

INEXPENSIVE

✪ **Crank's In London.** 8 Marshall St., W1. ☎ **0171/437-9431.** Main courses £3.95–£5.45 ($6.30–$8.70). AE, DC, MC, V. Mon–Tues 8am–8pm; Wed–Fri 8am–9pm. Tube: Oxford Circus. VEGETARIAN.

Located just off Carnaby Street, this is the headquarters of a chain of vegetarian restaurants with seven other branches in London. Outfitted in natural wood, wicker-basket lamps, pinewood tables, and handmade ceramic bowls and plates, Crank's is completely self-service: You carry your own tray to one of the tables. Organic-white and stone-ground flour is used for breads and rolls. The uncooked vegetable salad is especially good, and there's always a hot stew of savory vegetables (with "secret" seasoning), served in a hand-thrown stoneware pot with a salad. Homemade honey cake, cheesecake, tarts, and crumbles are featured. Bakery goods, nuts, and general health-food supplies are sold in an adjoining shop.

Hard Rock Cafe. 150 Old Park Lane, W1. ☎ **0171/629-0382.** Main courses £7.50–£15 ($12–$24). AE, MC, V. Sun–Thurs 11:30am–12:30am, Fri–Sat 11:30am–1am. Closed Dec 25–26. Tube: Green Park or Hyde Park Corner. AMERICAN.

This is the original Hard Rock, now a worldwide chain of rock-and-roll–themed American roadside diners serving up good food and service with a smile. Since it was established on June 14, 1971, more than 12 million people have eaten here. Almost every night there's a line waiting to get in. The portions are generous, and the price of a main dish includes not only a salad but also fries or a baked potato. The beef-laden menu has forced the restaurateurs to import the meat; the fajitas are always a good choice. The tempting dessert menu offers homemade apple pie and thick, cold shakes. There's also a good selection of beers. The collection of rock memorabilia is worth seeking out if you're a fan.

MARYLEBONE
MODERATE

Odin's. 27 Devonshire St., W1. ☎ **0171/935-7296.** Reservations recommended. 2-course set-price lunch or dinner £22.95 ($36.70); 3-course set-price lunch or dinner £24.95 ($39.90). AE, DC, MC, V. Mon–Fri 12:30–2:30pm and 7–11:30pm. Tube: Regent's Park. INTERNATIONAL.

This elegant restaurant is one of at least four in London owned by chef Richard Sheperd and actor Michael Caine (whose stable includes Langan's Brasserie). Set adjacent to its slightly less expensive twin, Langan's Bistro (see below), it features ample space between tables and an eclectic decor that includes evocative paintings and deco accessories. The menu changes with the seasons: Typical fare might include forest mushrooms in brioche, braised leeks glazed with mustard and tomato sauce, roast duck with apple sauce and sage and onion stuffing, or roast filet of sea bass with a juniper cream sauce.

INEXPENSIVE

Langan's Bistro. 26 Devonshire St., W1. ☎ **0171/935-4531.** Reservations recommended. 2-course set-price lunch or dinner £17.95 ($28.70); 3-course set-price lunch or dinner £19.95 ($31.90). AE, DC, MC, V. Mon–Fri 12:30–2:30pm; Mon–Sat 7–11:30pm. Tube: Regent's Park. BRITISH/FRENCH.

This deliberately unpretentious restaurant has been a busy fixture on the London restaurant scene since the mid-1960s, when it was established by the late restaurateur Peter Langan with chef Richard Shepherd and actor Michael Caine. Of the several restaurants within its chain (see Odin's, above), it's the least expensive (and the least spacious), but it's the most visually appealing. Set behind a brightly colored storefront on a residential street, the dining room's surfaces are richly covered with fanciful clusters of Japanese parasols, rococo mirrors, surrealistic paintings, and old photographs. The menu is defined as "mostly English with a French influence"; it changes with the seasons, but might include salmon and broccoli mousse, snails in a garlic-butter sauce, poached salmon in pastry served with a watercress sauce, pan-fried squid, and lamb stew. Chocaholics should finish off with the dessert extravaganza known as "Mrs. Langan's chocolate pudding."

ST. JAMES'S
VERY EXPENSIVE

♻ **Suntory.** 72–73 St. James's St., SW1. ☎ **0171/409-0201.** Reservations required. Main courses £18.20–£40.30 ($29.10–$64.50); set lunch £15–£35 ($24–$56); fixed-price dinner £49.80–£73 ($79.70–$116.80). AE, DC, MC, V. Mon–Sat noon–2pm and 6–10pm. Tube: Green Park. JAPANESE.

This is the best—and the most expensive—Japanese restaurant in London. Owned and operated by Japanese distillers and brewers, it offers a choice of dining rooms in a setting evocative of a Japanese manor house. First-time visitors seem to prefer the tappanyaki dining room downstairs, where iron grills are set on each table and you can watch the mastery of the high-hatted, knife-wielding chef up close. In other rooms you can dine on sukiyaki, tempura, and sushi (especially good is the delicately sliced raw tuna). Waitresses in traditional dress serve you with all the highly refined ritual of Japan. Appetizers are artful and delicate; even the tea is superior.

PICCADILLY CIRCUS & LEICESTER SQUARE
EXPENSIVE

♻ **Wiltons.** 55 Jermyn St., SW1. ☎ **0171/629-9955.** Reservations required. Main courses £15–£25 ($24–$40). AE, DC, MC, V. Mon–Fri 12:30–2:30pm and 6–10:30pm, Sun 6:30–10pm. Tube: Green Park or Piccadilly Circus. BRITISH.

This is one of the top purveyors of traditional British cuisine, and our favorite of London's current bunch. The thoroughly British menu is known for its fish and game. You might begin with an oyster cocktail and follow with Dover sole, plaice, salmon, or lobster, prepared in any number of ways. In season (from mid-Aug), there are such delights as roast partridge, pheasant, or grouse; you might even be able to order widgeon, a wild, fish-eating river duck (the chef might ask you if you want them "blue" or "black," a reference to roasting times). Game is often accompanied by bread sauce (milk thickened with bread crumbs). To finish, consider some Welsh rarebit, soft roes, or anchovies; if that's too much, try the sherry trifle or syllabub.

We consistently find the service, by a bevy of bosomy matrons, to be the most helpful in the West End. Since this is a bastion of traditionalism, however, don't show up in the latest Covent Garden fashions—you might not get in. Instead, don your oldest suit and look like you believe the Empire still exists.

MODERATE

Atlantic Bar & Grill. 20 Glasshouse St., W1. ☎ **0171/734-4888.** Reservations required. Main courses £9.50–£15 ($15.20–$24); fixed-price lunch £14.50

($23.20), including 2 glasses of wine. AE, MC, V. Mon–Fri noon–2:45pm, Mon–Sat 6pm–3am, Sun 6–10:30pm. Tube: Piccadilly Circus. BRITISH.

A titanic eatery installed in a former art deco ballroom off Piccadilly Circus, this 160-seat restaurant draws a trendy crowd to London's tawdry heartland. Hailed as the "restaurant of the year" when it opened in the spring of 1994, the Atlantic's business seems to have fallen off a bit recently. Not because the food is bad—it's quite good. But fickle hipsters are beginning to move on, even though on any given night you'll still find a bevy of yuppies; the after-theater crowd also makes a strong showing.

Classically trained chef Sanjay Dwidedi is at the helm, serving the world's most sublime potato-and-chive hash along with well-smoked salmon. Even American cuisine comes into focus here, especially the grilled tuna on mashed black beans with seared tomatoes, spiced avocado, and corn chips (the best this side of Santa Fe). The menu changes every 2 months, but is always strong on seafood: The pan-fried skate wing stuffed with black-olive purée is a delight. The desserts, however, are purposefully (and inexplicably) unsophisticated: rice pudding, *poire Belle Hélène* (poached pear). If you're rushed, you can drop into Dick's Bar, where they serve up everything from lamb burgers sparked with yogurt and fresh mint to Cashel blue cheese and pumpkin seeds on ciabatta bread, for a quick bite.

The Criterion Brasserie–Marco Pierre White. 224 Piccadilly, W1. ☎ **0171/930-0488.** Main courses £11–£14 ($17.60–$22.40); £14.95 ($23.90) fixed-price 2-course lunch, £17.95 ($28.70) fixed-price 3-course lunch. AE, MC, V. Daily noon–2:30pm and 6pm–midnight. Tube: Piccadilly Circus. BRITISH.

Known as the bad boy of British cookery, Michelin-starred Marco Pierre White runs what he calls his "junior" restaurant here. Designed by Thomas Verity in the 1870s, this palatial neo-Byzantine, mirrored marble hall is a glamorous backdrop for the master chef's cuisine, served under a golden ceiling, with theatrical peacock-blue draperies. The menu is wide ranging, from Paris brasserie food to "nouvelle-classical," and served by a mainly French staff. The food is excellent, but falls short of sublime. Still, the roast skate wing with deep-fried snails is delectable, as is the roast saddle of lamb stuffed with mushrooms and spinach.

Greens Restaurant & Oyster Bar. 36 Duke St., SW1. ☎ **0171/930-4566.** Reservations recommended. Main courses £9.50–£34 ($15.20–$54.40). AE, DC, MC, V. Restaurant daily 12:30–3pm, Mon–Sat 6–11pm; oyster bar Mon–Sat 11:30am–3pm and 5:30–11pm, Sun noon–3pm. Tube: Piccadilly Circus or Green Park. SEAFOOD.

ɪɪ **Family-Friendly Restaurants**

Chiaroscuro (Bloomsbury; *see p. 96*)   Here's a restaurant that kids *and* their parents love. The vision of rising star Sally James, Chiaroscuro has a playroom specially designed to amuse the kids— complete with a video screen and a library of Disney films—while their parents dine on terrific international fare. What's more, kids under 10 eat free at Sunday brunch—as long as they chaperone their parents.

Deal's Restaurant & Diner (Chelsea; *see p. 112*)   After enjoy- ing the boat ride down to Chelsea Harbour, kids will love the burgers and other American fare served here. Reduced-price children's portions are available.

Dickens Inn by the Tower (Docklands; *see p. 104*)   Even fussy kids will find something they like at this old former spice ware- house, now a three-story restaurant with sweeping Thames and Tower Bridge views. The fare ranges from parent-pleasing mod- ern British to yummy lasagna and pizza.

Hard Rock Cafe (Mayfair; *see p. 88*)   This is a great place for older children. Teenagers like the rock 'n' roll memorabilia as well as the juicy burgers with a heap of fries and a salad doused with Thousand Island dressing. Even über-vegetarian Linda McCartney has approved of the veggie dishes here.

Porter's English Restaurant (Covent Garden; *see p. 100*)   This restaurant serves traditional English meals that most kids love— especially the pies, stews, and steamed "puds." They'll get a real kick out of ordering wonderfully named food like bubble and squeak and mushy peas.

Ye Olde Cheshire Cheese (The City; *see p. 124*)   Fleet Street's most famous chop house, established in 1667, is an eternal family favorite. If "ye famous pudding" turns your kids off, the sandwiches and roasts will tempt them into digging in instead.

Critics say it's a triumph of tradition over taste but, as far as seafood goes in London, this is a tried-and-true favorite, thanks to an excel- lent menu, a central location, and a charming staff. This busy place has a cluttered entrance leading to a crowded bar where you can stand to sip fine wines and, from September to April, enjoy oysters. In the faux-Dickensian dining room, you can select from a long menu of seafood dishes, ranging from fish cakes with parsley sauce to poached Scottish lobster. For zesty starters, try either the smoked eel filets (Cockney) or the warm pigeon and bacon salad with a hazelnut vinaigrette (trendy). Desserts include black-currant sorbet and banana fritters.

INEXPENSIVE

✪ The Carvery. In the Regent Palace Hotel, Glasshouse St., W1. ☎ **0171/ 488-4600.** Reservations recommended. All-you-can-eat meals £14.95 ($23.90), or £11.95 ($19.10) from 5:15–7pm; 2-course buffet £10.95 ($17.50); half-price for children 5–16, free for those under 5. AE, DC, MC, V. Daily noon–2:30pm, Mon–Fri 5:15–9pm, Sat 5:15–9:30pm, Sun 6–9pm. Tube: Piccadilly Circus. BRITISH.

Just 20 feet from Piccadilly Circus, you can have all the fabulous roasts you can eat—that's the famous policy of this renowned establishment. There's a wide range of appetizers, and the buffet carving table boasts a roast leg of Southdown lamb with mint sauce and a roast leg of English pork with apple sauce. Your choice of roast will be carved for you by the chef; you'll then serve yourself buttered peas, roast potatoes, new carrots, and gravy. In another area is cold food and assorted salads, whatever's in season. Desserts might include chocolate fudge cake or a sherry trifle. Well-brewed coffee is included in the price.

The Granery. 39 Albemarle St., W1. ☎ **0171/493-2978.** Main courses £6.90–£7.90 ($11.05–$12.65). MC, V. Mon–Fri 11:30am–8pm, Sat–Sun noon–2:30pm. Tube: Green Park. BRITISH.

This family-operated country-style restaurant has served a simple but flavorful array of home-cooked dishes, listed daily on a blackboard, since 1974. The daily specials might include lamb casserole with mint and lemon; pan-fried cod; or avocado stuffed with prawns, spinach, and cheese. Vegetarian meals include mushrooms stuffed with mixed vegetables, stuffed eggplant with curry sauce, and vegetarian lasagna. Tempting desserts are bread-and-butter pudding and brown Betty (both served hot). The large portions guarantee that you won't go hungry.

SOHO
EXPENSIVE

Alastair Little. 49 Frith St., W1. ☎ **0171/734-5183.** Reservations recommended. Fixed-price dinner £28 ($44.80); fixed-price 3-course lunch £25 ($40). AE, DC, MC, V. Mon–Fri noon–3pm; Mon–Sat 6–11:30pm. Tube: Leicester Square or Tottenham Court Road. BRITISH.

In a circa-1830 brick-fronted town house—which for a brief period supposedly housed John Constable's art studio—this informal, cozy restaurant is a pleasant place to enjoy a well-prepared lunch or dinner. Some loyal critics still claim that Alastair Little is the best chef in London, but lately he's been buried under the avalanche of new talent. Actually, Little himself is not here a lot; he divides his time between his other enterprises and a cooking school in Umbria. The talented Juliet Peston is in charge, and she believes in keeping dishes simple but flavorful, with exceptional tastes and textures. For inspiration, the kitchen draws upon all corners of the globe, from Japan and Thailand to France and Scandinavia; the menu, which changes twice a day, reflects whatever's good and fresh at the market. You might enjoy a full-flavored roasted sea bass with parsley salad, a tender rack of lamb with rosemary, or Tuscan squab; dessert might be a créme brûlée or tarte tatin with créme fraîche. There's a nice wine list.

✪ **The Ivy.** 1–5 West St., WC2. ☎ **0171/836-4751.** Reservations required. Main courses £9.75–£21.75 ($15.60–$34.80); Sat–Sun lunch £14.50 ($23.20). AE, DC, MC, V. Daily noon–3pm and 5:30pm–midnight (last order). Tube: Leicester Square. BRITISH/FRENCH.

Effervescent and sophisticated, The Ivy has been intimately associated with the West End theater district since it opened in 1911. With its ersatz 1930s look and tiny bar near the entrance, this place is fun—and it hums with the energy of London's glamour scene. The menu may seem simple, but the kitchen has a solid appreciation for fresh ingredients and a talent for skillful preparation. Favorite dishes include white asparagus with sea kale and truffle butter; seared scallops with spinach, sorrel, and bacon; and salmon fish cakes. There's also Mediterranean fish soup, a great mixed grill, and such English desserts as sticky toffee and caramelized bread-and-butter pudding. Meals are served quite late to accommodate the post-theater crowd.

✪ **Quo Vadis.** 26–29 Dean St., W1. ☎ **0171/437-9585.** Reservations required. Main courses £13–£26 ($20.80–$41.60). Set lunches £14.75–£17.95 ($23.60–$28.70). AE, MC, V. Sun–Fri noon–3pm, Mon–Sat 6–11pm, Sun 6–10:30pm. Tube: Leicester Square or Tottenham Court Road. BRITISH.

This trendy restaurant occupies the former apartment house of Communist patriarch Karl Marx, who would never recognize it. It was a stodgy Italian restaurant (also called Quo Vadis) from 1926 until the mid-1990s, when its interior was ripped apart and reconfigured into the stylish, postmodern place you'll find today. The stark street-level dining room is a museum-style showcase for dozens of avant-garde paintings by the controversial Damien Hirst and other contemporary artists. But many bypass the restaurant altogether for the upstairs bar, where Hirst has put a severed cow's head and a severed bull's head on display in separate aquariums. Why? They're catalysts to conversation, satirical odes to the destructive effects of Mad Cow disease, and perhaps tongue-in-cheek commentaries on the flirtatious games going on here.

Quo Vadis is associated with Marco Pierre White, but don't expect to see the temperamental culinary superstar; as executive chef, he only functions as a consultant. The kitchen is actually overseen by Jeremy Hollingsworth. Also, don't expect that the harassed and overburdened staff will have the time to pamper you; they're too preoccupied dealing with the hysteria that follows when the glare of publicity makes you the hottest reservation in town. And the food? It's appealingly presented and very good, but not nearly as artful or innovative as the setting might lead you to believe. We suggest beginning with the mussel and saffron soup or the terrine of foie gras and duck confit before moving on to the escalope of tuna with tapenade and eggplant caviar (actually eggplant and black olives puréed and seasoned, which gives it the look of caviar), or the sage-scented roast rabbit with a tomato confit and ratatouille.

MODERATE

Dell'Ugo. 56 Frith St., W1. ☎ **0171/734-8300.** Reservations required. Main courses £8–£12 ($12.80–$19.20). AE, DC, MC, V. Mon–Fri noon–3pm, Mon–Sat 7pm–midnight. Tube: Tottenham Court Road. MEDITERRANEAN.

This immensely popular multistory restaurant is one of Soho's finest, serving very good food at affordable prices. Critics claim there's too long a wait between courses and dishes are overly contrived. But we have to agree with its legions of (mostly young) devotees: We've found the robust Mediterranean dishes to be prepared with the finest ingredients and packed with flavor. Most everything tastes fresh and appealing. Both the restaurant and bistro change their menus frequently, but generally feature an array of pasta, meat, fish, and vegetarian dishes. If you can, start with the goat cheese in a spicy tomato vinaigrette, and follow it with the linguini with langoustines or the rosemary-skewered lamb with a charred eggplant. Fish dishes, delectably seasoned and not allowed to dry out on the grill, range from monkfish to sea bass. Not everything works out—some dishes are tough (especially the duck) and lack spice. The crème brûlée (when it *finally* arrived) was excellent. All in all, not the spot for a romantic tete-à-tete, but immensely appealing. The ground-floor "caff" offers snacks all day, from tapas to meze.

BLOOMSBURY
MODERATE

Chiaroscuro. 24 Coptic St., WC1. ☎ **0171/636-2371.** Reservations recommended. Main courses £8.50–£15 ($13.60–$24); fixed-price menus £12.50 ($20). AE, MC, V. Mon–Fri noon–3pm, Mon–Sat 6–11:45pm; Sun brunch 11:30am–3:30pm. Tube: Tottenham Court Road or Holborn. BRITISH/PAN-PACIFIC.

Created by rising star Sally James, who's assisted in the dining rooms by her Cuban-born husband Carl, this well-recommended restaurant lies near the British Museum. Dining rooms are on three of the four floors of a Georgian town house, and include a playroom designed to amuse the kids while their parents dine. In a setting filled with modern accessories and copies of Renaissance paintings, you'll be fêted with a frequently changing menu whose compilation reads like a tour de force of culinary traditions from Scotland, Spain, Greece, Japan, and Thailand. Examples include purée of parsley with a tapenade of black olives, served with lemon butter on foccaccia; a tempting platter of mixed antipasti; steamed mussels with grilled chicken and chorizo sausage with French fries and *rouille* sauce; and shredded duck confit with rustic summer salad, lentils, and bacon.

✪ Museum Street Café. 47 Museum St., WC1. ☎ **0171/405-3211.** Reservations required. Lunch £13 ($20.80) for 2 courses, £16 ($25.60) for 3 courses; dinner £18 ($28.80) for 2 courses, £22 ($35.20) for 3 courses. AE, MC, V. Mon–Fri 12:30–2:15pm (last order) and 6:30–9:30pm (last order). Tube: Tottenham Court Road. BRITISH.

A 2-minute walk from the British Museum, this informal restaurant has been transformed from a greasy spoon to a charming dining room. You can sample creative, up-to-date dishes impeccably prepared with fresh ingredients, such as salmon and coconut soup with lime, chili, and coriander or a dill and leek tart with smoked salmon, followed by char-grilled corn-fed chicken with pesto, or else char-grilled quails with a Muscat sauce. Crispy polenta with wilted spinach, baked mushrooms, and a pomegranate-balsamic vinaigrette is another winning combination. And who can resist the blood-orange sorbet? Frills are few here, but the standard of cooking is quite high. The kitchen is at its best when it's char-grilling. The place has proven so popular in London that it has recently doubled in size.

IN NEARBY FITZROVIA
MODERATE

✪ Nico Central. 35 Great Portland St., W1. ☎ **0171/436-8846.** Reservations required. Fixed-price 2-course lunch £20 ($32); fixed-price 3-course

Restaurants from Bloomsbury to the Strand

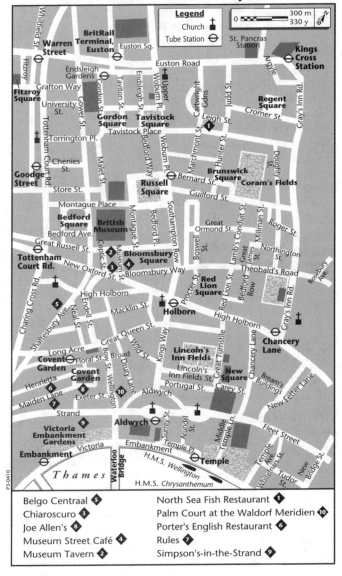

Legend

✝ Church
⊖ Tube Station

0 ▭▭▭ 300 m
        330 y

Belgo Centraal ❺
Chiaroscuro ❸
Joe Allen's ❽
Museum Street Café ❹
Museum Tavern ❷

North Sea Fish Restaurant ❶
Palm Court at the Waldorf Meridien ❿
Porter's English Restaurant ❻
Rules ❼
Simpson's-in-the-Strand ❾

dinner £27 ($43.20). AE, DC, MC, V. Mon–Fri noon–2:45pm, Mon–Sat 7–10:45pm. Tube: Oxford Circus. FRENCH/BRITISH.

This brasserie—founded and inspired by London's legendary chef, Nico Ladenis—who spends most of his time at Chez Nico at Ninety Park Lane—delivers earthy French cuisine that's been called "haute but not haughty" and consistently praised for its "absurdly good value." Of course, everything is handled with considerable culinary finesse. Guests sit on bentwood chairs at linen-covered tables. Nearly a dozen starters—the pride of the chef—will tempt you. The menu changes seasonally and according to the inspiration of the chef, but might include grilled duck served with risotto with *cèpes* (flap mushrooms) and Parmesan; pan-fried foie gras served with brioche and a caramelized orange; braised knuckle of veal; and baked filet of brill with assorted vegetables. Save room for one of the desserts—they are, in the words of one devotee, "divine."

HOLBORN
INEXPENSIVE

✪ **North Sea Fish Restaurant.** 7–8 Leigh St., WC1. ☎ **0171/387-5892.** Reservations recommended. Fish platters £6.30–£12.60 ($10.10–$20.15). AE, DC, MC, V. Mon–Sat noon–2pm and 5:30–10pm. Tube: Russell Square. SEAFOOD.

The fish served in this bright and clean restaurant is purchased fresh every day; the quality is high, and the prices low. It is, in fact, in the view of London's most diehard chippie devotees, the best in town. The fish is most often served battered and deep-fried, but you can also order it grilled. The menu is wisely limited. Students from the Bloomsbury area flock to the place.

COVENT GARDEN & THE STRAND
MODERATE

Belgo Centraal. 50 Earlham St., WC2. ☎ **0171/813-2233.** Reservations required for the restaurant. Main courses £6.95–£17.95 ($11.10–$28.70); set menus £6–£12 ($9.60–$19.20). AE, DC, MC, V. Mon–Sat noon–11:30pm, Sun noon–10:30pm. Closed Christmas. Tube: Covent Garden. BELGIAN.

Chaos reigns supreme in this audacious and cavernous basement, where mussels marinière with frites and 100 Belgian beers capture the spotlight. You'll take a freight elevator down past the busy kitchen and into a converted cellar, which has been divided into two large eating areas. One is a beer hall seating about 250; the menu here is the same as in the restaurant, but reservations aren't needed. The restaurant side has three nightly seatings: 5:30, 7:30, and 10pm. Between 5:30 and 8pm you can choose one of three set menus and you pay based on the time of your order: the earlier you order, the less you pay. Although tons of fresh mussels are the big attraction here, you can also opt for fresh Scottish salmon, roast chicken, a perfectly done steak, or one of the vegetarian specialties. Gargantuan plates of wild-boar sausages arrive with *stoemp* (Belgian mashed spuds and cabbage). Belgian stews called *waerzooï* are also served. With waiters dressed in maroon monks' habits with black aprons and barking orders into headset microphones, it's all a bit bizarre.

Rules. 35 Maiden Lane, WC2. ☎ **0171/836-5314.** Reservations recommended. Main courses £13.95–£16.95 ($22.30–$27.10). AE, DC, MC, V. Daily noon–11:30pm. Tube: Covent Garden. BRITISH.

If you're looking for London's most quintessentially British restaurant, eat here or at Wiltons. London's oldest restaurant was established in 1798 as an oyster bar; today, on the site of the original premises, it rambles through a series of antler-encrusted Edwardian dining rooms exuding patriotic nostalgia. You can order such classic dishes as Irish or Scottish oysters, jugged hare, and mussels. Game dishes are offered from mid-August to February or March. There's also wild Scottish salmon or wild sea trout; wild Highland red deer; and game birds like grouse, snipe, partridge, pheasant, and woodcock. As a finale, the "great puddings" continue to impress decade after decade.

Simpson's-in-the-Strand. 100 The Strand (next to the Savoy Hotel), WC2. ☎ **0171/836-9112.** Reservations required. Jacket and tie for men. Main courses £12.50–£22.50 ($20–$36); fixed-price 2-course lunch and pretheater dinner £10 ($16); set breakfasts £11.50 ($18.40). AE, DC, MC, V. Mon–Fri 7am–noon, daily noon–2:30pm and 6–11pm. Tube: Charing Cross or Embankment. BRITISH.

Simpson's is more of an institution than a restaurant—it's been in business since 1828. This very Victorian place boasts Adam paneling, crystal, and an army of grandly formal waiters to whom nouvelle cuisine means anything after Henry VIII. But most diners agree that Simpson's serves the best roasts in London, an array that includes roast sirloin of beef, roast saddle of mutton with red-currant jelly, roast Aylesbury duckling, and steak, kidney, and mushroom pie. (Remember to tip the tail-coated carver.) For a pudding, you might order the treacle roll and custard or Stilton with vintage port.

Taking advantage of the recent upsurge in popularity of traditional British cooking, Simpson's recently started serving the traditional breakfasts. The most popular one, curiously enough, is called "the ten deadly sins": a plate of sausage, fried egg, streaky and back bacon, black pudding, lamb's kidneys, fried bread, bubble and squeak, baked beans, lamb's liver, and fried mushrooms and tomatoes. That will certainly fortify you for the day. Simpson's now also features late-night jazz.

INEXPENSIVE

✪ **Joe Allen's.** 13 Exeter St., WC2. ☎ **0171/836-0651.** Reservations required. Main courses £6.50–£13.50 ($10.40–$21.60); Sun brunch £13.50–£15.50 ($21.60–$24.80). AE, V. Mon–Fri noon–1am, Sat 11:30am–1am, Sun 11:30am–midnight. Tube: Covent Garden or Embankment. AMERICAN.

This fashionable American restaurant near the Savoy attracts primarily theater crowds. Like the New York branch, it's decorated with theater posters. The menu has grown increasingly sophisticated and might include dishes such as grilled corn-fed chicken with sunflower-seed pesto, marinated sweet peppers, and garlic roast new potatoes, as well as specialties like black-bean soup and pecan pie. The Sunday brunch is one of the best in London. You get such main dishes as a mixed grill with lamb chop, calf's liver, and Cumberland sausage, and a choice of a Bloody Mary, Bucks Fizz, or a glass of champagne. The food here has been called "unimaginative." Loyal patrons say, "Who cares?"

✪ **Porter's English Restaurant.** 17 Henrietta St., WC2. ☎ **0171/836-6466.** Reservations recommended. Main courses £7.95–£8 ($12.70–$12.80); fixed-price menu £16.50 ($26.40). AE, DC, MC, V. Mon–Sat noon–11:30pm, Sun noon–10:30pm. Tube: Covent Garden or Charing Cross. ENGLISH.

In 1979 the 7th Earl of Bradford opened this restaurant, stating "it would serve real English food at affordable prices," and he has succeeded notably—and not just because Lady Bradford turned over her carefully guarded recipe for banana and ginger steamed pudding. A comfortable, two-story restaurant with a friendly, informal, and lively atmosphere, Porter's specializes in classic English pies, including Old English fish pie; lamb and apricot; ham, leek, and cheese; and of course, bangers and mash. Main courses are so generous, and accompanied by vegetables and side dishes, that you hardly need appetizers. The puddings, including bread-and-butter pudding or steamed syrup sponge, are the real puddings (in the American sense); they're served hot or cold, with whipped cream or custard. The bar does quite a few exotic cocktails, as well as beers, wine, or traditional English mead. A traditional English tea is also served for £3.50 ($5.60) per person. Who knows? You may even bump into his Lordship.

WESTMINSTER/VICTORIA
MODERATE

The Atrium. 4 Millbank, SW1. ☎ **0171/233-0032.** Reservations recommended for lunch, not for dinner. 2 courses for £16.95 ($27.10), 3 courses for £19.95 ($31.90). AE, DC, MC, V. Mon–Fri noon–3pm and 6–11pm. Tube: Westminster. BRITISH/IRISH.

In a soaring six-story atrium of a Westminster office building, this restaurant is surviving the departure of fabled restaurateur Antony Worall Thompson—it even seems to be doing quite well without his august supervision. The media has been unkind, ranting against the bland British cookery (actually British/Irish) and the terrible venue. However, the restaurant fills an important gap in a district of London where the pickings are slim. You might begin with a warm onion tart with a green tomato pickle. There's always a meat pie, maybe beef-and-Guinness, or a roast of the day, such as leg of lamb, in addition to the regularly featured rib of beef with mashed potatoes and fresh veggies. Other mains are likely to include dill-flavored salmon fish cakes, pot roast, or even vegetable dishes. Satisfyingly good desserts include apple charlotte or tipsy trifle. There's also has a good selection of British and Irish cheeses and a most decent wine list, with several whites and reds served by the glass. A pianist entertains in the evening.

✪ **Ken Lo's Memories of China.** 67–69 Ebury St., SW1. ☎ **0171/730-7734.** Reservations recommended. Main courses £9.80–£29.50 ($15.70–$47.20); fixed-price lunch £9.50–£21.50 ($15.20–$34.40); 3-course fixed-price dinner £27.80 ($44.50), 5-course fixed-price dinner £32.50 ($52), 3-course after-theater dinner £23.80 ($38.10). AE, DC, MC, V. Mon–Sat noon–2:30pm; daily 7–11:15pm. Tube: Victoria Station. CHINESE.

Many food critics consider this the finest Chinese restaurant in London—and so do we. It was founded by the late Ken Lo, whose grandfather was the Chinese ambassador to the Court of St. James's (he was knighted by Queen Victoria in 1880). Mr. Lo wrote more than 30 cookbooks and a well-known autobiography, and once hosted his own TV cooking show. The restaurant, which is impeccably staffed and outfitted in an appealing minimalist decor, has been called "a gastronomic bridge between London and China." The menu spans broadly divergent regions of China, and might include Cantonese quick-fried beef in oyster sauce, lobster with handmade noodles, pomegranate-prawn balls, and "bang-bang chicken" (a Szechuan dish), among many others. This restaurant should not be confused with its less expensive branch of the same name in Chelsea Harbour.

♦ Simply Nico. 48A Rochester Row, SW1. ☎ **0171/630-8061.** Reservations required. 2-course set lunch £22 ($35.20); 3-course set lunch £25 ($40); 3-course fixed-price dinner £27 ($43.20). AE, DC, MC, V. Mon–Fri 12:30–2pm, Mon–Sat 7–11pm. Tube: Victoria Station or St. James's. FRENCH.

This place is the brainchild of Nico Ladenis, of the much grander and more expensive Chez Nico at Ninety Park Lane. Run by his sous-chef, Simply Nico is, in Nico's own words, "cheap and cheerful." We think it's the best value in town. The wood floors reverberate the din of contented diners, who pack in daily at snug tables to enjoy the simply prepared—and invariably French-inspired—food. The set menu changes frequently, but options might include starters such as poached egg tartlet with hollandaise and marinated puréed mushrooms, followed by crispy duck with plum sauce.

♦ Tate Gallery Restaurant. Millbank, SW1. ☎ **0171/887-8877.** Reservations recommended. Main courses £9.50–£16 ($15.20–$25.60); 2-course set lunch £14.95 ($23.90). MC, V. Mon–Sat noon–3pm. Tube: Pimlico. Bus: 77 or 88. BRITISH.

This traditional restaurant is particularly attractive to wine fanciers; it offers what may be the best bargains for superior wines anywhere in Britain. Bordeaux and Burgundies are in abundance, and the management keeps the markup between 40% and 65%, rather than the 100% to 200% added to the wholesale price in other restaurants. In fact, the prices here are even lower than they are in most retail wine shops. Wine begins at £12.50 ($20) per bottle, or £3 ($4.80) per glass. Oenophiles frequently come just for lunch, heedless of the art. The restaurant's menu changes about every month. Dishes might include pheasant casserole; Oxford sausage with mashed potatoes; pan-fried skate with black butter and capers; and a selection of vegetarian dishes. Access to the restaurant is through the museum's main entrance on Millbank.

3 The City

MODERATE

♦ Café Spice Namaste. 16 Prescot St., E1. ☎ **0171/488-9242.** Reservations required. Main courses £8–£10 ($12.80–$16). AE, DC, MC, V. Mon–Sat noon–3pm and 6–10:30pm. Tube: Tower Hill. INDIAN.

This is Frommer's favorite Indian restaurant in London, where the competition is stiff, with Tamarind, Chutney Mary, and Bombay Brasserie also vying for top honors. It's cheerfully housed in a landmark Victorian hall near Tower Bridge. The chef, Cyrus Todiwala, is a Parsi and former resident of Goa, where he learned many of his culinary secrets. As a result, he concentrates on spicy southern and northern Indian dishes with a strong Portuguese influence, such as the signature dish of Goa, *sorpotel:* diced kidney, liver, and pork slow cooked and served in a brown-colored stew heavy with onions. Chicken and lamb are prepared a number of ways, from mild to spicy-hot. The homemade chutneys alone are worth the trip; our favorite is made with kiwi. All dishes come with fresh vegetables and Indian bread.

INEXPENSIVE

The George & Vulture. 3 Castle Court, Cornhill, EC3. ☎ **0171/626-9710.** Reservations accepted if you agree to arrive by 12:45pm. Main courses £6.45–£12.45 ($10.30–$19.90). AE, DC, MC, V. Mon–Fri noon–2:30pm. Tube: Bank. BRITISH.

Dickens enthusiasts should seek out this old Pickwickian place. Founded in 1660, it claims that it's "probably" the world's oldest tavern, and refers to an inn on this spot in 1175. They no longer puts up overnight guests here, but English lunches are still served on the tavern's three floors. Besides the daily specials, the menu includes a mixed grill, a loin chop, and fried Dover sole filets with tartar sauce. Potatoes and buttered cabbage are the standard vegetables, and the apple tart is always reliable. The system is to arrive and give your name, then retire to the Jamaican pub opposite for a drink; you're fetched when your table is ready. After, be sure to explore the mazes of pubs, shops, wine houses, and other old buildings near the tavern.

By the way, the Pickwick Club meets in this pub about six times a year for reunion dinners. This literary club is headed by Cedric Dickens, a great-great-grandson of Charles Dickens.

FOR AN ENGLISH BREAKFAST NEAR THE BARBICAN

✪ **Fox & Anchor.** 115 Charterhouse St., EC1. ☎ **0171/253-4838.** Reservations recommended. "Full house" breakfast £6.50 ($10.40); steak breakfast £5–£9 ($8–$14.40). AE, DC, MC, V. Mon–Fri 7–10:30am and noon–2:15pm. Tube: Barbican. BRITISH.

For British breakfast at its best, try this place, which has been serving traders from the nearby famous Smithfield meat market since the pub was built in 1898. Breakfasts are gargantuan, especially if you order the "full house"—a plate with at least eight items, including sausage, bacon, mushrooms, kidneys, eggs, beans, white pudding, and a fried slice of bread, along with unlimited tea or coffee, toast, and jam. Add a Black Velvet (champagne with Guinness) and the day is yours. (Of course, in the modern British view, Guinness ruins the champagne, but some people order it anyway—just to be traditional.) More fashionable is a Bucks Fizz, with orange juice and champagne (we usually call it a Mimosa). The Fox & Anchor is noted for its range of fine English ales, all available at breakfast. Butchers from the meat market, spotted with blood, still appear, as do nurses getting off their shifts, and clerks and tycoons from the City who've been working at bookkeeping chores (or making millions) all night.

4 On the Thames: Docklands & South Bank

ST. KATHARINE'S DOCK
INEXPENSIVE

☼ **Dickens Inn by the Tower.** St. Katharine's Way, E1. ☎ **0171/488-2208.** Reservations recommended. In Pickwick Grill, main courses £9.75–£15.50 ($15.60–$24.80); in Tavern Room, snacks and platters £3.75–£4.95 ($6–$7.90); in pizza restaurant, pizzas £4.25–£23 ($6.80–$36.80). AE, DC, MC, V. Restaurant, daily noon–3pm and 6:30–10:30pm; bar and pizza restaurant, daily 11:30am–4:30pm and 5:30–10pm. Tube: Tower Hill. BRITISH.

This three-floor restaurant is in an 1830 brick warehouse initially used to house spices imported from afar. It's deliberately devoid of carpets, curtains, or anything that might conceal its unusual antique trusses, including a set of massive redwood timbers that were part of the original construction. Large windows afford a sweeping view of the nearby Thames and Tower Bridge. On the ground level, you'll find a bar and the **Tavern Room,** serving sandwiches, platters of lasagna, steaming bowls of soup and chili, bar snacks, and other foods kids love. On the floor above is **Pizza on the Dock,** offering four sizes of pizzas that should also make the kids happy when they have a craving for the familiar. Above that, you'll find a relatively formal dining room, **The Pickwick Grill,** serving more elegant modern British meals; specials include steaks, char-grilled brochette of wild mushrooms, pan-fried calf's kidney with tangy lime and ginger sauce, and baked filet of cod.

BUTLER'S WHARF
MODERATE

Butler's Wharf Chop House. 36E Shad Thames, SE1. ☎ **0171/403-3403.** Reservations recommended. 3-course set lunch £36 ($57.60); dinner, main courses £11–£18 ($17.60–$28.80). AE, DC, MC, V. Sun–Fri noon–3pm (last order); Mon–Sat 6–11pm. Tube: Tower Hill. BRITISH.

Of the four restaurants housed in the renovated warehouse complex known as Butler's Wharf, this one is the closest to Tower Bridge, and is most committed to moderate prices. There's an even cheaper restaurant, la Cantina del Ponte, but most diners consider that merely a place for pastas. The Chop House was modeled after a large boathouse, with russet-colored banquettes, lots of exposed wood, flowers, candles, and big windows overlooking Tower Bridge and the Thames.

Dishes are largely adaptations of British recipes, some (but not all) geared for modern tastes: roast rack of lamb with champ and spiced lentils; a warm salad of mushrooms, soft poached egg, and tarragon hollandaise; roast salmon with tarragon and saffron cream sauce; and Dublin bay prawns and salmon wrapped in bacon. To follow, there might be a dark-chocolate tart with whisky cream or sticky toffee pudding. The bar offers such stiff-upper-lip choices as Theakston's best bitter, several English wines, and a half-dozen French clarets served by the jug.

5 In & Around Knightsbridge

VERY EXPENSIVE

✪ Marco Pierre White: The Restaurant. In the Hyde Park Hotel, 66 Knightsbridge, SW1. ☎ **0171/259-5380.** Reservations required. Fixed-price lunch £29.50 ($47.20); fixed-price dinner £75 ($120). AE, DC, MC, V. Mon–Fri noon–2:15pm, Mon–Sat 7–11:15pm. Tube: Knightsbridge. MODERN BRITISH.

Simply put, Marco Pierre White is the best chef in London. Creative, bold, and sophisticated, this daring young talent—the *enfant terrible* of the British kitchen—claims he never apprenticed in France, other than 2 weeks of eating in Paris restaurants. Lavish in his choice of ingredients—as you peruse the dozen or so appetizers, you'll note that most feature foie gras, caviar, and truffles—White explores the depths of flavor in food. Tantalizing mains include Bressole of Bresse pigeon (with foie gras again), and braised pig's trotter (inspired by Pierre Koffmann's masterpiece at Chelsea's La Tante Claire). As many critics have said, such explosive flavors make enduring the dull dining room more than worth it. Some plates, such as the gratinée of brill with a soft herb crust, young spinach, and a sabayon of chives, are arranged to best show off their brilliant colors as well. In spite of all this fancy fare, MPW makes the world's greatest mashed potatoes. One diner hailed his virtuosity with the mighty spud by declaring that they're "sieved, puréed, and squeezed through silk stockings." White's clearly a magician; if you can afford it, try to catch his show.

Restaurants from Knightsbridge to Kensington

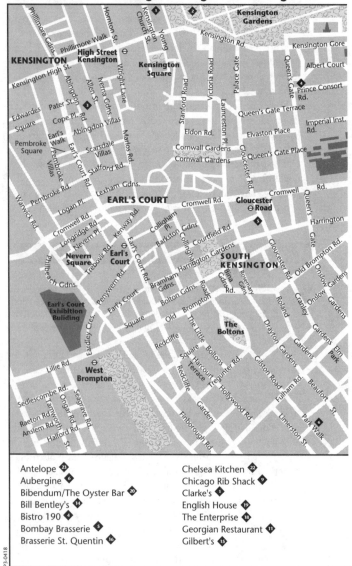

Antelope 🔶23	Chelsea Kitchen 🔶22
Aubergine 🔶6	Chicago Rib Shack 🔶9
Bibendum/The Oyster Bar 🔶20	Clarke's 🔶1
Bill Bentley's 🔶14	English House 🔶19
Bistro 190 🔶4	The Enterprise 🔶18
Bombay Brasserie 🔶5	Georgian Restaurant 🔶11
Brasserie St. Quentin 🔶16	Gilbert's 🔶15

P3-0418

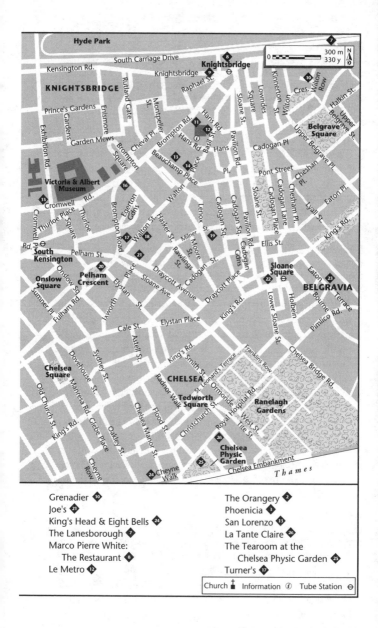

Grenadier ⑩

Joe's ㉑

King's Head & Eight Bells ㉔

The Lanesborough ⑦

Marco Pierre White:
    The Restaurant ⑧

Le Metro ⑫

The Orangery ②

Phoenicia ③

San Lorenzo ⑬

La Tante Claire ㉖

The Tearoom at the
    Chelsea Physic Garden ㉕

Turner's ⑰

Church ⛪ Information ⓘ Tube Station ⊖

MODERATE

Georgian Restaurant. On the 4th floor of Harrods, 87–135 Brompton Rd., SW1. ☎ **0171/225-5390** or 0171/225-6800. Reservations recommended for lunch and tea. Main courses £16–£20 ($25.60–$32); set lunch £22–£26.50 ($35.20–$42.40); sandwiches and pastries at teatime £13.50 ($21.60) per person. AE, DC, MC, V. Mon–Sat noon–3pm; tea Mon–Sat 3:45–5:15pm. Tube: Knightsbridge. BRITISH.

The Georgian Restaurant, set under elaborate ceilings and *belle époque* skylights atop London's fabled emporium, is one of the neighborhood's most appealing places for lunch and afternoon tea. One of the rooms, big enough for a ball, features a pianist whose music trills among the crystal of the chandeliers. A lunchtime buffet features cold meats and an array of fresh salads. If you want a hot meal, head for the carvery, where a uniformed crew of chefs dishes out such offerings as poultry, fish, and pork.

✪ **San Lorenzo.** 22 Beauchamp Place, SW3. ☎ **0171/584-1074.** Reservations required. Main courses £14.50–£20 ($23.20–$32). No credit cards. Mon–Sat 12:30–3pm and 7:30–11:30pm. Tube: Knightsbridge. ITALIAN.

This fashionable restaurant, a favorite of the late Princess Di, specializes in regional cuisines from Tuscany and the Piedmont. Frequently mentioned in the London tabloids thanks to its high-profile clients, San Lorenzo is the domain of effervescent owners Lorenzo and Mara Berni. Reliability is the keynote of the seasonal cuisine, which often includes homemade fettuccine with salmon; risotto with fresh asparagus; veal piccata; and partridge in white-wine sauce. Regional offerings might include salt cod with polenta. Some critics have dismissed this as a once-great place that had its heyday in the 1970s, but its continuing popularity is illustrated by how difficult it is to get a table. The food is really good, although attitudes and service need improvement. Nevertheless, it's still a great choice, especially if you're doing some upscale shopping along Beauchamp Place.

INEXPENSIVE

Chicago Rib Shack. 1 Raphael St., SW7. ☎ **0171/581-5595.** Reservations accepted, except Sat. Main courses £6.45–£14.95 ($10.30–$23.90). AE, MC, V. Daily 11:45am–11:45pm. Tube: Knightsbridge. AMERICAN.

This restaurant, just 100 yards from Harrods, specializes in real American barbecue, cooked in imported smoking ovens and marinated in a sauce made with 15 ingredients. Their decadent onion loaf is a famous treat. Visitors are encouraged to eat with their fingers, and bibs and hot towels are provided. A TV screen is suspended in the bar showing American sports games. The British touch is an overwhelming number of Victorian architectural antiques, which have been salvaged from demolished buildings all over the country. The 45-foot-long ornate mahogany and mirrored bar was once part of a Glasgow pub, and eight massive stained-glass windows came from a chapel in Lancashire.

6 Chelsea

VERY EXPENSIVE

✪ **La Tante Claire.** 68–69 Royal Hospital Rd., SW3. ☎ **0171/352-6045.** Reservations required at least 2 weeks in advance. Main courses £26.50–£28.50 ($42.40–$45.60) 3-course fixed-price lunch £27–£35 ($43.20–$56); minimum charge £50 ($80) per person. AE, DC, MC, V. Mon–Fri 12:30–2pm and 7–11pm. Tube: Sloane Square. FRENCH.

This is a culinary monument of the highest order. Thanks to a chef who's far more interested in turning out food of the highest order than he is in creating a media frenzy, the quality of the cuisine is so legendary that "Aunt Claire" is one of London's best—and most popular—French restaurants, even though the setting is far from grand. The ring of a doorbell set discreetly into the Aegean blue and white facade prompts an employee to usher you politely inside, where you can settle in and prepare yourself for one of London's finest dining experiences.

Pierre Koffman is the celebrated chef behind such culinary fireworks as ravioli langoustine and pigs' trotters stuffed with morels—who would've thought that the lowly pig trotter (long a staple of menus in Paris's Les Halles district) could be transformed into such a sublime creation as this? Other favorites include grilled scallops on squid-ink sauce; baked filet of turbot with mustard-seed sauce on a bed of roasted leeks; and duck in red-wine sauce and confit. The sauces that complement many of Koffman's dishes are exquisite.

EXPENSIVE

✪ **Aubergine.** 11 Park Walk, SW10. ☎ **0171/352-3449.** Reservations required 5 weeks in advance. 2-course fixed-price lunch £24 ($38.40); fixed-price dinner £45 ($72); menu prestige £55 ($88). AE, DC, MC, V. Mon–Fri noon–2:15pm, Mon–Sat 7–10:30pm. Tube: South Kensington. FRENCH.

"The Eggplant" is luring savvy diners down to the lower reaches of Chelsea where Gordon Ramsay continues to deliver some of the best food in London. Ramsay trained with some of Europe's greatest chefs, including Marco Pierre White and Joël Robuchon, but here he forges ahead with his own creative statement. Celebrities don't seem to impress him, whether it's Princess Margaret complaining that the air-conditioning is too cold (he lent her his cardigan) or Madonna calling for a late-night booking (Evita was turned down). Ramsay is a perfectionist, but not pretentious.

Subtlety and delicacy—without any sacrifice of the food's natural essence—are the keynotes of this genius's cuisine: Every dish is satisfyingly flavorsome, including his celebrated cappuccino of white beans with grated truffle. The fish and lighter, Mediterranean-style dishes are stunning achievements, as are the Bresse pigeon with a wild-mushroom ravioli and the filet of venison with braised baby turnips. There are only 14 tables, so bookings are imperative.

MODERATE

✪ **Chutney Mary.** 535 King's Rd., SW10. ☎ **0171/351-3113.** Reservations recommended. Main courses £9.95–£12.50 ($15.90–$20); fixed-price lunch Mon–Fri £9 ($14.40); 3-course brunch Sat–Sun £15 ($24). AE, DC, MC, V. Daily 12:30–3pm and 7–11pm. Tube: Fulham Broadway. BRITISH/INDIAN.

This multiple-award winner is often cited as the best Indian restaurant in England, although we think Café Spice Namaste (see above) poses a serious challenge, and wins by a small margin. Originally, Chutney Mary billed itself as "the world's first Anglo-Indian restaurant"; the chefs kept the English palate in mind and didn't go wholeheartedly ethnic. But, realizing that today's patrons are more adventuresome, they've turned the tide and now offer an authentic cuisine, served in a smart setting evocative of the days of Raj, that evokes the best of southern and southwestern Indian cooking. Specialties include Mangalore prawn curry, Hyderabad lamb korma (a curried diced lamb dish with spices), and scallop kedgeree with lentils; some dishes, such as green chicken curry, are inspired by the old Portuguese colony of Goa (now controlled by India). We love the stuffed eggplant in sesame with a tamarind sauce. Of course, the chefs prepare homemade chutneys based on decades-old recipes.

English House. 3 Milner St., SW3. ☎ **0171/584-3002.** Reservations required. Main courses £13.50–£17.25 ($21.60–$27.60); fixed-price set lunch £15.75 ($25.20); set dinner (Sun only) £20.75 ($33.20). AE, DC, MC, V. Mon–Sat 12:30–2:30pm and 7:30–11:15pm, Sun 12:30–2pm and 7:30–9:45pm. Tube: Sloane Square. BRITISH.

Another design creation of Roger Wren (who did the English Garden), this tiny restaurant will make you feel like you're a guest in an elegant but cozy Victorian house. The food is British, the menu seasonal, and each dish is given a subtle, modern treatment. Some savvy foodies find the cuisine outdated, but year after year—based on the mail we get—readers find it immensely satisfying. Begin with the pumpkin-and-rosemary soup (which sounds almost medieval), or grilled pigeon breast with a bean compote. For a main dish, try either the roast chump of lamb with bubble and squeak (cabbage and potatoes), or the braised ham hock with corn and mashed apples. Game is available in season, as is a fresh fish of the day. Summer berries in season predominate on the pudding menu, including fresh berries laced with elderflower syrup. Other offerings include a "Phrase of Apples," the chef's adaptation of a 17th-century recipe for a delectable apple pancake. London is filled with trendy places these days; every time we visit, we're newly pleased that there's still at least one place that focuses on rescuing long-forgotten recipes and bringing them to a new audience.

INEXPENSIVE

Chelsea Kitchen. 98 King's Rd., SW3. ☎ **0171/589-1330.** Reservations recommended. Main courses £2–£5.50 ($3.20–$8.80), fixed-price menu £6 ($9.60). No credit cards. Daily 8–11:15pm. Tube: Sloane Square. INTERNATIONAL.

This simple restaurant feeds large numbers of Chelsea residents in a setting that's changed very little since in 1961. The food and the clientele move fast, almost guaranteeing that the entire inventory of ingredients is sold out at the end of each day. Menu items usually include leek-and-potato soup, chicken Kiev, chicken parmigiana, steaks, sandwiches, and burgers. The clientele includes a broad cross-section of patrons—all having a good and cost-conscious time.

IN NEARBY CHELSEA HARBOUR
INEXPENSIVE

✪ **The Canteen.** Unit G4, Harbour Yard, Chelsea Harbour, SW10. ☎ **0171/351-7330.** Cover charge £1 ($1.60) per person. Reservations recommended. Main courses £13–£14 ($20.80–$22.40). AE, MC, V. Mon–Sat noon–3pm and 6:30pm–midnight (last order), Sun noon–3pm and 7–10:30pm (last order). Chelsea Harbour Hoppa Bus C3 from Earl's Court. On Sun, take a taxi. INTERNATIONAL.

This is the most viable and popular of the several restaurants in the Chelsea Harbour Complex, the multimillion-dollar development of formerly abandoned piers and wharves southwest of central London. You'll dine in a whimsical setting influenced by *Alice in Wonderland*— very fantastical and the kind of thing that children as well as adults love. The cuisine is exceptional, too. The menu changes every 2 months, but may include risotto of butternut squash, mascarpone, and coriander; pappardelle with field mushrooms and truffle oil; Roquefort and endive salad with honey-mustard dressing; escalope of calf's liver with Alsace bacon, black pudding, and pomme purée; and monkfish sauté with creamed peas, bacon, and potatoes.

Deal's Restaurant and Diner. Harbour Yard, Chelsea Harbour, SW10. ☎ **0171/795-1001.** Reservations recommended. Main courses £6.75–£16.50 ($10.80–$26.40). MC, V. Mon–Fri noon–3:30pm and 5:30–11pm, Sat noon–11:30pm, Sun noon–10pm. Chelsea Harbour Hoppa Bus C3 from Earl's Court. On Sun, take a taxi. INTERNATIONAL.

Deal's is co-owned by Princess Margaret's son, Viscount Linley, and Lord Lichfield. As soon as the Queen Mother arrived here on a barge to order a Deal's burger, the success of this place was assured. The early 1900s atmosphere includes ceiling fans and bentwood banquettes. The food is American-diner style, with a strong Eastern influence: Try a teriyaki burger, the prawn curry, spareribs, or a vegetarian dish, and finish with New England–style apple pie.

7 Kensington

EXPENSIVE

Turner's. 87–89 Walton St., SW3. ☎ **0171/584-6711.** Reservations required. Weekday set lunch £12.50–£15 ($20–$24); Sun fixed-price lunch £19.50 ($31.20); set dinner £32.50 ($52). AE, DC, MC, V. Mon–Fri and Sun 12:30–2:30pm; Mon–Sat 7:30–11:15pm, Sun 6–8:30pm. Tube: Knightsbridge. INTERNATIONAL.

This is the domain of Brian J. Turner, a Yorkshire native–turned–accomplished London chef who gained fame at a number of establishments, including the Capital Hotel, before acquiring his own place in the culinary sun. As one critic has aptly put it, his food comes not only fresh from the market each day but also "from the heart." He doesn't imitate anyone; he sets his own goals and standards. The set menus change every day, and the à la carte listings at least every season, but you might find chicken liver pâté with foie gras, a terrine of fresh salmon with a dill sauce, roast rack of lamb with herb crust, smoked and roast breast of duck in a port and green-peppercorn sauce, or sea bass on a bed of stewed leeks with a bacon dressing.

MODERATE

Joe's. 126 Draycott Ave., SW3. ☎ **0171/225-2217.** Reservations required. Main courses £10–£15.50 ($16–$24.80). AE, DC, MC, V. Mon–Sat noon–3pm and 7–11pm, Sun 10am–5pm. Tube: South Kensington. BRITISH.

This is one of three London restaurants established by fashion designer Joseph Ettedgui. Thanks to its sense of glamour and fun, it's often filled with well-known names from the British fashion, music, and entertainment industries. You can enjoy crab-crusted halibut, breast of duck with roasted root vegetables, char-grilled swordfish with cracked wheat and *salsa verde* (green sauce), or tiger prawns and monkfish kabobs with a sesame-balsamic dressing. It's all safe, but a bit unexciting. No one will mind if your meal is composed exclusively of appetizers. There's a bar near the entrance, a cluster of tables for quick meals near the door, and more leisurely (and gossipy) dining available in an area a few steps up. Brunch is served on Sunday, which is the cheapest way to enjoy this place. The atmosphere remains laid back and unstuffy, just like trendsetters in South Ken prefer it. With a name like Joe's, what else could it be?

INEXPENSIVE

✪ **Phoenicia.** 11–13 Abingdon Rd., W8. ☎ **0171/937-0120.** Reservations required. Main courses £9.50–£10.95 ($15.20–$17.50); buffet lunch £9.95–£11.95 ($15.90–$19.10); fixed-price dinner £15.30–£28.30 ($24.50–$45.30). AE, CB, DC, MC, V. Daily noon–midnight; buffet lunch, Mon–Sat 12:15–2:30pm, Sun 12:15–3:30pm. Tube: High Street Kensington. LEBANESE.

Phoenicia is highly regarded for the quality of its Lebanese cuisine—outstanding in presentation and freshness—and for its moderate prices. For the best value, go for lunch, when you can enjoy a buffet of more than two dozen *meze* (appetizers), presented in little pottery dishes. Each day at lunch, the chef prepares two or three home-cooked dishes to tempt your taste buds, including chicken in garlic sauce or stuffed lamb with vegetables. Many Lebanese patrons begin their meal with the *apéritif arak,* a liqueur some have compared to ouzo. To start, you can select from such classic Middle Eastern dishes as hummus or stuffed vine leaves. The chefs bake fresh bread and two types of pizza daily in a clay oven. Minced lamb, spicy and well flavored, is an eternal favorite. Various charcoal-grilled dishes are also offered.

SOUTH KENSINGTON
EXPENSIVE

Bibendum/The Oyster Bar. 81 Fulham Rd., SW3. ☎ **0171/581-5817.** Reservations required in Bibendum; not accepted in Oyster Bar. Main courses £17–£23 ($27.20–$36.80); 3-course fixed-price lunch £28 ($44.80); cold seafood platter in Oyster Bar £22 ($35.20) per person. AE, MC, V. Bibendum, Mon–Fri 12:30–2:30pm and 7–11:15pm, Sat 12:30–3pm and 7–11:15pm, Sun 12:30–3pm and 7–10:15pm; Oyster Bar, Mon–Sat noon–11:30pm, Sun noon–3pm and 7–10:30pm. Tube: South Kensington. FRENCH/MEDITERRANEAN.

In trendy Brompton Cross, this still-fashionable restaurant occupies two floors of a garage—the former home of the Michelin tire company—that's an art deco masterpiece. Although it's still going strong, Bibendum's heyday was in the early 1990s; it no longer enjoys the top berth on the lists of London's food critics. The white-tiled art deco–inspired room, with stained-glass windows, streaming sunlight, and a chic clientele, is an extremely pleasant place to dine. The fabulously eclectic cuisine, known for its freshness and simplicity, is comprised of carefully planned interpretations of what's available seasonally. Dishes might include roast quail flavored with Marsala and thyme, braised oxtail with prunes and almonds, and *ris de veau* (sweetbreads) with black butter and capers. Some of the best dishes are for dining *a deux:* Bresse pullet flavored with fresh tarragon, or roast lamb with a soubise sauce and onion rings.

Simpler meals and cocktails are available on the building's street level, in the Oyster Bar. The bar-style menu stresses fresh shellfish presented in the traditional French style, on ice-covered platters occasionally adorned with strands of seaweed. It's a crustacean lover's lair.

Bombay Brasserie. Courtfield Close, adjoining Bailey's Hotel, SW7. ☎ **0171/ 370-4040.** Reservations required. Main courses £12.50–£20.95 ($20–$33.50); buffet lunch £14.95 ($23.90). MC, V. Daily 7:30pm–midnight; buffet, daily 12:30–3pm. Tube: Gloucester Road. INDIAN.

This was London's best, most popular, and most talked-about Indian restaurant in the early 1990s, although lately it seems to have fallen off somewhat. It's still an impressive place, if a bit frayed here and there, and most visitors still find the cuisine "fabulous." It remains one of the best places in London for late-night dining. Before heading in to dinner, you might enjoy a drink amid the wicker of the pink-and-white bar; the bartender's specialty is a mango Bellini.

The waitstaff is professional and accommodating, each willing to advise you on the spice-laden delicacies. One look at the menu and you're launched on a grand culinary tour of the subcontinent: tandoori trout, fish with mint chutney, chicken tikka, and vegetarian meals. One corner of the menu is reserved for Goan cookery, representing that part of India seized from Portugal in 1961. The cookery of North India is represented by Mughlai specialties, including chicken biryani, the famous Muslim pilaf dish. Under the category "Some Like It Hot," you'll find such main courses as lamb korma, prepared Kashmiri style.

MODERATE

Gilbert's. 2 Exhibition Rd., SW7. ☎ **0171/589-8947.** Reservations recommended. Fixed-price lunch £7.50–£12.50 ($12–$20); main courses £17.20–£21.50

($27.50–$34.40). AE, DC, MC, V. Mon–Fri noon–2pm and 5:30–10pm. Closed Sat–Sun. Tube: South Kensington. BRITISH/FRENCH.

Gilbert's changes its menu every 4 weeks, based on the fresh ingredients of the season. Virtually everything is prepared on the premises of this small restaurant, including fudge with coffee and homemade bread at dinner. The cuisine is known as "new English," but much of it is comprised of adaptations of French dishes. The menu is normally limited to six choices per course, and there are often additional specials. At dinner, there's also a two- or three-course fixed-price meal. For dessert, try, if featured, Mrs. Beeton's lemon tart or chocolate tipsy cake. The wine list also changes frequently.

Brasserie St. Quentin. 243 Brompton Rd., SW3. ☎ **0171/581-5131.** Reservations required. Main courses £8–£15.30 ($12.80–$24.50); 2-course set-price lunch £10 ($16). AE, DC, MC, V. Mon–Sat noon–3pm and 7–11:30pm, Sun noon–3:30pm and 6:30–11pm. Tube: Knightsbridge or South Kensington. FRENCH.

St. Quentin is the most authentic-looking French brasserie in London. It attracts many members of London's French community, all of whom seem to talk at once (which tends to raise the level of noise and conviviality here to a dull roar). The decor of mirrors and crystal chandeliers reflects a fashion- and trend-conscious clientele who enjoy the social hubbub. The waiters take it all in stride, usually with seemingly effortless Gallic tact. Try the baked sea bass with thyme, the scallops and Bayonne ham, or the duck confit with lentils. Look also for a salad of crab and baby spinach or the artichoke heart with poached egg and mushrooms.

INEXPENSIVE

Bistro 190. In the Gore Hotel, 190 Queen's Gate, SW7. ☎ **0171/581-5666.** Reservations not accepted. Main courses £8.95–£12.95 ($14.30–$20.70). AE, DC, MC, V. Mon–Sat noon–12:30am, Sun noon–11pm. Tube: Gloucester Road. MEDITERRANEAN.

Set in the airy front room of the Gore hotel, this restaurant features a light Mediterranean cuisine much appreciated by the hip music and media crowd that keeps the place hopping. In an artfully simple setting of wood floors, potted plants, and framed art accented by a convivial but gossipy roar, you can dine on such dishes as lamb grilled over charcoal and served with deep-fried basil; salmon fish cakes with chips; a cassoulet of fish with chili toast; Mediterranean chowder with pesto toast; and—if it's available—a rhubarb crumble based loosely on an old-fashioned British dessert. Service isn't particularly fast, and the policy on reservations is confusing: Although membership is required for reservations, nonmembers may leave their name at the door and have a drink at the bar while they wait for a table. In the crush of peak dining hours, your waiter may or may not remember the special requests you made while placing your order, but the restaurant is nonetheless memorable. Go down to Downstairs 190 for a seafood or vegetarian meal.

8 Bayswater

VERY EXPENSIVE

✪ **I-Thai.** In the Hempel Hotel, Hempel Sq., 31035 Craven Hill Gardens, W2. ☎ **0171/298-9000.** Reservations required. Main courses £21–£27 ($33.60–$43.20). AE, DC, MC, V. Daily noon–2:30pm and 7–10pm. Tube: Lancaster Gate. ITALIAN/THAI.

Part of the aggressively minimalist Hempel Hotel, our favorite newcomer of the year specializes in upscale clients, upscale Thai and Italian food, and upscale prices. The antithesis of the kind of showy, lushly decorated restaurants of the 1980s that it was designed to compete with, I-Thai prides itself on a Zen-like calm. The menu is sparse but innovative, and expensive—dining here is more fun if you're on an expense account. We suggest beginning with one of the soups, either the spicy squid-ink version with lemongrass and coconut cream, or the chicken, coconut, and foie gras soup flavored with Thai basil. Main dishes are prepared exquisitely; we loved the truffle and mascarpone risotto and the stir-fried cellophane noodles with tiger prawns in a black-ink parcel. On our most recent trip, we tried a to-die-for breadcrumb-encrusted halibut with Thai eggplant, shiitake mushrooms, and lime-flavored rice—a dish made all the more flavorful with a pineapple and tamarind sauce. For dessert, try almost anything, especially the steamed Pandan pudding garnished with a warm coconut and blueberry sauce.

INEXPENSIVE

✪ **Veronica's.** 3 Hereford Rd., W2. ☎ **0171/229-5079.** Reservations required. Main courses £9.50–£15.50 ($15.20–$24.80); fixed-price meals £12.50 ($20). AE, DC, MC, V. Mon–Fri noon–3pm; Mon–Sat 6:30pm–midnight. Tube: Bayswater or Queensway. BRITISH.

Called the "market leader in cafe salons," Veronica's offers some of the finest British cuisine in London at tabs you won't mind paying. It's a celebration of British food; some dishes are even based on medieval and Tudor-age recipes, but all are given an imaginative modern twist by owner Veronica Shaw. One month she'll focus on Scotland, another month on Victorian foods, yet another on Wales, and the next on Ireland. Your appetizer might be a salad called salmagundy, made with crunchy pickled vegetables, that Elizabeth I enjoyed in her day. Another concoction might be watersouchy, a medieval stew crammed with mixed seafood. Many dishes are vegetarian, and everything tastes better when followed with one of the British farmhouse cheeses or a pudding. The restaurant is brightly and attractively decorated, and the service warm and ingratiating.

9 Teatime

Everyone should indulge in a formal afternoon tea at least once while in London. It's a relaxing, drawn-out, civilized affair that usually consists of three courses, all elegantly served on delicate china: first, dainty finger sandwiches (with the crusts cut off, of course); then fresh-baked scones served with jam and deliciously decadent clotted cream (also known as Devonshire cream); and, lastly, an array of bite-sized sweets. All the while, an indulgent server keeps the pot of tea of your choice fresh at hand. Sometimes, ports and aperitifs are on offer to accompany your final course. It's a quintessential British experience; we've listed our favorites below. We've also included a handful of less formal alternatives, in case high tea just isn't your style.

MAYFAIR

✪ **Brown's Hotel.** 30–34 Albemarle St., W1. ☎ **0171/493-6020.** Reservations not accepted. Afternoon tea £16.95 ($27.10). AE, DC, MC, V. Daily 3–5:45pm. Tube: Green Park.

Along with the Ritz, Brown's ranks as one of the most chic venues for tea in London. Tea is served in the drawing room; done in English antiques, oil paintings, and floral chintz—much like the drawing room of a country estate—it's an appropriate venue for such an affair. Give your name to the concierge upon arrival; he'll seat you at one of the clusters of sofas and settees or at low tables. There's a choice of 10 teas, plus sandwiches, scones, and pastries (all made right in the hotel kitchens) that are rolled around on a trolley for your selection.

Claridge's. Brook St., W1. ☎ **0171/629-8860.** Reservations recommended. Jacket and tie for men. High tea £16.50 ($26.40). AE, DC, MC, V. Daily 3–5pm. Tube: Bond Street.

Claridge's teatime rituals have managed to persevere through the years with as much pomp and circumstance as the British Empire itself. It's never stuffy, though; you'll feel very welcomed. Tea is served in The Reading Room. A portrait of Lady Claridge gazes benevolently from above as a choice of 17 kinds of tea is served ever so politely. The various courses are served consecutively, including finger sandwiches with cheese savories, apple and raisin scones, and yummy pastries.

✪ **Goode's.** 19 South Audley St., Mayfair Sq., W1. ☎ **0171/409-7242.** Mon–Fri noon–3pm and 4–6pm (tea). Fixed-price lunch £30 ($48) for 2 courses, £37.50 ($60) for 3; afternoon pot of tea £3 ($4.80); high tea £16 ($25.60); high tea with glass of champagne £23.50 ($37.60). AE, DC, MC, V. Tube: Bond Street or Green Park.

Few other teatime choices capture so accurately the charm and verve of the Edwardian age. The high-ceilinged gold and blue salon is housed on the premises of that prestigious British emporium of fine porcelain, Thomas Goode. The real charm of Goode's, which also serves elegant lunches, emerges during teatime, when any overt reference to the ever-so-polite commerce in the adjoining china shop is swept under the rugs. Indeed, all the trappings of the Empire are present, but with none of the staid cucumber-with-wilted-lettuce sandwiches you'd expect. You'll enjoy about a half-dozen types of tea; sandwiches made with poached chicken with red onion and compôte of pear, or tuna with sweet corn and arugula; and scones with gingered rhubarb preserves and clotted cream. A hostess and battallion of formally dressed butlers in tails present their fare on Thomas Goode porcelain at lunch (Versailles) and teatime (Pink Carousel).

Palm Court Lounge. In the Park Lane Hotel, Piccadilly, W1. ☎ **0171/499-6321.** Reservations required. Afternoon tea £15 ($24). AE, DC, MC, V. Daily 3:30–6pm. Tube: Hyde Park Corner or Green Park.

This is one of the great London favorites for tea. Restored to its former charm, the lounge has an atmosphere straight from 1927, with a domed yellow-and-white-glass ceiling, torchères, and palms in Compton stoneware *jardinières*. A delightful afternoon tea that includes a long list of different teas is served daily. Many guests come here after the theater for a sandwich and drink. A pianist plays every weekday afternoon. However, on Saturday and Sunday a popular tea dance is presented, costing £15 to £18 ($24–$28.80) per person, the latter with a glass of champagne.

ST. JAMES'S

Ritz Palm Court. In the Ritz Hotel, Piccadilly, W1. ☎ **0171/493-8181.** Reservations required at least 8 weeks in advance. Afternoon tea £21 ($33.60). AE, DC, MC, V. Daily 2–6pm. Jeans and sneakers not acceptable. Tube: Green Park.

This is the most fashionable place in London to order afternoon tea—and the hardest to get into without reserving way in advance. Its spectacular setting is straight out of *The Great Gatsby*, complete with marble steps and columns and a baroque fountain. You have your choice of a long list of teas, served with delectable sandwiches and luscious pastries.

✪ **St. James Restaurant & The Fountain Restaurant.** In Fortnum & Mason, 181 Piccadilly, W1. ☎ **0171/734-8040.** In the St. James, full tea £10.50–£12.25 ($16.80–$19.60). In The Fountain, full teas £6.95–£9.95 ($11.10–$15.90). AE, DC, MC, V. St. James, Mon–Sat 3–5:30pm; The Fountain, Mon–Sat 3–6pm. Tube: Piccadilly Circus.

This pair of tea salons functions as a culinary showplace for London's most prestigious grocery store, Fortnum & Mason, so the tea-drinking ritual is pretty spiffy.

The more formal of the two venues, the St. James, on the venerable store's fourth floor, is a pale-green and beige homage to formal Edwardian taste. More rapid, less formal, and better-tuned to the hectic pace of London shoppers and London commuters is the Fountain Restaurant, on the street level, where a sense of tradition and manners is very much a part of the teatime experience, but in a less opulent setting. The quantities of food served in both venues are usually ample enough to be defined as full-fledged early suppers for most theatregoers.

COVENT GARDEN & THE STRAND

✪ **Palm Court at the Waldorf Meridien.** In the Waldorf Hotel, Aldwych, WC2. ☎ **0171/836-2400.** Reservations required. Jacket and tie for men. Afternoon tea £15–£18 ($24–$28.80); tea dance £22–£25 ($35.20–$40). AE, DC, MC, V. Afternoon tea Mon–Fri 3:30–6pm; tea dance Sat–Sun 3:30–6pm. Tube: Covent Garden.

The Waldorf's Palm Court combines afternoon tea with afternoon dancing (such as the fox-trot, quickstep, and the waltz). The Palm Court is aptly compared to a 1920s movie set (which it has been several times in its long life). You can order tea on a terrace or in a pavilion the size of a ballroom lit by skylights. On tea-dancing days, the orchestra leader will conduct such favorites as "Ain't She Sweet" and "Yes, Sir, That's My Baby," as a butler in a cutaway inquires if you want a cucumber sandwich.

KNIGHTSBRIDGE

✪ **The Georgian Restaurant.** On the 4th floor of Harrods, 87–135 Brompton Rd., SW1. ☎ **0171/581-1656.** High tea £12.75 ($20.40) per person. AE, DC, MC, V. Teatime, Mon–Sat 3:45–5:30pm (last order).

As long as anyone can remember, teatime at Harrods has been one of the most distinctive features of Europe's most famous department store. A flood of visitors is somehow gracefully herded into a high-volume but nevertheless elegant room. Many come here expressly for the tea ritual, where staff haul silver pots and trolleys laden with pastries and sandwiches through the cavernous dining hall. The list of teas available (at least 50) is sometimes so esoteric that choosing one might remind you of selecting one of the vintages of a sophisticated wine cellar. Most exotic is Betigala, a rare blend from China, similar to Lapsang Souchong.

BELGRAVIA

The Lanesborough. Hyde Park Corner, SW1. ☎ **0171/259-5599.** Reservations recommended, especially on weekends. High tea £14.50 ($23.20); high tea with strawberries and champagne £21.50 ($34.40); cup of tea £3.10 ($4.95). AE, DC, MC, V. Daily 3:30–5:30pm (last order). AE, DC, MC, V. Tube: Hyde Park Corner.

You'll suspect that many of the folk sipping exotic teas here have dropped in to inspect the public areas of one of London's most expensive hotels. The staff here rises to the challenge with aplomb, offering a selection of seven teas that include the Lanesborough special blend and such herbal esoteria as Rose Cayou. The focal point for this ritual is the Conservatory, a glass-roofed Edwardian fantasy filled with potted plants and a sense of the long-gone majesty of empire. The finger sandwiches, scones, and sweets are all appropriately lavish and endlessly correct.

CHELSEA

The Tearoom at the Chelsea Physic Garden. 66 Royal Hospital Rd., SW3. ☎ **0171/352-5646.** Tea with cake is £3 ($4.80). MC, V (in shop only). Wed 2–5pm, Sun 2–6pm. Closed late Nov–Mar. Tube: Sloane Square.

It encompasses only 3½ spectacular acres, crisscrossed with gravel paths and ringed with a high brick wall that shuts out the roaring traffic of Royal Hospital Road. On the 2 days a week it's open, its tearoom is likely to be filled with botanical enthusiasts merrily sipping cups of tea as fortification for their garden treks. The setting is a rather banal-looking Edwardian building. Since the tearoom is only an adjunct to the glories of the garden itself, don't expect lavish rituals. But you can carry your cakes and cups of tea outside, into a garden that, despite meticulous care, always looks a bit unkempt. (Herbaceous plants within its hallowed precincts are left untrimmed to encourage bird life and seed production.) Botanists and flower lovers in general find the place fascinating.

KENSINGTON

✪ **The Orangery.** In the gardens of Kensington Palace, W8. ☎ **0171/376-0239.** Reservations not accepted. Pot of tea £1.60 ($2.55); summer cakes and puddings £1.95–£3.50 ($3.10–$5.60), sandwiches £5.95 ($9.50). MC, V. Mar–Oct 10am–6pm; Nov–Mar 10am–4pm. Tube: High Street Kensington or Queensway.

In its way, the Orangery is the most amazing place for midafternoon tea in the world. Set about 50 yards north of Kensington Palace, it occupies a long and narrow garden pavilion built in 1704 by Queen Anne as a site for her tea parties. In homage to that monarch's original intentions, rows of potted orange trees bask in the sunlight from soaring windows, and tea is still served amid Corinthian columns, ruddy-colored bricks, and a pair of Grinling Gibbons woodcarvings.

To help accessorize the place, there are even some urns and statuary that the Royal Family imported to the site from Windsor Castle. The menu includes lunchtime soups and sandwiches, which come with a salad and a portion of upscale potato chips known as "kettle chips." There's also an array of different teas, served with high style, usually accompanied by freshly baked scones with clotted cream and jam, and Belgian chocolate cake.

10 Pubs & Wine Bars

IN THE WEST END
MAYFAIR

Shepherd's Tavern. 50 Hertford St., W1. ☎ **0171/499-3017.** Reservations recommended. Main courses from £7 ($11.20). AE, DC, MC, V. Restaurant, daily noon–3pm, Mon–Sat 6:30–10pm; Sun 7–10:30pm; bar, Mon–Sat noon–11pm, Sun noon–3pm and 7–10:30pm. Tube: Green Park. BRITISH.

This pub is one of the focal points of the all-pedestrian shopping zone of Shepherd's Market. It's set amid a warren of narrow, cobble-covered streets behind Park Lane, in an 18th-century town house very similar to many of its neighbors.

The street-level bar is cramped but congenial, with many luxurious touches, including a collection of memorabilia and antiques. Many of the regulars recall this tavern's popularity with the pilots of the Battle of Britain. Bar snacks include simple platters of shepherd's pie and fish-and-chips. More formal dining is available upstairs in the cozy, cedar-lined Georgian-style restaurant; the classic British menu probably hasn't changed much since the 1950s. If you're a little leery of the roast beef with Yorkshire pudding, go with the Oxford ham instead.

St. James's

Bubbles. 41 N. Audley St., W1. ☎ **0171/491-3237.** Reservations recommended. Main courses £4.50–£12.50 ($7.20–$20); fixed-price dinner £14.50 ($23.20); fixed-price vegetarian menu £5.50–£6.25 ($8.80–$10). AE, DC, MC, V. Daily 11am–11pm. Tube: Marble Arch or Bond Street. BRITISH/INTERNATIONAL VEGETARIAN.

This interesting wine bar lies between Upper Brook Street and Oxford Street (in the vicinity of Selfridges). The owners attach equal importance to their food and to their impressive wine list (some wines are sold by the glass). On the ground floor, you can enjoy not only fine wines but also draft beer and liquor, along with a limited but well-chosen selection of bar food, such as smoked salmon on brown bread, or a homemade steak burger with fries, salad, and cheese. Downstairs, the restaurant serves both English and continental dishes, including an appealing vegetarian selection. You might begin with French onion soup, followed by bangers and mash with onion gravy, Dover sole, or grilled chicken breast with apple rice and creamed leeks.

Red Lion. 2 Duke of York St. (off Jermyn St.), SW1. ☎ **0171/930-2030.** Sandwiches £2.30 ($3.70); fish-and-chips £8 ($12.80). No credit cards. Mon–Sat noon–11pm. Tube: Piccadilly Circus. BRITISH.

This little Victorian pub, with its early 1900s decorations and mirrors 150 years old, has been compared in spirit to Edouard Manet's painting *A Bar at the Folies-Bergère* (on display at the Courtauld Institute Galleries). You can order premade sandwiches, but once they're gone you're out of luck. On Friday and Saturday, homemade fish-and-chips are also served. Wash down your meal with Ind Coope's fine ales or the house's special beer, Burton's, an unusual brew made of spring water from the Midlands town of Bourton-on-Trent.

Leicester Square

✪ **Cork & Bottle Wine Bar.** 44–46 Cranbourn St., WC2. ☎ **0171/734-7807.** Reservations recommended. Main courses £5.95–£8.95 ($9.50–$14.30); glass of wine from £2.50 ($4). AE, DC, MC, V. Mon–Sat 11am–midnight, Sun noon–10:30pm. Tube: Leicester Square. INTERNATIONAL.

Don Hewitson, a connoisseur of fine wines for more than 30 years, presides over this trove of blissful fermentation. The metamorphic wine list features an excellent selection of Beaujolais crus from Alsace, 30 selections from Australia, 30 champagnes, and a good selection of California labels. If you want something to wash down, the most successful dish is a raised cheese-and-ham pie, with a cream cheese–like filling and crisp well-buttered pastry—not your typical quiche. There's also chicken and apple salad, Lancashire hot pot, Mediterranean prawns with garlic and asparagus, lamb in ale, and tandoori chicken.

Salisbury. 90 St. Martin's Lane, WC2. ☎ **0171/836-5863.** Reservations not accepted. Buffet meal £3.90–£5.99 ($6.25–$9.60). AE, DC, MC, V. Mon–Sat 11am–11pm, Sun noon–10:30pm. Tube: Leicester Square. BRITISH.

Salisbury's glittering cut-glass mirrors reflect the faces of English stage stars (and hopefuls) sitting around the curved buffet-style bar. A less prominent place to dine is the old-fashioned wall banquette with its copper-topped tables and art nouveau decor. The pub's specialty—home-cooked pies set out in a buffet cabinet with salads—is really quite good and inexpensive. Hot food is served from noon until 7:30pm, cold sandwiches from noon to 10pm.

SOHO

Old Coffee House. 49 Beak St., W1. ☎ **0171/437-2197.** Main courses £4–£4.50 ($6.40–$7.20). No credit cards. Restaurant, Mon–Sat noon–3pm; pub, Mon–Sat 11am–11pm, Sun noon–3pm and 7–10:30pm. Tube: Oxford Circus or Piccadilly Circus. BRITISH.

Once honored as "Soho Pub of the Year," the Old Coffee House takes its name from the coffeehouse heyday of 18th-century London, when coffee was called "the devil's brew." The pub still serves pots of filtered coffee. The place is heavily decorated with bric-a-brac, including archaic musical instruments and World War I recruiting posters. Have a drink at the long, narrow bar, or retreat to the upstairs restaurant, where you can enjoy good pub food at lunch, including steak-and-kidney pie, one of three vegetarian dishes, scampi and chips, or a burger and fries.

BLOOMSBURY

Museum Tavern. 49 Great Russell St., WC1. ☎ **0171/242-8987.** Bar snacks £2–£6 ($3.20–$9.60). AE, DC, MC, V. Mon–Sat 9:30am–11pm, Sun 10:30–10:30pm. Tube: Holborn or Tottenham Court Road. BRITISH.

Across the street from the British Museum, this circa-1703 pub retains most of its antique trappings: velvet, oak paneling, and cut glass. It lies right in the center of the University of London area and is popular with writers, publishers, and researchers from the museum. (Supposedly, Karl Marx wrote in the pub over meals.) Traditional English food is served, with steak-and-kidney pie, sausages cooked in English cider, and chef's specials on the hot-food menu. Cold fare includes turkey-and-ham pie, ploughman's lunch, and salads. Several English ales, cold lagers, cider, Guinness, wines, and spirits are available. Food and coffee are served all day; the pub gets crowded at lunchtime.

WESTMINSTER (NEAR TRAFALGAR SQUARE)

Sherlock Holmes. 10 Northumberland St., WC1. ☎ **0171/930-2644.** Reservations recommended for restaurant. Main courses £7.95–£13.95 ($12.70–$22.30); fixed-price menus £10.95–£15.95 ($17.50–$25.50); ground-floor snacks £3.95–£4.75 ($6.30–$7.60). AE, DC, MC, V. Restaurant, Mon–Thurs noon–3pm and 5:30–10:45pm, Fri–Sun noon–10:30pm; pub, Mon–Sat 11am–11pm, Sun noon–10:30pm. Tube: Charing Cross or Embankment. BRITISH.

It would be rather strange if the Sherlock Holmes were not the old gathering spot for the Baker Street Irregulars, a once-mighty clan of mystery lovers who met here to honor the genius of Sir Arthur Conan Doyle's most famous fictional character. Upstairs, you'll find a re-creation of the living room at 221B Baker St. and such "Holmes-iana" as the serpent of *The Speckled Band* and the head of *The Hound of the Baskervilles.* In the upstairs dining room, you can order complete meals with wine. Try "Copper Beeches" (grilled butterfly chicken breasts with lemon and herbs). You select dessert from the trolley. The downstairs is mainly for drinking, but there's a good snack bar with cold meats, salads, cheeses, and wine and ales sold by the glass.

THE CITY

✪ **Ye Olde Cheshire Cheese.** Wine Office Court, 145 Fleet St., EC4. ☎ **0171/353-6170.** Main courses £12.95–£15.95 ($20.70–$25.50). AE, DC, MC, V. Daily noon–2:30pm and 6–9:30pm; drinks and bar snacks, daily 11:30am–11pm. Tube: St. Paul's or Blackfriars. BRITISH.

Set within a recently remodeled, carefully preserved building whose foundation was laid in the 13th century, this is the most famous of the old city chop houses and pubs. Established in 1667, it claims to be the spot where Dr. Samuel Johnson (who lived nearby) entertained admirers with his acerbic wit. Charles Dickens and other literary lions also patronized the place. Later, many of the ink-stained journalists and scandalmongers of 19th- and early–20th-century Fleet Street made it their local. You'll find six bars and two dining rooms here. The house specialties include "ye famous pudding" (steak, kidney, mushrooms, and game) and Scottish roast beef with Yorkshire pudding and horseradish sauce. Sandwiches, salads, and standby favorites like steak-and-kidney pie are also available.

Ye Olde Cock Tavern. 22 Fleet St., EC4. ☎ **0171/353-8570.** Reservations recommended. Main courses £9–£14 ($14.40–$22.40); fixed-price 2-course lunch £12 ($19.20). AE, DC, MC, V. Carvery, Mon–Fri noon–3pm; pub, Mon–Fri 11am–11pm. Tube: Temple or Chancery Lane. BRITISH.

Dating back to 1549, this tavern boasts a long line of literary patrons: Samuel Pepys mentioned the pub in one of his diaries; Dickens frequented it, and Tennyson referred to it in one of his poems, a copy of which is framed and proudly displayed near the front entrance. It's one of the few buildings in London to have survived the Great Fire of 1666. At street level, you can order a pint as well as snack-bar food, steak-and-kidney pie, or a cold chicken-and-beef plate with salad. At the Carvery upstairs, a meal includes a choice of appetizers, followed by lamb, pork, beef, or turkey.

KNIGHTSBRIDGE

Bill Bentley's. 31 Beauchamp Place, SW3. ☎ **0171/589-5080.** Reservations recommended. Main courses £8–£16.90 ($12.80–$27.05). AE, MC, V. Mon–Sat noon–2:30pm and 6–10:30pm. Tube: Knightsbridge. BRITISH.

Bill Bentley's, on fashionable Beauchamp Place, has a varied and reasonable wine list that has a good selection of Bordeaux. Many visitors come here just to sample the wines, including some New World choices along with popular French selections. In summer, a garden patio opens to patrons. If you don't prefer the formality of the restaurant, you can order from the wine-bar menu that begins with a half-dozen oysters, or you can enjoy the chef's fish soup with croûtons and *rouille*. Main dishes include the famous salmon cakes, served with tomato sauce, and daily specialties. In keeping with contemporary trends, the restaurant menu has been simplified and is rather less expensive than before. It changes frequently, but typical dishes might include avocado, crab, and prawn salad as an appetizer, followed by supreme of chicken with oyster mushrooms and a madeira jus, or else grilled rainbow trout with a petit garni and lemon sauce. A large selection of bottled beers and spirits is also available.

Le Metro. 28 Basil St., SW3. ☎ **0171/589-6286.** Reservations recommended. Main courses £7.50–£8.50 ($12–$13.60). AE, DC, MC, V. Mon–Sat 7:30am–10:30pm. Tube: Knightsbridge. INTERNATIONAL.

Located just around the corner from Harrods, Le Metro draws a fashionable crowd to its basement precincts. Owned by David and Margaret Levin, the place serves good, solid, and reliable food prepared with flair. The menu changes frequently, but try the chicken satays or confit of duck with lentils, garlic, and shallots if you can. You can order special wines by the glass.

IN NEARBY BELGRAVIA

Antelope. 22 Eaton Terrace, SW1. ☎ **0171/730-7781.** Reservations recommended for upstairs dining room. Main courses £6–£8 ($9.60–$12.80). AE, MC, V. Daily noon–2:30pm; pub, Mon–Fri 11am–11pm, Sat 11am–3pm and 6–11pm, Sun noon–3pm and 7–10:30pm. Tube: Sloane Square. BRITISH.

Located on the fringe of Belgravia, at the gateway to Chelsea, this eatery caters to a hodgepodge of clients, aptly described as people of all classes, colors, and creeds (including English rugby aficionados). At lunchtime, the ground-floor bar provides hot and cold pub food, but in the evening, only drinks are served there. Upstairs, the lunch menu includes principally English dishes: fish-and-chips, jugged hare, and the like.

✪ **Grenadier.** 18 Wilton Row, SW1. ☎ **0171/235-3074.** Reservations recommended. Main courses £10.95–£19.95 ($17.50–$31.90). AE, DC, MC, V. Daily noon–3pm; Mon–Sat 6–10pm, Sun noon–3:30pm and 7–10:30pm. Tube: Hyde Park Corner. BRITISH.

Tucked away in a mews, the Grenadier is one of London's reputedly haunted pubs. Aside from the poltergeist, the basement houses the original bar and skittles alley used by the Duke of Wellington's officers on leave from fighting Napoléon. The scarlet front door of the one-time officers' mess is guarded by a scarlet sentry box and shaded by a vine. The bar is nearly always crowded. Lunch and dinner is offered daily—even on Sunday, when it's a tradition to drink Bloody Marys here. In the stalls along the side, you can order good-tasting fare based on seasonal ingredients. Good dishes include pork Grenadier, and chicken and Stilton roulade.

CHELSEA

King's Head & Eight Bells. 50 Cheyne Walk, SW3. ☎ **0171/352-1820.** Main courses £4.95–£6 ($7.90–$9.60). MC, V. Mon–Sat 11am–11pm, Sun noon–10:30pm. Tube: Sloane Square. BRITISH.

Many distinguished personalities once lived near this historic Thameside pub; a short stroll will take you to the former homes of Carlyle, Swinburne, and George Eliot. In other days, press gangs used to roam these parts of Chelsea seeking lone travelers to abduct for a life at sea. Today, it's popular with stage and TV celebrities as well as writers. The best English beers are served here, as well as a good selection of reasonably priced wine. The menu features homemade specials of the day, such as fish 'n' chips or sausage 'n' chips, and including at least one vegetable main dish. On Sunday, a roast of the day is served. You can also enjoy live music while you sip your beer.

5

Exploring London

*D*r. Samuel Johnson said, "When a man is tired of London, he is tired of life, for there is in London all that life can afford." Indeed, it would take a lifetime to explore every alley, court, street, and square in this vast city (and volumes to discuss them). Since you don't have a lifetime to spend here, we've discussed the best of what London has to offer in this chapter. Still, what's included is more than enough to keep you busy on a dozen trips to the city by the Thames.

A Note about Admission and Open Hours: In the listings below, children's prices generally apply to those 16 and under. To qualify for a senior discount, you must be 60 or older. Students must present a student ID to get discounts, where available. Also note that many attractions, in addition to shutting down for bank holidays, close for some days around Christmas and New Year's (and, in some cases, early in May), so be sure to call ahead if you're visiting in those seasons.

1 The Top Attractions

✪ **The British Museum.** Great Russell St., WC1. ☎ **0171/323-8599,** or 0171/636-1555 for recorded information. Free admission. Mon–Sat 10am–5pm, Sun 2:30–6pm. Tube: Holborn or Tottenham Court Road.

Set in scholarly Bloomsbury, this immense museum grew out of a private collection of manuscripts purchased in 1753 with the proceeds of a lottery. It grew and grew, fed by legacies, discoveries, and purchases, until it became one of the most comprehensive collections of art and artifacts in the world. It's utterly impossible to take in this museum in 1 day.

The overall storehouse splits basically into the national collections of antiquities; prints and drawings; coins, medals, and banknotes; and ethnography. Even on a cursory first visit, be sure to see the Asian collections (the finest assembly of Islamic pottery outside the Islamic world), the Chinese porcelain, the Indian sculpture, and the Prehistoric and Romano-British collections. Special treasures you might want to seek out on your first visit include the Rosetta Stone,

Central London Sights

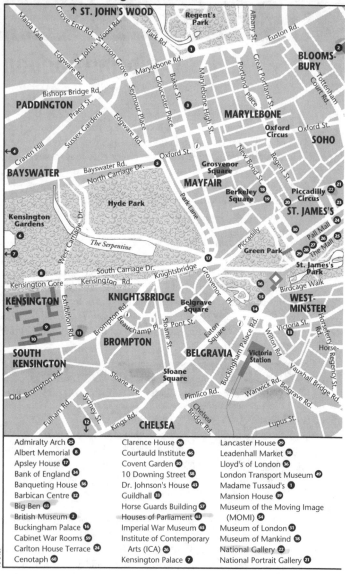

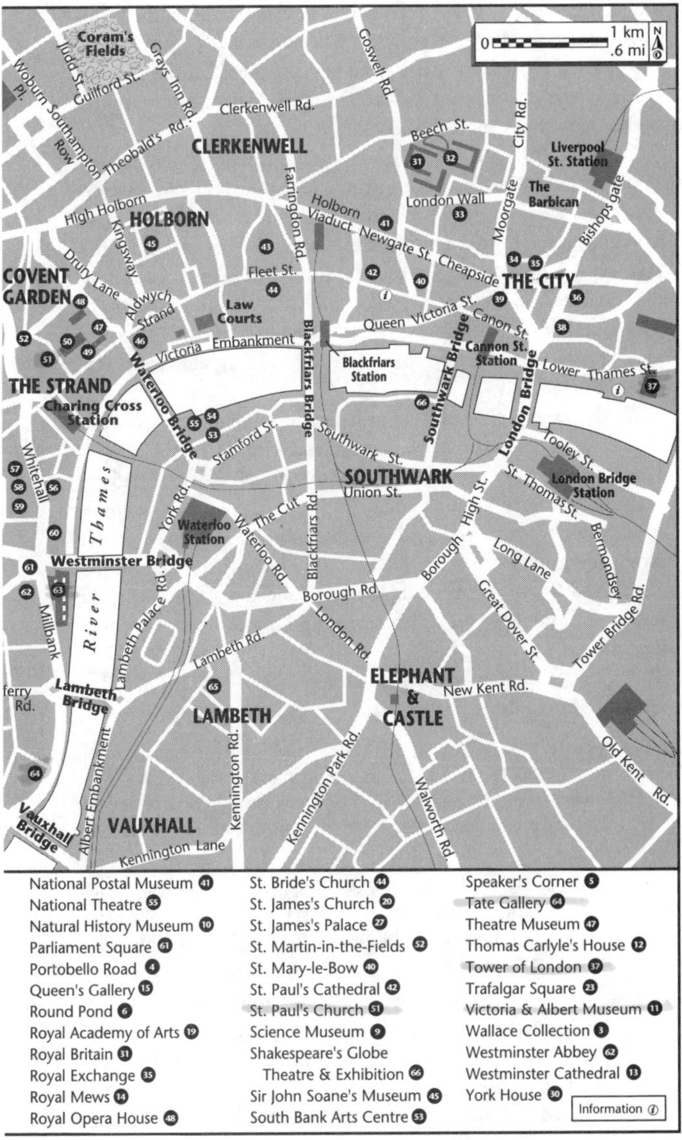

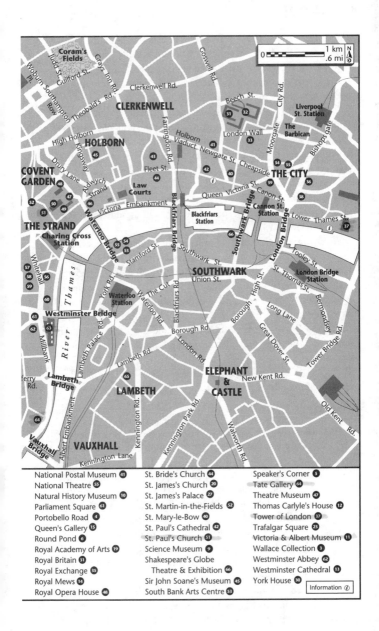

National Postal Museum 41
National Theatre 55
Natural History Museum 10
Parliament Square 61
Portobello Road 4
Queen's Gallery 15
Round Pond 6
Royal Academy of Arts 19
Royal Britain 31
Royal Exchange 35
Royal Mews 14
Royal Opera House 48

St. Bride's Church 44
St. James's Church 20
St. James's Palace 27
St. Martin-in-the-Fields 52
St. Mary-le-Bow 40
St. Paul's Cathedral 42
St. Paul's Church 51
Science Museum 9
Shakespeare's Globe Theatre & Exhibition 66
Sir John Soane's Museum 45
South Bank Arts Centre 53

Speaker's Corner 5
Tate Gallery 64
Theatre Museum 47
Thomas Carlyle's House 12
Tower of London 37
Trafalgar Square 23
Victoria & Albert Museum 11
Wallace Collection 3
Westminster Abbey 62
Westminster Cathedral 13
York House 30

Information ⓘ

whose discovery led to the deciphering of hieroglyphs, in the Egyptian Room; the Elgin Marbles, a priceless series of pediments, metopes, and friezes of the Parthenon in Athens, in the Duveen Gallery; and the legendary Black Obelisk, dating from around 860 B.C., in the Nimrud Gallery.

Other treasures include the contents of Egyptian royal tombs (including mummies); fabulous arrays of 2,000-year-old jewelry, cosmetics, weapons, furniture, and tools; Babylonian astronomical instruments; and winged lions (in the Assyrian Transept) that once guarded Ashurna-sirpal's palace at Nimrud. The latest additions include a Mexican Gallery, a Hellenistic Gallery, and a History of Money exhibit. The exhibits change throughout the months, so if your heart is set on seeing a specific treasure, call ahead to make sure it's on display.

Insider tip: With 2$\frac{1}{2}$ miles of galleries, the museum is overwhelming. To get a handle on it, we recommend taking a 1$\frac{1}{2}$-hour overview tour for £6 ($9.60) Monday to Saturday at 10:45am, 11:15am, 1:45pm, and 2:15pm, or Sunday at 3pm, 3:20pm, and 3:45pm. After, you can return to the galleries that most interested you. If you have only minutes to spare for the museum, concentrate on the Greek and Rome rooms (1–15), which hold the golden hoard of booty both bought and stolen from the Empire's once far-flung colonies.

For information on the British Library, see p. 148; for the Museum of Mankind, see p. 150.

✪ **Buckingham Palace.** At end of The Mall (on the road running from Trafalgar Sq.). ☎ **0171/839-1377.** Palace tours (usually offered in Aug and Sept) £9 ($14.40) adults to age 60, £6.50 ($10.40) seniors, £5 ($8) children under 17. Changing of the Guard free. Tube: St. James's Park, Green Park, or Victoria.

This massive, graceful building is the official residence of the Queen. The redbrick palace was built as a country house for the notoriously rakish duke of Buckingham. In 1762, it was bought by King George III, who needed room for his 15 children; it didn't become the official royal residence, though, until Queen Victoria took the throne; she preferred it over St. James's Palace. From George III's time, the building was continuously expanded and remodeled, faced with Portland stone, and twice bombed (during the Blitz). Located in a 40-acre garden, it's 360 feet long and contains 600 rooms. You can tell whether Her Majesty is at home by the Royal Standard flying at the masthead.

For most of the year, you can't visit the palace unless you're officially invited. Since 1993, though, much of it has been open for tours during an 8-week period in August and September, when the Royal Family is usually vacationing outside London. Elizabeth II agreed to allow visitors to tour the State Room, Grand Staircase, Throne Room, and other areas designed by John Nash for George IV, as well as the huge Picture Gallery, which displays masterpieces by Van Dyck, Rembrandt, Rubens, and others. The admission charges help pay for repairing Windsor Castle, badly damaged by fire in 1992. The Queen has decided that the palace will remain open to the public until 2000, at which time a decision to continue will be reviewed.

Insider tip: You can avoid the long queues by purchasing tickets before you go through **Edwards & Edwards** (☎ **800/223-6108** or 212/328-2150). Disabled visitors can reserve tickets directly through the palace by calling ☎ **0171/930-5526.** You can, however, peep through the railings into the front yard at any time.

Buckingham Palace's most famous spectacle is the **Changing of the Guard.** This ceremony begins (when it begins) at 11:30am and lasts for a half-hour. It's been called the finest example of military pageantry extant. The new guard, marching behind a band, comes from either the Wellington or Chelsea Barracks and takes over from the old guard in the forecourt of the palace.

Warning: Any schedule announced here is not written in stone. Officials of the ceremony never announce their plans a year in advance, which poses a dilemma for guidebook writers. In theory at least, the guard is changed daily from some time in April to mid-July, at which time it goes on its "winter" schedule—that is, every other day. The cutback is said to be because of budget constraints. In any case, always check locally with the tourist office to see if it's likely to be staged at the time of your visit. The ceremony has been cut at the last minute and on short notice, leaving thousands of tourists angry, feeling they have missed out on a London must-see.

✪ **Houses of Parliament.** Bridge St. and Parliament Sq., SW1. House of Commons ☎ **0171/219-4272;** House of Lords ☎ **0171/219-3107.** Free admission. House of Lords open to public Mon–Thurs from 3:30pm and some Fridays (check by phone). House of Commons open to public Mon–Tues and Thurs from 3:30pm, Wed and Fri from 9:30am. Join line at St. Stephen's entrance. Tube: Westminster.

The Houses of Parliament, along with their trademark clock tower, are the ultimate symbol of London. They're the stronghold of

Britain's democracy, the assemblies that effectively trimmed the sails of royal power. Both the House of Commons and the House of Lords are in the former royal Palace of Westminster, the king's residence until Henry VIII moved to Whitehall. The current Gothic Revival buildings date from 1840 and were designed by Charles Barry. (The earlier buildings were destroyed by fire in 1834.) Assisting Barry was Augustus Welby Pugin, who designed the paneled ceilings, tiled floors, stained glass, clocks, fireplaces, umbrella stands, and even the inkwells. There are more than 1,000 rooms and 2 miles of corridors.

The clock tower at the eastern end houses the world's most famous timepiece. **"Big Ben"** refers not to the clock tower itself, but to the largest bell in the chime, which weighs close to 14 tons and is named for the first commissioner of works. At night a light shines in the tower whenever Parliament is in session.

You may observe parliamentary debates from the **Stranger's Galleries** in both houses. Sessions usually begin in mid-October and run to the end of July, with recesses at Christmas and Easter. Although we can't assure you of the oratory of a Charles James Fox or a William Pitt the Elder, the debates are often lively and controversial in the House of Commons (seats are at a premium during crises). The chances of getting into the House of Lords when it's in session are generally better than for the more popular House of Commons, where even the Queen isn't allowed. Many political observers maintain that the peerage speak their minds more freely and are less likely to adhere to the party line than their counterparts in the Commons; they do behave, however, in a much more civilized fashion, without the yelling that sometimes accompanies Commons debates.

The general public is admitted to the Strangers' Galleries on "sitting days." You have to join a public line outside the St. Stephen's entrance on the day in question, and there's often considerable delay before the public is admitted. The line forms on the left for the House of Commons, on the right for the Lords. You can speed matters up somewhat by applying at the American Embassy or the Canadian High Commission for a special pass, which should be issued well in advance of your trip, but this is too cumbersome for many people. Besides, the embassy has only four tickets for daily distribution, so you might as well stand in line. It's usually easier to get in after about 5:30pm; debates often continue until about 11pm. To arrange a tour before you leave home, you can write **House of Commons Information Office,** 1 Derby Gate, Westminster, London SW1A 2DG. Tours are usually conducted on Friday.

Kensington Palace. The Broad Walk, Kensington Gardens, W8. ☎ **0171/ 937-9561.** Admission £6.50 ($10.40) adults, £4.50 ($7.20) children, £5 ($8) students and senior citizens. May–Oct 5, daily 10am–6pm by guided tour (last tour leaves at 4:45pm). Closed Oct 6–Apr for ongoing restoration. Tube: Queensway or Bayswater on north side of gardens; High Street Kensington on south side.

Once the residence of British monarchs, Kensington Palace hasn't been the official home of reigning kings since George II. The palace was acquired in 1689 by William and Mary as an escape from the damp royal rooms along the Thames. Since the end of the 18th century, the palace has been home to various members of the royal family. It was here in 1837 that a young Victoria was roused from her sleep with the news that her uncle, William IV, had died and that she was now queen of England. You can view a nostalgic collection of Victoriana, including some of her memorabilia. In the apartments of Queen Mary II, wife of William III, there's a striking piece of furniture, a 17th-century writing cabinet inlaid with tortoise shell. Paintings from the Royal Collection literally line the walls of the apartments.

A rare ladies' court dress of 1750 and splendid examples of male court dress from the 18th century are on display in rooms adjacent to the State Apartments.

Kensington Gardens are open daily to the public for leisurely strolls through the manicured grounds and around the Round Pond. One of the most famous sights here is the controversial Albert Memorial, a lasting tribute not only to Victoria's consort but also to the questionable artistic taste of the Victorian era. There's a wonderful afternoon tea offered in the Orangery; see "Teatime" in chapter 4.

Madame Tussaud's. Marylebone Rd., NW1. ☎ **0171/935-6861.** Admission £8.95 ($14.30) adults, £6.75 ($10.80) senior citizens, £5.90 ($9.45) children under 16, under 5 free. Combination tickets including the new planetarium cost £11.20 ($17.90) adults, and £7.10 ($11.35) children under 16. Mon–Sun 10am–5:30pm. Tube: Baker Street.

Madame Tussaud's is not so much a wax museum as an enclosed amusement park. A weird, moving, sometimes terrifying collage of exhibitions, panoramas, and stage settings, it manages to be most things to most people, most of the time.

Madame Tussaud attended the court of Versailles and learned her craft in France. She personally took the death masks from the guillotined heads of Louis XVI and Marie Antoinette (which you'll find among the exhibits). She moved her original museum from Paris to England in 1802. Her exhibition has been imitated in every part of the world, but never with the realism and imagination on hand here. Madame herself molded the features of Benjamin Franklin, whom she met in Paris. All the rest—from George Washington to John F. Kennedy, Mary Queen of Scots to Sylvester Stallone—have been subjects for the same painstaking (and breathtaking) replication.

In the well-known Chamber of Horrors—a kind of underground dungeon—there are all kinds of instruments of death, along with figures of their victims. The shadowy presence of Jack the Ripper lurks in the gloom as you walk through a Victorian London street. Present-day criminals are portrayed within the confines of prison. The latest attraction to open here is "The Spirit of London," a musical ride that depicts 400 years of London's history, using special effects that include audio-animatronic figures that move and speak. Visitors take "time-taxis" that allow them to see and hear "Shakespeare" as he writes and speaks lines, be received by Queen Elizabeth I, and feel and smell the Great Fire of 1666 that destroyed London.

❂ **The National Gallery.** Northwest side of Trafalgar Sq., WC2. ☎ **0171/ 839-3321.** Free admission. Mon, Tues, Thurs–Sat 10am–6pm; Wed 10am– 8pm; Sun noon–6pm. Tube: Charing Cross, Embankment, or Leicester Square.

This stately neoclassical building contains an unrivaled collection of Western art that spans 7 centuries—from the late 13th to the early 20th—and covers every great European school. For sheer skill of display and arrangement, it surpasses its counterparts in Paris, New York, Madrid, and Amsterdam.

The largest part of the collection is devoted to the Italians, including the Sienese, Venetian, and Florentine masters. They're now housed in the Sainsbury Wing, which was designed by noted Philadelphia architects Robert Venturi and Denise Scott Brown and opened by Elizabeth II in 1991. On display are such works as da Vinci's *Virgin of the Rocks;* Titian's *Bacchus and Ariadne;* Giorgione's *Adoration of the Kings;* and unforgettable canvases by Bellini, Veronese, Botticelli, and Tintoretto. Botticelli's *Venus and Mars* is eternally enchanting. (The Sainsbury Wing is also used for large temporary exhibits.)

Of the early Gothic works, the *Wilton Diptych* (French or English school, late 14th century) is the rarest treasure; it depicts Richard II being introduced to the Madonna and Child by John the Baptist and the Saxon king, Edward the Confessor.

Then there are the Spanish giants: El Greco's *Agony in the Garden,* and portraits by Goya and Velázquez. The Flemish-Dutch school is represented by two Brueghels, Jan van Eyck, Vermeer,

Rubens, and de Hooch; the Rembrandts include two of his immortal self-portraits. There's also an immense French impressionist and postimpressionist collection that includes works by Manet, Monet, Degas, Renoir, and Cézanne. Particularly charming is the peep-show cabinet by Hoogstraten in one of the Dutch rooms: It's like spying through a keyhole.

British and modern art are the specialties of the Tate Gallery (see below), but the National Gallery does have some fine 18th-century British masterpieces, including works by Hogarth, Gainsborough, Reynolds, Constable, and Turner.

Insider tip: The National Gallery has a computer information center where you can design your own personal tour map. The computer room, located in the Micro Gallery, includes a dozen hands-on work stations. The on-line system lists 2,200 paintings and has background notes for each artwork. The program includes four indexes that are cross-referenced for your convenience. Using a touch-screen computer, you design your own personalized tour by selecting a maximum of 10 paintings that you would like to view. Once you have made your choices, you print a personal tour map with your selections; this mapping service is free.

✪ **St. Paul's Cathedral.** St. Paul's Churchyard, EC4. ☎ **0171/236-4128**, 0171/248-8348, or 0171/236-4128. Cathedral £3.50 ($5.60) adults, £2 ($3.20) children 6–16; galleries £3 ($4.80) adults, £1.50 ($2.40) children; guided tours £2.50 ($4). Children 5 and under free. Sightseeing, Mon–Sat 8:30am–4pm; galleries Mon–Sat 9:30am–4pm. No sightseeing Sun (services only). Tube: St. Paul's.

During World War II, newsreel footage reaching America showed St. Paul's Cathedral standing virtually alone among the rubble of the City, its dome lit by fires caused by bombings all around it. That it survived at all is a miracle, since it was badly hit twice during the early years of the Nazi bombardment of London. But St. Paul's is accustomed to calamity, having been burned down three times and destroyed once by invading Norsemen. It was during the Great Fire of 1666 that the old St. Paul's was razed, making way for a new Renaissance structure designed by Sir Christopher Wren and built between 1675 and 1710. It's the architectural genius's ultimate masterpiece.

The classical dome of St. Paul's dominates the City's square mile. The golden cross surmounting it is 365 feet above the ground; the golden ball on which the cross rests measures 6 feet in diameter yet looks like a marble from below. Surrounding the interior of the dome is the Whispering Gallery, an acoustic marvel in which the faintest whisper can be heard clearly on the opposite side—so be careful of what you say. You can climb to the top of the dome for a spectacular 360° view of London.

Although the interior looks almost bare, it houses a vast number of monuments. The Duke of Wellington (of Waterloo fame) is entombed here, as are Lord Nelson and Sir Christopher Wren himself. At the east end of the cathedral is the American Memorial Chapel, honoring the 28,000 U.S. service personnel who lost their lives while stationed in Britain in World War II.

Guided tours last 1¹/₂ hours and include parts of the cathedral not open to the general public. They take place Monday to Saturday at 11am, 11:30am, 1:30pm, and 2pm. Recorded tours lasting 45 minutes are available throughout the day.

St. Paul's is an Anglican cathedral with daily services at the following times: matins at 7:30am Monday to Friday and 8:30am on Saturday, Holy Communion Monday to Saturday at 8am and 12:30pm, and evensong Monday to Saturday at 5pm. On Sunday, there's Holy Communion at 8am and again at 11am, matins at 8:45am, and evensong at 3:15pm. Admission charges don't apply if you're attending a service.

Insider's Tip: If you're here in spring, take a stroll through the free gardens of St. Paul's when the roses are in bloom.

The Tate Gallery. Millbank, SW1. ☎ **0171/887-8725.** Free admission; special exhibitions £3–£5 ($4.80–$8). Daily 10am–5:50pm. Tube: Pimlico. Bus: 77A, 88, or C10.

Fronting the Thames near Vauxhall Bridge in Pimlico, the Tate looks like a smaller and more graceful relation of the British Museum, and its paintings are a lot more controversial than those at the National Gallery (see above). The most prestigious gallery in Britain, it houses the national collections, covering British art from the 16th century on, plus an international array of moderns. The Tate's holdings are split between the traditional and the contemporary. Since only a portion of the collections can be displayed at any one time, the works on view change from time to time. Because it's difficult to take in all the exhibits, we suggest that you try to schedule two visits—the first to see the classic British works, the second to take in the modern collection—or concentrate on whichever section interests you more, if your time is limited.

The older works include some of the best of Gainsborough, Reynolds, Stubbs, Blake, and Constable. William Hogarth is well represented, particularly by his satirical *O the Roast Beef of Old*

England (known as *Calais Gate*). The collection of works by J. M. W. Turner is its largest collection of works by a single artist; Turner himself willed most of the paintings and watercolors here to the nation.

Also on display are the works of many major 19th- and 20th-century painters, including Paul Nash. The drawings of William Blake, the incomparable mystical poet and illustrator of such works as *The Book of Job, The Divine Comedy,* and *Paradise Lost,* attract the most attention. In the modern collections are works by Matisse, Dalí, Modigliani, Munch, Bonnard, and Picasso. Truly remarkable are the room devoted to several enormous abstract canvases by Mark Rothko; the group of paintings and sculptures by Giacometti; and the paintings of one of England's best-known modern artists, the late Francis Bacon. Sculptures by Henry Moore and Barbara Hepworth are also occasionally displayed.

Insider tip: Spare a little time for the Art Now Gallery, which houses recent works of both new and established artists, some highly controversial. There's always something new, different, and on the cutting edge of the art world here.

Downstairs is the internationally renowned restaurant (see chapter 4), with murals by Whistler, as well as a coffee shop.

✪ **The Tower of London.** Tower Hill, EC3. ☎ **0171/709-0765.** Admission £8.50 ($13.60) adults, £6.40 ($10.25) students and senior citizens, £5.60 ($8.95) children, free for those under 5; family ticket for 5 (but no more than 2 adults) £25.40 ($40.65). Gates open Mar–Oct, Mon–Sat 9am–5pm, Sun 10am–5pm; off-season Tues–Sat 9am–4pm, Mon and Sun 10am–4pm. Tube: Tower Hill.

This ancient fortress continues to pack in the crowds, largely because of its macabre associations with all the legendary figures who were imprisoned and/or executed here. James Street once wrote, "There are more spooks to the square foot than in any other building in the whole of haunted Britain. Headless bodies, bodiless heads, phantom soldiers, icy blasts, clanking chains—you name them, the Tower's got them." Even today, centuries after the last head rolled on Tower Hill, a shivery atmosphere of impending doom lingers over the mighty walls. Plan on spending a lot of time here.

The Tower is actually an intricately patterned compound of structures built throughout the ages for varying purposes, mostly as expressions of royal power. The oldest is the **White Tower,** begun by William the Conqueror in 1078 to keep London's native Saxon population in check. Later rulers added other towers, more walls, and fortified gates, until the building became something like a small town within a city. Until the reign of James I, the Tower was also one of the royal residences. But above all, it was a prison for distinguished captives. *Warning:* The White Tower will be closed for refurbishment throughout 1998.

Every stone of the Tower tells a story—usually a gory one. In the **Bloody Tower,** according to Shakespeare, the two little princes (the sons of Edward IV) were murdered by henchmen of Richard III. (Modern historians, however, tend to think that Richard may not have been the guilty party.) Here, too, Sir Walter Raleigh spent 13 years before his date with the executioner. On the walls of the **Beauchamp Tower,** you can actually read the last messages scratched by despairing prisoners. Through **Traitors' Gate** passed such ill-fated, romantic figures as Robert Devereux, the second earl of Essex, a favorite of Elizabeth I. A plaque marks the eerie place at **Tower Green** where two wives of Henry VIII, Anne Boleyn and Catherine Howard; Sir Thomas More; and the 4-day queen, Lady Jane Grey, all lost their lives. Lady Jane's husband, Lord Guildford Dudley, was executed across the way at Tower Hill.

The Tower, besides being a royal palace, a fortress, and a prison, was also an armory, a treasury, a menagerie, and in 1675 an astronomical observatory. To reopen in 1999, the White Tower holds the **Armouries,** which date from the reign of Henry VIII, as well as a display of instruments of torture and execution that recalls some of the most ghastly moments in the Tower's history. In the Jewel House, you'll find the tower's greatest attraction, the **Crown Jewels.** Here, some of the world's most precious stones are set into the robes, swords, sceptres, and crowns. The Imperial State Crown is the most famous crown on earth; made for Victoria in 1837, it's worn today by Queen Elizabeth when she opens Parliament. Studded with some 3,000 jewels (principally diamonds), it includes the Black Prince's Ruby, worn by Henry V at Agincourt. The 530-carat Star of Africa, a cut diamond on the Royal Sceptre with Cross, would make Harry Winston turn over in his grave. You'll have to stand in long lines to catch just a glimpse of the jewels as you and hundreds of others scroll by on moving sidewalks, but the wait is worth it.

A **palace** once inhabited by King Edward I in the late 1200s, stands above Traitor's Gate. It's the only surviving medieval palace in Britain. Guides are dressed in period costumes. Reproductions of furniture and fittings, including Edward's throne, evoke the era, along with burning incense and candles.

Oh, yes—and don't forget to look for the ravens. Six of them (plus two spares) are all registered as official Tower residents.

According to a legend, the Tower of London will stand as long as those black, ominous birds remain; so, to be on the safe side, one of the wings of each raven is clipped.

One-hour guided tours of the entire compound are given by the Yeoman Warders (also known as "Beefeaters") every half-hour, starting at 9:25am from the Middle Tower near the main entrance. The last guided walk starts about 3:30pm in summer, 2:30pm in winter, weather permitting, of course.

You can attend the nightly **Ceremony of the Keys,** the ceremonial locking-up of the Tower by the Yeoman Warders. For free tickets, write to the Ceremony of the Keys, Waterloo Block, Tower of London, London EC3N 4AB, and request a specific date, but also list alternate dates. At least 6 weeks' notice is required. All requests must be accompanied by a stamped, self-addressed envelope (British stamps only) or two International Reply Coupons. With ticket in hand, you'll be admitted by a Yeoman Warder at 9:35pm.

Insider tip: The secret to avoid the notoriously long lines here is to come early. The hordes descend in the afternoon. Arrive the moment the gates open. Choose a day other than Sunday if you can—crowds are at their worst then.

The Victoria & Albert Museum. Cromwell Rd., SW7. ☎ **0171/938-8500.** Admission £5 ($8) adults, £3 ($4.80) senior citizens, free for children under 18 and persons with disabilities. Mon noon–5:50pm, Tues–Sun 10am–5:50pm. Tube: South Kensington. Bus: C1, 14, or 74.

The Victoria and Albert is the greatest museum in the world devoted to the decorative arts. It's also one of the liveliest and most imaginative museums in London—where else would you find the quintessential "little black dress" in the permanent collection?

The medieval holdings include such treasures as the Early English Gloucester Candlestick; the Byzantine Veroli Casket, with its ivory panels based on Greek plays; and the Syon Cope, a highly valued embroidery made in England in the early 14th century. An area devoted to Islamic art houses the Ardabil carpet from 16th-century Persia.

The Victoria and Albert houses the largest collection of Renaissance sculpture outside Italy, including a Donatello marble relief, *The Ascension;* a small terra-cotta Madonna and Child by Antonio Rossellino; a marble group, *Samson and a Philistine,* by Giovanni Bologna; and a wax model of a slave by Michelangelo. A highlight of the 16th-century collection is the marble group *Neptune with Triton* by Bernini. The cartoons by Raphael, which were conceived as designs for tapestries for the Sistine Chapel, are owned by the Queen and on display here. A most unusual, huge, and impressive exhibit is the Cast Courts, life-size plaster models of ancient and medieval statuary and architecture.

The museum has the greatest collection of Indian art outside India, plus Chinese and Japanese galleries as well. In complete contrast are suites of English furniture, metalwork, and ceramics, and a superb collection of portrait miniatures, including the one Hans Holbein the Younger made of Anne of Cleves for the benefit of Henry VIII, who was again casting around for a suitable wife. The dress collection includes a collection of corsetry through the ages that's sure to make you wince, and there's also a remarkable collection of musical instruments.

In a major redevelopment plan, some 10% of the entire gallery space closed in the summer of 1997. The entire run of British Galleries won't reopen again until 2001. But the museum has a lively program of changing exhibitions and displays, so there's always something new to see.

Insider tip: As incongruous as it sounds, the museum hosts a jazz brunch on Sunday from 11am to 3pm that's worth attending. You'll get some of the hottest jazz in the city, accompanied by a full English breakfast or lunch for only £8 ($12.80). And don't miss the Victoria Albert's most bizarre gallery, "Fakes and Forgeries." The impostors here are amazingly authentic—in fact, we'd judge some of them as better than the Old Masters themselves.

✪ **Westminster Abbey.** Broad Sanctuary, SW1. ☎ **0171/222-7110** or 0171/222-5897. Free admission to abbey, donation invited; Royal Chapels, Royal Tombs, Coronation Chair, Lady Chapel £4 ($6.40) adults, £2 ($3.20) students and seniors, £1 ($1.60) children under 16. Mon–Fri 9am–3:45pm, Sat 9:15am–1:45pm and 4–4:45pm. Tube: Westminster or St. James's Park.

With its square twin towers and superb archways, this early English Gothic abbey is one of the greatest examples of ecclesiastical architecture on earth. But it's far more than that: It's the shrine of a nation, the symbol of everything Britain has stood for and stands for, the place in which most of its rulers were crowned and where many lie buried.

Nearly every figure in English history has left his or her mark on Westminster Abbey. Edward the Confessor founded the Benedictine abbey in 1065 on this spot overlooking Parliament Square. The first English king crowned in the abbey was Harold in 1066. The man who defeated him at the Battle of Hastings the next year, William the Conqueror, was also crowned here. The coronation tradition has continued to the present day, broken only twice (Edward V and Edward VIII). The essentially early English Gothic structure existing today owes more to Henry III's plans than to those of any other sovereign, although many architects, including Wren, have contributed to the abbey.

Built on the site of the ancient lady chapel in the early 16th century, the **Henry VII Chapel** is one of the loveliest in Europe, with its fan vaulting, Knights of Bath banners, and Torrigiani-designed tomb of the king himself, over which hangs a 15th-century Vivarini painting, *Madonna and Child.* Also here are the feuding half-sisters, ironically buried in the same tomb, Catholic Mary I and Protestant Elizabeth I (whose archrival, Mary Queen of Scots, is entombed on the other side of the Henry VII Chapel). In one end of the chapel, you can stand on Cromwell's memorial stone and view the **Royal Air Force Chapel** and its Battle of Britain memorial window, unveiled in 1947 to honor the RAF.

You can also visit the most hallowed spot in the abbey, the **shrine of Edward the Confessor** (canonized in the 12th century). In the chapel is the Coronation Chair, made at the command of Edward I in 1300 to display the Stone of Scone. Scottish kings were once crowned on it (it has since been returned to Scotland).

When you enter the transept on the south side of the nave and see a statue of the Bard with one arm resting on a stack of books, you've arrived at **Poets' Corner.** Shakespeare himself is buried at Stratford-upon-Avon, but resting here are Dickens, Chaucer, Ben Jonson, John Dryden, William Wordsworth, Milton, Kipling, Shelley, Goldsmith, Thackeray, Hardy, and Alfred, Lord Tennyson; there's even an American, Henry Wadsworth Longfellow, as well as monuments to just about everybody: Chaucer, Shakespeare, "O Rare Ben Johnson" (his name misspelled), Samuel Johnson, the Brontë sisters, George Eliot, Thackeray, Dickens, Tennyson, Kipling. The most stylized monument is Sir Jacob Epstein's sculptured bust of William Blake. More recent tablets commemorate poet Dylan Thomas and Sir Laurence Olivier.

Statesmen and men of science—such as Disraeli, Newton, Charles Darwin—are also interred in the abbey or honored by monuments. Near the west door is the 1965 memorial to Sir Winston Churchill. In the vicinity of this memorial is the tomb of the **Unknown Soldier,** commemorating the British dead in World War I.

Off the Cloisters, the **College Garden** is the oldest garden in England, under cultivation for more than 900 years. Surrounded by high walls, flowering trees dot the lawns and park benches provide comfort where you can hardly hear the roar of passing traffic. It's open only on Tuesday and Thursday. In the Cloisters, you can make a rubbing at the **Brass Rubbing Centre** (☎ 0171/222-2085).

Insider Tip: Far removed from the pomp and glory is the **Abbey Treasure Museum,** with a bag of oddities. They're displayed in the undercroft or crypt, part of the monastic buildings erected between 1066 and 1100. Here are royal effigies that were used instead of the real corpses for lying-in-state ceremonies because they smelled better. You'll see the almost lifelike effigy of Admiral Nelson (his mistress arranged his hair) and even that of Edward III, his lip warped by the stroke that felled him. Other oddities include a Middle English lease to Chaucer, the much-used sword of Henry VI, and the Essex Ring Elizabeth I gave to her favorite earl when she was feeling good about him.

The only time photography is allowed in the abbey is Wednesday evening from 6 to 7:45pm. On Sunday, the Royal Chapels are closed, but the rest of the church is open unless a service is being conducted. For times of services, phone the **Chapter Office** (☎ 0171/222-5152). Up to six supertours of the abbey are conducted by the vergers Monday to Saturday, beginning at 10am and costing £7 ($11.20) per person.

2 More Central London Attractions

CHURCHES & CATHEDRALS

Many of London's churches offer free **lunchtime concerts;** a full list of churches offering them is available from the London Tourist Board. It's customary to leave a small donation.

All Hallows Barking by the Tower. Byward St., EC3. ☎ 0171/481-2928. Free admission. Museum, Mon–Fri 11am–4:30pm, Sat 10am–4:30pm, Sun 1–4:30pm; church, Mon–Fri 9am–6pm, Sat–Sun 10am–5pm. Tube: Tower Hill.

The brass-rubbing center at this fascinating church, next door to the Tower, has a crypt museum, Roman remains, and traces of early London, including a Saxon arch predating the Tower. Samuel Pepys, the famed diarist, climbed to the spire of this church to watch the raging fire of London in 1666. In 1644, William Penn was baptized here, and in 1797, John Quincy Adams was married here. Bombs destroyed the church in 1940, leaving only the tower and walls standing. Rebuilt from 1949 to 1958, the church is now home to the **London Brass Rubbing Centre.** Materials and instructions are supplied, and the charges range from £1.50 to £11.50 ($2.40 to $18.40) for the largest.

✪ **Brompton Oratory.** Brompton Rd., SW7. ☎ **0171/589-4811.** Free admission. Daily 6:30am–8pm. Tube: South Kensington.

Converts are supposedly the most zealous adherents of any faith. The Oxford Movement, a group of Victorian intellectuals turned Catholic, certainly didn't go halfway when they created this church in 1884. Done in the Italian Renaissance style, this dramatic Roman Catholic church is famous for its musical services and its organ with nearly 4,000 pipes. After Westminster Cathedral (see below) and York Minster, this is the widest nave in England.

Westminster Cathedral. Ashley Place, SW1. ☎ **0171/798-9055.** Cathedral free; tower, £2 ($3.20). Cathedral, daily 7am–8pm; tower, Apr–Nov, daily 9am–1pm and 2–5pm; otherwise Thurs–Sun only. Tube: Victoria.

This spectacular brick-and-stone church (1903) is the headquarters of the Roman Catholic church in Britain. Adorned in high Byzantine style, it's massive: 360 feet long and 156 feet wide. One hundred different marbles compose the richly decorated interior, and eight marble columns support the nave. The huge balacchino over the high altar is lifted by eight yellow marble columns. Mosaics emblazon the chapels and the vaulting of the sanctuary. If you take the elevator to the top of the 273-foot-tall campanile, you're rewarded with sweeping views that take in Buckingham Palace, Westminster Abbey, and St. Paul's Cathedral.

HISTORIC BUILDINGS

Cabinet War Rooms. Clive Steps, at end of King Charles St. (off Whitehall near Big Ben), SW1. ☎ **0171/930-6961.** Admission £4.40 ($7.05) adults, £2.20 ($3.50) children, £3.30 ($5.30) senior citizens, and £3 ($4.80) for students. Apr–Sept, daily 9:30am–6pm (last admission at 5:15pm); Oct–Mar, daily 10am–5:30pm. Tube: Westminster or St. James's.

This is the bombproof bunker from which Winston Churchill and his government ran the nation during World War II. Many of the rooms are exactly as they were in September 1945: Imperial War Museum curators studied photographs to put notepads, files, typewriters, even pencils, pins, and clips, in their correct places.

Along the tour, you'll have a step-by-step personal sound guide that provides a detailed account of the function and history of each room of this WWII nerve center. They include the Map Room, with its huge wall maps. Next door is Churchill's bedroom-cum-office; it has a very basic bed and a desk with two BBC microphones for those famous broadcasts that stirred the nation. The Transatlantic Telephone Room is little more than a broom closet, but it held the extension linked to the special scrambler phone (called "Sig-Saly") that allowed Churchill to confer with Roosevelt. (The scrambler equipment itself was actually too large to house in the bunker, so it was placed in the basement of Selfridges department store on Oxford Street.)

✪ **Horse Guards.** Whitehall, SW1. ☎ **0171/414-2396.**

North of Downing Street, on the west side of Whitehall, is the building of the Horse Guards, designed by William Kent, chief architect to George II, as the headquarters of the British Army (John Vardy took over and completed the structure in 1758). The real draw here are the Horse Guards themselves: Their unit is the Household Cavalry Mounted Regiment, which is a union of the two oldest and most senior regiments in the British Army: the Life Guards and the Blues and Royals. In theory, their duty is to protect the sovereign. Life Guards wear red tunics and white plumes and the Blues and Royals are attired in blue tunics with red plumes. Two much-photographed mounted members of the Household Cavalry keep watch daily from 10am to 5pm. The mounted sentries change duty every hour as a benefit to the horses. The sentries on foot change every 2 hours. The chief guard rather grandly inspects the troops here daily at 4pm. The guard, with flair and fanfare, dismounts at 5pm.

Some visitors prefer the **changing of the guards** here to the more famous ceremony at Buckingham Palace. Guards are changed around 10:30am Monday to Saturday and 9:30am on Sunday. A new guard leaves the Hyde Park Barracks, rides down Pall Mall, and arrives at the Horse Guards building all in about 30 minutes. The old guard then returns to the barracks.

If you pass through the arch at Horse Guards, you'll find yourself at the **Horse Guards Parade,** which opens onto St. James's Park. This spacious court provides the best view of the various architectural styles that make up Whitehall. Regrettably, the parade ground itself is now a parking lot.

The military pageant—the most famous in Britain—known as the **Trooping the Colour,** which celebrates the Queen's birthday, takes place in June at the Horse Guards Parade (see the "Calendar of Events" in chapter 1). The "Colour" refers to the flag of the regiment. For devotees of pomp and circumstance, "Beating the

Retreat" is staged here 3 or 4 evenings a week during the first 2 weeks of June. It's only a dress rehearsal, though, for Trooping the Colour.

LEGAL LONDON

The smallest borough in London, bustling **Holborn** (pronounced *ho*-burn) is often referred to as "Legal London," as it's home to the majority of the city's barristers, solicitors, and law clerks as well as the ancient **Inns of Court** (Tube: Holborn or Chancery Lane). All barristers must belong to one of these institutions, and many work from their dignified ancient buildings: **Lincoln's Inn** (the best preserved of the three) and the **Middle** and **Inner Temple.** They were severely damaged during World War II, and the razed buildings were replaced with modern offices, but the borough still retains pockets of its former days.

Law Courts. The Strand, WC2. Free admission. No cameras or tape recorders allowed during sessions, Mon–Fri 10:30am–1pm and 2–4pm. Tube: Holborn or Temple.

At these 60 or more courts presently in use, all civil and some criminal cases are heard. Designed by G. E. Street, the neo-Gothic buildings (1874–82) contain more than 1,000 rooms and 3^1/$_2$ miles of corridors. Sculptures of Christ, King Solomon, and King Alfred grace the front door; Moses is depicted at the back entrance. On the second Saturday in November, the annually elected lord mayor is sworn in by the lord chief justice.

Lincoln's Inn. Carey St., WC1. ☎ **0171/405-1393.** Free admission. Mon–Thurs 9am–5:30pm, Fri–Sat 9am–5pm. Tube: Holborn or Chancery Lane.

Lincoln's Inn is the oldest of the four Inns of Court. Between the City and the West End, Lincoln's Inn comprises 11 acres, including lawns, squares, gardens, a 17th-century chapel, a library, and two halls. One of these, Old Hall, dates from 1490 and has remained almost unaltered with its linenfold paneling, stained glass, and wooden screen by Inigo Jones. It was once the home of Sir Thomas More, and it was where barristers met, ate, and debated 150 years before the *Mayflower* sailed on its epic voyage. Old Hall set the scene for the opening chapter of Charles Dickens's *Bleak House.* The other hall, Great Hall, remains one of the finest Tudor Revival buildings in London, and was opened by Queen Victoria in 1843. It's now the center of the inn and is used for the formal ceremony of calling students to the bar.

Middle Temple Tudor Hall. Middle Temple Lane, EC4. ☎ **0171/427-4800.** Free admission. Mon–Fri 10:30am–noon and 3–4pm. Tube: Temple.

From the Victoria Embankment, Middle Temple Lane runs between Middle and Inner Temple Gardens to the area known as The Temple, named after the medieval order of the Knights Templar (originally formed by the Crusaders in Jerusalem in the 12th century). It was in the Middle Temple Garden that Henry VI's barons are supposed to have picked the blooms of red and white roses and started the Wars of the Roses in 1430; today only members of the Temple and their guests are allowed to enter the gardens. But the Middle Temple contains a Tudor hall, completed in 1570, that's open to the public. It's believed that Shakespeare's troupe played *Twelfth Night* here for the first time in 1602. A table on view is said to have been built of timber from Sir Francis Drake's *The Golden Hind.*

LITERARY LANDMARKS

Carlyle's House. 24 Cheyne Row, SW3. ☎ **0171/352-7087.** Admission £3 ($4.80) adults, £1.50 ($2.40) children. Easter–Oct, Wed–Sun 11am–4:30pm. Tube: Sloane Square. Bus: 11, 19, 22, or 23.

From 1834 to 1881, Thomas Carlyle, author of *The French Revolution,* and Jane Baillie Welsh Carlyle, his noted letter-writing wife, resided in this modest 1708 terraced house. Furnished essentially as it was in Carlyle's day, the house is located about three-quarters of a block from the Thames, near the Chelsea Embankment, along King's Road.

The house was described by his wife as being "of most antique physiognomy, quite to our humour; all wainscotted, carved, and queer-looking, roomy, substantial, commodious, with closets to satisfy any Bluebeard." The second floor contains Mrs. Carlyle's drawing room, but the most interesting chamber is the not-so-soundproof "soundproof" study in the skylit attic. Filled with Carlyle memorabilia—his books, a letter from Disraeli, personal effects, a writing chair, even his death mask—this is where the author labored on his *Frederick the Great* manuscript.

Dickens House. 48 Doughty St., WC1. ☎ **0171/405-2127.** Admission £3.50 ($5.60) adults, £2.50 ($4) students, £1.50 ($2.40) children, £7 ($11.20) families. Mon–Sat 10am–5pm. Tube: Russell Square.

Here in Bloomsbury stands the simple abode in which Charles Dickens wrote *Oliver Twist* and finished *The Pickwick Papers* (his American readers actually waited at the dock for the ship that brought in each new installment). The place is almost a shrine: It contains his study, manuscripts, and personal relics, as well as reconstructed interiors.

Samuel Johnson's House. 17 Gough Sq., EC4. ☎ **0171/353-3745.** Admission £3 ($4.80) adults, £2 ($3.20) students and senior citizens, £1 ($1.60) children, 10 and under free. May–Sept Mon–Sat 11am–5:30pm; Oct–Apr Mon–Sat 11am–5pm. Tube: Blackfriars. Walk up New Bridge St. and turn left onto Fleet; Gough Sq. is tiny and hidden, north of Fleet St.

Dr. Johnson and his copyists compiled his famous dictionary in this Queen Anne house, where the lexicographer, poet, essayist, and fiction writer lived from 1748 to 1759. Although Johnson also lived at Staple Inn in Holborn and at a number of other places, the Gough Square house is the only one of his residences remaining in London. The 17th-century building has been painstakingly restored, and it's well worth a visit.

After you're done touring the house, you might want to stop in at **Ye Olde Cheshire Cheese,** Wine Court Office Court, 145 Fleet St. (☎ **0171/353-6170**), Johnson's favorite local. He must have had some lean nights at the pub, because by the time he had compiled his dictionary, he'd already spent his advance of 1,500 guineas. G. K. Chesterton, author of *What's Wrong with the World* (1910) and *The Superstition of Divorce* (1920), was also a familiar patron at the pub.

Shakespeare's Globe Theatre & Exhibition. New Globe Walk, Bankside, SE1. ☎ **0171/928-6406.** Exhibition admission £5 ($8) adults, £3 ($4.80) children 15 and under; guided tours £5 ($8) adults, £4 ($6.40) students and seniors, £3 ($4.80) children. Daily 10am–5pm (guided tours every 30 min. or so). Tube: Mansion House.

This is a re-creation of what was probably the most important public theater ever built—on the exact site where many of Shakespeare's plays were originally staged in the 17th century. The late American filmmaker, Sam Wanamaker, worked for some 20 years to raise funds to re-create the theater as it existed in Elizabethan times, thatched roof and all. A fascinating exhibit tells the story of the Globe's re-creation in modern times, using the material (including goat's hair in the plaster), techniques, and craftsmanship of 400 years ago. The new Globe isn't actually an exact replica: It seats 1,500 patrons, not the 3,000 that regularly squeezed in during the early 1600s; and this thatched roof has been specially treated with a fire retardant. Guided tours of the facility are offered throughout the day.

In May 1997, the Globe's company staged its first slate of plays. See "The Play's the Thing: The London Theater Scene" in chapter 7 for details on attending a play here.

Plans also call for an archival library, shops, an auditorium, and an exhibition gallery, but the full complex may not be fully operational until September 1999.

Sherlock Holmes Museum. 221B Baker St., NW1. ☎ **0171/935-8866.** Admission £5 ($8) adults, £3 ($4.80) children. Daily 9:30am–6pm. Tube: Baker Street.

Where but on Baker Street would there be a museum displaying mementos of this famed fictional detective? Museum officials call it "the world's most famous address" (although 10 Downing St. is a rival for the title); it was here that mystery writer Sir Arthur Conan Doyle created a residence for Sherlock Holmes and his faithful Dr. Watson. These sleuths "lived" here from 1881 to 1904. In Victorian rooms, you can examine a range of exhibits, including published Holmes adventures and letters written to Holmes. This is a very commercial and artificial museum, but Holmes buffs don't seem to mind.

MUSEUMS & GALLERIES

Apsley House, The Wellington Museum. 149 Piccadilly, Hyde Park Corner, W1. ☎ **0171/499-5676.** Admission £4 ($6.40) adults, £2.50 ($4) seniors and children 12–17, under 12 free; £7 ($11.20) family ticket. Tues–Sun 11am–5pm. Tube: Hyde Park Corner.

This was the mansion of the Duke of Wellington, one of Britain's greatest generals. The "Iron Duke" defeated Napoléon at Waterloo, but later, for a short period while prime minister, he had to have iron shutters fitted to his windows to protect him from the mob outraged by his autocratic opposition to reform. (His unpopularity soon passed, however.)

The house is crammed with art treasures, including three original Velázquez paintings, and military mementos that include the duke's medals and battlefield orders. Apsley House also holds some of the finest silver and porcelain pieces in Europe in the Plate and China Room. Grateful to Wellington for saving their thrones, European monarchs endowed him with treasures. The collection includes a Sèvres Egyptian service that was intended as a divorce present from Napoléon to Josephine (but she refused it, foolish woman); Louis XVIII eventually presented it to Wellington. The Portuguese Silver Service, created between 1812 and 1816, has been hailed as the single greatest artifact of Portuguese neoclassical silver.

British Library. British Museum, 96 Euston Rd., NW1. ☎ **0171/412-7000.** Free admission. Mon–Sat 10am–5pm, Sun 2:30–6pm. Tube: Holborn or Tottenham Court Road.

One of the world's greatest libraries is no longer at the British Museum but has moved to St. Pancras. Although it will be open in part in 1998, the entire library may not be fully functioning until the dawn of the millennium. The move began in December 1996, and will continue for some $2^1/2$ years, as the library moves some 12 million books, manuscripts, and other items. Call ahead if you're looking for a specific exhibition or manuscript; special phone lines are dedicated to providing detailed information about the moves of specific parts of its collection.

Most people visit the library to view its rare books. The fascinating collection includes such items of historical and literary interest as two of the four surviving copies of King John's Magna Carta (1215), the Gutenberg Bible, Nelson's last letter to Lady Hamilton, and the journals of Captain Cook. Almost every major author—Dickens, Jane Austen, Charlotte Brontë, Keats, hundreds of others—is represented in the section devoted to English literature. Beneath Roubiliac's 1758 statue of Shakespeare stands a case of documents relating to the Bard, including a mortgage bearing his signature and a copy of the First Folio of 1623. The rare-books room is slated to open in the spring of 1998. There's also an unrivaled collection of philatelic items.

Imperial War Museum. Lambeth Rd., SE1. ☎ **0171/416-5000.** Admission £4.70 ($7.50) adults, £3.70 ($5.90) senior citizens and students, £2.35 ($3.75) children; free daily 4:30–6pm. Daily 10am–6pm. Tube: Lambeth North or Elephant and Castle.

One of the few major sights south of the Thames, this museum occupies 1 city block the size of an army barracks, greeting you with 15-inch guns from the battleships *Resolution* and *Ramillies.* The large domed building, constructed in 1815, was the former Bethlehem Royal Hospital for the insane, known as Bedlam.

A wide range of weapons and equipment is on display, along with models, decorations, uniforms, posters, photographs, and paintings. You can see a Mark V tank, a Battle of Britain Spitfire, and a German one-man submarine, as well as a rifle carried by Lawrence of Arabia. In the documents room, you can view the self-styled "political testament" that Hitler dictated in the chancellery bunker in the closing days of World War II in Europe, witnessed by henchmen Joseph Goebbels and Martin Bormann, as well as the famous "peace in our time" agreement that Neville Chamberlain brought back from Munich in 1938. (Of his signing the agreement, Hitler later said, "[Chamberlain] was a nice old man, so I decided to give him my autograph.") It's a world of espionage and clandestine warfare in the major new permanent exhibit known as the Secret War Exhibition, where you can discover the truth behind the image of James Bond—and find out why the real secret war is even stranger and more fascinating than fiction. Displays include many items never before on public display: coded messages, forged documents, secret wirelesses, and equipment used by spies from World War I to the present day.

Museum of the Moving Image. South Bank (underneath Waterloo Bridge), SE1. ☎ 0171/401-2636. Admission £5.95 ($9.50) adults, £4 ($6.40) children and senior citizens, £4.85 ($7.75) students, £16 ($25.60) family ticket (up to 2 adults and 2 children). Daily 10am–6pm (last admission 5pm). Tube: Waterloo or Embankment.

Museum of the Moving Image, part of the South Bank complex, traces the history of cinema and TV, taking you on an incredible journey from cinema's earliest experiments to modern animation, from Charlie Chaplin to the operation of a TV studio. There are artifacts to handle, buttons to push, and a cast of actors to tell visitors more.

Three to four changing exhibitions are presented yearly; it's wise to allow 2 hours for a visit.

✪ The Museum of London. 150 London Wall, EC2. ☎ **0171/600-3699.** Admission £4 ($6.40) adults; £2 ($3.20) children, students, and senior citizens; £9.50 ($15.20) family ticket. Tues–Sat 10am–5:50pm, Sun noon–5:50pm. Tube: St. Paul's, Barbican, Bank, or Moorgate.

In London's Barbican district near St. Paul's Cathedral, overlooking the city's Roman and medieval walls, the museum traces the history of London from prehistoric times to the 20th century through archeological finds; paintings and prints; social, industrial, and historical artifacts; and costumes, maps, and models. Exhibits are arranged so that you can begin and end your chronological stroll through 250,000 years at the main entrance to the museum.

You can see the death mask of Oliver Cromwell, but the pièce de résistance is the Lord Mayor's Coach, a gilt-and-scarlet fairy-tale coach built in 1757 and weighing in at 3 tons. You can also see the Great Fire of London in living color and sound; cell doors from Newgate Prison made famous by Charles Dickens; and most amazing of all, a shop counter with pre–World War II prices.

Museum of Mankind. In the British Museum, Great Russell St., WC1. ☎ 0171/323-8599. Free admission. Mon–Sat 10am–5pm, Sun 2:30–6pm. Tube: Holborn or Tottenham Court Road.

This is the finest ethnographic collection in the world. It has it all—Eskimo polar-bear pants, an Amazonian's human-head mascot, a painted skull from Mexico honoring the Day of the Dead, British Columbian stone carvings, Sioux war bonnets—and it continues to grow. A chief curiosity is a Hawaiian god with a Mohawk, brought back from the islands by Captain Cook. The Beninese bronzes are stunning, as are the gold jewelry and ornaments from West Africa.

Following the departure of the British Library from its British Museum site, this ethnographic collection is set to close its Burlington Gardens location in December 1997 and move back to the main museum location. However, since schedules do change, it's best to call before you go; for the current status of displays, call the information number above. The collection is scheduled to be closed for some days in early May, so call ahead.

✪ **National Portrait Gallery.** St. Martin's Place, WC2. ☎ **0171/306-0055.** Free admission; fee charged for certain temporary exhibitions. Mon–Sat 10am–6pm, Sun noon–6pm. Tube: Charing Cross or Leicester Square.

In a gallery of remarkable and unremarkable pictures (they're collected here for their notable subjects rather than their artistic quality), a few paintings tower over the rest, including Sir Joshua Reynolds's first portrait of Samuel Johnson ("a man of most dreadful appearance"). Among the best are Nicholas Hilliard's miniature of a handsome Sir Walter Raleigh and a full-length Elizabeth I, along with the Holbein cartoon of Henry VIII. There's also a portrait of William Shakespeare (with gold earring, no less) by an unknown artist that bears the claim of being the "most authentic contemporary likeness" of its subject. One of the most famous pictures in the gallery is the group portrait of the Brontë sisters (Charlotte, Emily, and Anne) painted by their brother, Branwell. An idealized portrait of Lord Byron by Thomas Phillips is also on display.

The galleries of Victorian and early–20th-century portraits were radically redesigned recently. Occupying the whole of the first floor, they display portraits from 1837 (when Victoria took the throne) to present day; later 20th-century portraiture include major works by such artists as Warhol and Hambling. Some of the more flamboyant personalities of the last 2 centuries are on show: T. S Eliot, Disraeli, Macmillan, Iris Murdoch, Sir Richard Burton, Elizabeth Taylor, the Baroness Thatcher, and our two favorites: G. F. Watts' famous portrait of his great actress wife, Ellen Terry, and Vanessa Bell's portrait of her sister, Virginia Woolf. The portrait of Princess Diana is on the Royal Landing.

The Natural History Museum. Cromwell Rd., SW7. ☎ **0171/938-9123.** Admission £5.50 ($8.80) adults, £2.80 ($4.50) children 5–17, £3 ($4.80) seniors and students, children 4 and under free, £15 ($24) family ticket. Free to everyone Mon–Fri after 4:30pm and Sat–Sun after 5pm. Tube: South Kensington.

This is the home of the national collections of living and fossil plants, animals, and minerals, with many magnificent specimens on display. Exciting exhibits designed to encourage people of all ages to learn about natural history include "Human Biology—An Exhibition of Ourselves," "Our Place in Evolution," "Origin of the Species," "Creepy Crawlies," and "Discovering Mammals." The Mineral Gallery displays marvelous examples of crystals and gemstones. Also in the museum is the Meteorite Pavilion, which exhibits fragments of rock that have crashed into the earth, some from the farthest reaches of the galaxy. What attracts the most attention is the huge dinosaur exhibit, displaying 14 complete skeletons. The center of the show depicts a trio of full-size robotic Deinonychus enjoying a freshly killed Tenontosaurus for lunch. The latest addition is "Earth Galleries," an exhibition outlining man's relationship with planet Earth.

Queen's Gallery, Buckingham Palace. Entrance on Buckingham Palace Rd., SW1. ☎ **0171/879-1377** or 0171/839-1377. Admission £3.60 ($5.75) adults, £2.50 ($4) seniors, £2 ($3.20) children under 17. Daily 9:30am–4:30pm. Closed late Dec to early Mar. Tube: Green Park, St. James's, or Victoria.

Here you can see a sampling of the Royal Family's art collection. We can't predict what works will be on display during your visit, as they change yearly, but we can tell you that the Queen's collection contains an unsurpassed range of Royal portraits, including the well-known profile of Henry V; companion portraits of Elizabeth I as a girl and her brother, Edward VI; two portraits of Queen Alexandra from Sandringham; plus paintings of Elizabeth II and other members of the present House of Windsor.

Royal Academy of Arts. Burlington House, Piccadilly, W1. ☎ **0171/439-7438.** Admission varies, depending on the exhibition. Daily 10am–6pm (last admission 5:30pm). Tube: Piccadilly Circus or Green Park.

Established in 1768, this organization included Sir Joshua Reynolds, Thomas Gainsborough, and Benjamin West among its founding members. Since its beginning, each member had to donate a work of art, and so over the years the academy has built up a sizable collection. The outstanding treasure is Michelangelo's beautiful relief of *Madonna and Child.* The annual Summer Exhibition has been held for more than 200 years; see the "Calendar of Events" in chapter 1 for details.

Royal Mews, Buckingham Palace. Buckingham Palace Rd., SW1. ☎ **0171/ 839-1377.** Admission £3.60 ($5.75) adults, £2.50 ($4) seniors, £2 ($3.20) children under 17. Daily noon–4pm (restricted hrs in winter). Tube: Green Park, St. James's, or Victoria.

This is where you can get a close look at Her Majesty's State Coach, built in 1761 to the designs of Sir William Chambers and decorated with paintings by Cipriani. Traditionally drawn by eight gray horses, it was formerly used by sovereigns when they traveled to open Parliament and on other state occasions; Queen Elizabeth II traveled in it to her 1953 coronation and in 1977 for her Silver Jubilee Procession. The Queen's carriage horses are also housed here, as well as other state coaches.

Science Museum. Exhibition Rd., SW7. ☎ **0171/938-8000.** Admission £5.50 ($8.80) adults, £2.90 ($4.65) children 5–17, under 5 free; free to all Mon– Fri after 4:30pm and Sat–Sun after 5pm. Daily 10am–6pm. Tube: South Kensington.

This museum traces the development of science and industry, and their influence on everyday life. These are among the largest, most comprehensive, and most significant scientific collections anywhere. On display is Stephenson's original Rocket, the tiny prototype railroad engine; you can also see Whittle's original jet engine and the Apollo 10 space module.

The King George III Collection of scientific instruments is the highlight of a gallery on science in the 18th century. Health Matters is a permanent gallery on modern medicine. The museum has two hands-on galleries, as well as working models and video displays.

✪ Sir John Soane's Museum. 13 Lincoln's Inn Fields, WC2. ☎ **0171/430- 0175.** Free admission (donations invited). Tues–Sat 10am–5pm, first Tues of each month 6–9pm. Tours given Sat at 2:30pm; free tickets given out at 2pm on a first-come, first-served basis (group tours by appointment only; call ☎ 0171/405-2107). Tube: Chancery Lane or Holborn.

This is the former home of Sir John Soane (1753–1837), an architect who rebuilt the Bank of England (not the present structure). With his multiple levels, fool-the-eye mirrors, flying arches, and domes, Soane was a master of perspective and a genius of interior space (his picture gallery, for example, is filled with three times the number of paintings a room of similar dimensions would be likely to hold). Don't miss William Hogarth's satirical series *The Rake's Progress*, which includes his much-reproduced *Orgy* and *The Election*, a satire on mid–18th-century politics. Soane also filled his house with classical sculpture. Be sure to see the sarcophagus of Pharaoh

Seti I, found in a burial chamber in the Valley of the Kings. Also on display are architectural drawings from Soane's collection of 30,000.

Theatre Museum. Russell St., WC2. ☎ **0171/836-7891.** £3.50 ($5.60) adults, £2 ($3.20) seniors and children 5–17. Tues–Sun 11am–7pm. Tube: Covent Garden or Charing Cross.

This branch of the Victoria and Albert Museum contains the national collections of the performing arts, encompassing theater, ballet, opera, music-hall pantomime, puppets, circus, and rock and pop music. Daily make-up demonstrations and costume workshops are run using costumes from the Royal Shakespeare Company and the Royal National Theatre. The museum also has a major Diaghilev archive.

Insider tip: The box office inside offers tickets to West End plays—including the hot ones—a well as to concerts, dramas, and musicals, with almost no mark-up in most cases.

PARKS & GARDENS

London's parks are the greatest, most advanced system of "green lungs" of any large city on the globe. Although not as rigidly maintained as those of Paris (Britons traditionally prefer a more natural look), they're cared for with a loving and lavishly artistic hand that puts their American equivalents to shame.

The largest of the central London parks—and one of the biggest in the world—is **Hyde Park** (tube: Marble Arch, Hyde Park Corner, Lancaster Gate), once a favorite deer-hunting ground of Henry VIII. With the adjoining Kensington Gardens (see below), it covers 615 acres of central London with velvety lawns interspersed with ponds, flower beds, and trees. Running through its width is a 41-acre lake known as the Serpentine, where you can row, sail model boats, or swim (provided you don't mind sub–Florida water temperatures). Rotten Row, a 1¹/₂-mile sand track, is reserved for horseback riding; on Sunday, it attracts some skilled equestrians. At the northeastern tip, near Marble Arch, is Speakers' Corner.

Well-manicured **Kensington Gardens** (tube: High Street Kensington, Queensway), blending with Hyde Park and bordering on the grounds of Kensington Palace (see "The Top Attractions," above), contains the famous statue of Peter Pan, with the bronze rabbits that toddlers are always trying to kidnap. It's also home to the Albert Memorial, that Victorian extravaganza. The Orangery is a wonderful place to take afternoon tea (see "Teatime" in chapter 4).

East of Hyde Park, across Piccadilly, stretch **Green Park** (tube: Green Park) and **St. James's Park** (tube: St. James's Park), forming an almost unbroken chain of landscaped beauty. This is an ideal area for picnics; you'll find it hard to believe that this was once a festering swamp near a leper hospital. There's a romantic lake stocked with a variety of ducks and some surprising pelicans, descendants of the pair that the Russian ambassador presented to Charles II back in 1662.

Regent's Park (tube: Regent's Park, Baker Street), covers most of the district of that name, north of Baker Street and Marylebone Road. Designed by the 18th-century genius John Nash to surround a palace for the prince regent that never materialized, this is the most classically beautiful of London's parks. Its core is a rose garden planted around a small lake alive with waterfowl and spanned by Japanese bridges; in early summer, the rose perfume in the air is as heady as wine. The park is home to the Open-Air Theatre (see chapter 7) and the London Zoo (see "Especially for Kids," below). As at all the local parks, hundreds of deck chairs are scattered around the lawns, just waiting for sunbathers. The deck-chair attendants, who collect a small fee, are mostly college students on break.

Chelsea Physic Garden, 66 Royal Hospital Rd., SW3 (☎ 0171/ 352-5646; tube: Sloane Square), founded in 1673 by the Worshipful Society of Apothecaries, is the second-oldest surviving botanical garden in England. Sir Hans Sloane, doctor to George II, required the apothecaries of the empire to develop 50 plant species a year for presentation to the Royal Society. The objective was to grow plants for medicinal study; plant specimens and even trees arrived at the gardens by barge. Many plants grew here in English soil for the first time. Cotton seeds from this garden launched an industry in the new colony of Georgia. Some 7,000 plants still grow here, everything from the pomegranate to the willow Pattern tree; there's even exotic cork oak, as well as England's earliest rock garden. The garden is open April to October, Wednesday from 2 to 5pm and Sunday from 2 to 6pm. Admission is £3.50 ($5.60) for adults, £1.80 ($2.90) for children 5 to 15 and students. The garden is also the setting for a well-recommended afternoon tea, where you can carry your cuppas on promenades through the garden (see "Teatime" in chapter 4).

3 Sightseeing & Boat Tours Along the Thames

There's a row of fascinating attractions lying on, across, and alongside the River Thames. All of London's history and development is linked with this winding ribbon of water: The Thames connects the city with the sea, from which it drew its wealth and its power, and it was London's chief commercial thoroughfare and royal highway (the only regal one in the days of winding cobblestone streets). Every royal procession was undertaken on gorgeously painted and gilded barges. All important state prisoners were delivered to the Tower of London by water, eliminating the chance of an ambush by their friends in one of those narrow, crooked alleys surrounding the fortress. Much of the commercial traffic disappeared when London's streets were widened enough for horse-drawn coaches to maintain a decent pace.

RIVER CRUISES

A trip up or down the river will give you an entirely different view of London from the one you get from dry land. You'll see exactly how the city grew along and around the Thames and how many of its landmarks turn their faces toward the water. It's like seeing Manhattan from a ferry. Several companies operate motor launches from the Westminster piers (tube: Westminster), offering panoramic views of one of Europe's most historic waterways en route.

The **Westminster–Greenwich Thames Passenger Boat Service,** Westminster Pier, Victoria Embankment, SW1 (☎ 0171/930-4097), concerns itself only with downriver traffic from Westminster Pier to such destinations as Greenwich. The most popular excursion departs for Greenwich (a 50-minute ride) at half-hour intervals between 10:30am and 4:30pm in April, May, September, and October, and between 10:30am and 5pm from June to August; from November to March, boats depart from Westminster Pier at hourly intervals daily between 10:30am and 3:30pm. One-way fares are £4.80 ($7.70) for adults, £2.40 ($3.85) for children under 16. Round-trip fares are £5.80 ($9.30) for adults, £3 ($4.80) for children. A family ticket for two adults and up to three children under 15 costs £12.50 ($20) one way, £15 ($24) round-trip.

The **Westminster Passenger Association (Upriver) Ltd.,** Westminster Pier, Victoria Embankment, SW1 (☎ 0171/930-2062 or 0171/930-4721), offers the only riverboat service upstream from Westminster Bridge to Kew, Richmond, and Hampton Court. There are regular daily sailings from the Monday before Easter until the end of October, on traditional river boats, all with licensed bars. Trip time, one way, can be as little as $1^1/_2$ hours to Kew and between $2^1/_2$ to 4 hours to Hampton Court, depending on the tide. Cruises from Westminster Pier to Hampton Court via Kew Gardens leave daily at 10:30am, 11:15am, and noon. Round-trip tickets are £8 to £12 ($12.80–$19.20) adults, £6 to £10 ($9.60–$16) senior citizens, and £4 to £7 ($6.40–$11.20) children 4 to 14; one child under 4 accompanied by an adult goes free. Evening cruises from May to September are also available departing Westminster Pier at 7:30pm and 8:30pm (9:30pm on demand) for £5 ($8) adults and £3.50 ($5.60) for children.

THE BRIDGES

Some of the Thames bridges are household names. **London Bridge,** contrary to the nursery rhyme, never fell down, but it has been replaced a number of times. The one that you see is the ugliest of the bunch. The previous one was dismantled and shipped to Lake Havasu, Arizona, in the 1960s.

Its neighbor to the east is the still-standing—and *much* more beautiful—**Tower Bridge,** SE1 (☎ **0171/403-3761;** tube: Tower Hill), one of the city's most celebrated landmarks and possibly the most photographed and painted bridge on earth. Its outward appearance is familiar to Londoners and visitors alike. (This is the one that a certain American thought he'd purchased instead of the one farther up the river that really ended up in the middle of the desert). In spite of its medieval appearance, Tower Bridge was actually built in 1894.

In 1993 an exhibition opened inside the bridge to commemorate its century-old history; it takes you up the north tower to high-level walkways between the two towers with spectacular views of St. Paul's, the Tower of London, and the Houses of Parliament—a photographer's dream. You're then led down the south tower and on to the bridge's original engine room, with its Victorian boilers and steam-pumping engines that used to raise and lower the roadway across the river. Exhibits housed in the bridge's towers used advanced technology, including animatronic characters, video, and computers to illustrate the history of the bridge. Admission to the **Tower Bridge Experience** (☎ **0171/378-1928**) is £5.70 ($9.10) for adults and £3.90 ($6.25) for children 5 to 15, students, and senior citizens; it's free for children 4 and under. Open April to October daily 10am to 6:30pm, November to March daily 9:30am to 6pm; last entry is $1^{1}/_{4}$ hours before closing. Closed Good Friday and January 1 to 28 as well as a few days around Christmas.

4   Especially for Kids

The attractions that follow are fun places for kids of all ages. In addition to what's listed below, kids also love **Madame Tussaud's,** the **Science Museum,** the **Natural History Museum,** the **Tower of**

London, and the **National Maritime Museum** in Greenwich, all discussed above.

Kidsline (☎ **0171/222-8070**) offers computerized information about current events that might interest kids. The line is open 4pm to 6pm during school-term time, 9am to 4pm on holidays. Only problem is, every parent in London is calling for information; it's almost impossible to get through.

London Dungeon. 28–34 Tooley St., SE1. ☎ **0171/403-0606.** Admission £7.95 ($12.70) adults, £6.95 ($11.10) students and senior citizens, £5.50 ($8.80) children under 15. Admission includes 2 shows. Apr–Sept, daily 10am–5:30pm; Oct–Mar, daily 10am–4:30pm. Tube: London Bridge.

This ghoulish place was deliberately designed to chill the blood while reproducing the conditions of the Middle Ages. Set under the arches of London Bridge Station, the dungeon is a series of tableaux that are more grisly than the ones in Madame Tussaud's. The rumble of trains overhead adds to the horror of the place, and tolling bells bring a constant note of melancholy to the background; dripping water and live rats (caged!) make for even more atmosphere. The murder of Thomas à Becket in Canterbury Cathedral is depicted, among others: Naturally, there's a burning at the stake, as well as a torture chamber with racking, branding, and fingernail extraction. For the first time in a British attraction, you can now experience special effects originally conceived for major film and TV productions. The "Jack the Ripper Experience" is spine-chilling! If you survive, there's a Pizza Hut on premises (for a little taste of home), and a souvenir shop selling certificates that testify that you've made it through the works.

London Planetarium. Marylebone Rd., NW1. ☎ **0171/935-6861.** £5.65 ($9.05) adult, £4.45 ($7.10) seniors, £3.70 ($5.90) children 5–17. Daily from 10am weekdays, 9:30am Sat–Sun with shows beginning at 12:20pm (10:20am on weekends). Tube: Baker Street.

Next door to Madame Tussaud's, the planetarium explores the mysteries of the stars and the night sky. The most recent star show starts with a spaceship of travelers forced to desert their planet when a neighboring star explodes; accompanying them on their journey, the audience travels through the solar system, visiting its major landmarks and witnessing spectacular cosmic activity. There are also several hands-on exhibits that relate to planets and space; for example, you can see what shape or weight you'd be on other planets. You can also hear Stephen Hawking talk about the mysterious black holes.

✪ **London Zoo.** Regent's Park, NW1. ☎ **0171/722-3333.** Admission £8.50 ($13.60) adults, £7.50 ($12) children (under 4 free). Mar–Sept, daily 10am–5:30pm; Oct–Feb, daily 10am–4pm. Tube: Regent's Park; or Camden Town, then bus Z1 or 274.

One of the greatest zoos in the world, the London Zoo is more than a century and a half old. This 36-acre garden houses about 8,000 animals, including some of the rarest species on earth. Separate houses are reserved for various species: the insect house (incredible bird-eating spiders, a cross-sectioned ant colony); the reptile house (huge dragonlike monitor lizards and a fantastic 15-foot python); and others, such as the Sobell Pavilion for Apes and Monkeys and the Lion Terraces. In the Moonlight World, special lighting effects simulate night for the nocturnal beasties, while rendering them clearly visible to onlookers, so you can see all the night rovers in action.

Unicorn Theatre for Children. The Arts Theatre, 6–7 Great Newport St., WC2. ☎ **0171/379-3280;** box office 0171/836-3334. Admission £8.75 ($14), £7 ($11.20), £5 ($8) depending on seat locations. Show times Sept–June, Sat 11am and 2:30pm; Sun and holidays 2:30pm. Tube: Leicester Square.

Situated in the heart of London's theater district in the West End, the Unicorn is its only theater just for children. Founded in 1947 and going stronger than ever, it presents a season of plays for 4- to 12-year-olds from September to June. The schedule includes specially commissioned plays and adaptations of old favorites, all performed by adult actors. You can also become a temporary member while you're in London and join in an exciting program of weekend workshops.

5 Organized Tours

BUS TOURS   For the first-timer, the quickest and most economical way to bring the big city into focus is to take a bus tour. One of the most popular is **The Original London Sightseeing Tour,** which passes by all the major sights in just about 1¹/₂ hours. London unfolds from a traditional double-decker bus, with live commentary by a guide. The sightseeing tour costs £12 ($19.20) for adults, £6 ($9.60) for children under 16, free for those under 5. The tour plus admission to Madame Tussaud's is £21 ($33.60) for adults, £12 ($19.20) for children; with a River Thames trip, the tour costs £12.50 ($20) for adults and £6.50 ($10.40) for children. You might prefer the London Plus Hop On/Hop Off ticket, which allows you to hop on and off guided tour buses all day long; it's

£12 ($19.20) for adults and £6 ($9.60) for children 5 to 15, free
for those under 5.

Departures are from various convenient points within the city;
you can choose your departure point when you purchase your ticket.
Tickets can be purchased on the bus or from any London Transport
or London Tourist Board Information Centre, where you can receive a discount. Most hotel concierges also sell tickets. For **information or ticket purchases** by phone, call ☎ **0181/877-1722.**
It's also possible to write for tickets: **London Coaches,** Jews Row,
London SW18 1TB.

The **Big Bus Company Ltd.,** Waterside Way, London SW17
7AB (☎ **0181/944-7810**), operates a 2-hour tour in summer, departing every 5 to 15 minutes from 9am to 6pm daily (in winter,
every 15–30 minutes from 9am–6pm daily) from Marble Arch by
Speakers' Corner, Green Park by the Ritz Hotel, and Victoria Station (Buckingham Palace Road by the Royal Westminster Hotel).
Tours cover the highlights—18 in all—ranging from the Houses of
Parliament and Westminster Abbey to the Tower of London and
Buckingham Palace (exterior looks only), accompanied by live commentary. The cost is £12 ($19.20) for adults, £6 ($9.60) for children. There's also a 1-hour tour that follows the same route, but
covers only 13 sights. Tickets are valid all day; you can hop on and
off the bus as you wish.

Of the companies operating a daily program of regularly scheduled public walks, **The Original London Walks,** 87 Messina Ave.,
London NW6 4LG (☎ **0171/624-3978**), is the best, hands down.
The oldest established walking-tour company in London, it's run by
an Anglo-American couple, David and Mary Tucker (he's an American journalist, she's an English actress). Their hallmarks are a variety of routes, reliability, reasonably sized groups, and—above all—
superb guides, including renowned crime historian Donald
Rumbelow (internationally recognized as the leading authority on
Jack the Ripper), a distinguished BBC producer, the foremost au-
thority on the Regent's Canal, the author of the classic guidebook
London Walks, a London Historical Society officer, and several
prominent actors and actresses (including classical actor Edward
Petherbridge). They offer more than 100 walks a week, year-round.
Their repertoire ranges from Greenwich to Ghost Walks; Beatles to
Bloomsbury; Dickens to Docklands; Hampstead to Hidden Lon-
don; Old Westminster to the Old Jewish Quarter; Legal London to
Little Venice to the "London Nobody Knows"; Covent Garden to

Camden Town; Shakespeare to Soho; the Famous Square Mile to the Footsteps of Sherlock Holmes; the "Undiscovered City" to the "Secret Village"; and Aristocratic London to Along the Thames. Walks cost £4.50 ($7.20) for adults, £3.50 ($5.60) for students and seniors; children under 15 go free. Call for schedule; no reservations needed.

6

Shopping

When Prussian Field Marshal Blücher, Wellington's stout ally at Waterloo, first laid eyes on London, he allegedly slapped his thigh and exclaimed, "Herr Gott, what a city to plunder!" He was gazing at what, for the early 19th century, was a phenomenal mass of shops and stores—overwhelming to Herr Blücher's unsophisticated eyes. Since those days, other cities may have equaled London's status as a shopping mecca, but none has ever surpassed it.

TAXES & SHIPPING

Value-added tax (VAT) is the British version of sales tax. VAT is a whopping 17.5% on most goods, but it's already included in the price, so the number you see on the price tag is exactly what you'll pay at the register. Non-European Community residents can get back much of the tax they pay by applying for a VAT refund.

One of the first secrets of shopping in London is that the minimum expenditure needed to qualify for a refund on value-added tax is a mere £50. Not every single store honors this minimum (it's £100 at Harrods, £75 at Selfridges, £62 at Hermès), but it's far easier to qualify for a tax refund in Britain than almost any other country in the European Union. (See the box below for details on how to get your refund.)

Vendors at flea markets might not be equipped to provide the paperwork for a refund, so if you're contemplating a major purchase and really want that refund, ask before you buy. Be suspicious of any dealer who tells you there's no VAT on antiques. There wasn't before, but there is now. The European Union has now made the British add VAT to antiques. Since dealers still have mixed stock, pricing should reflect this fact. So ask if it's included—before you bargain on a price. Get to the price you're comfortable with first, then ask for the VAT refund.

VAT is not charged on goods shipped out of the country, whether you spend £50 or not. Many London shops will help you beat the VAT rap by shipping for you. But watch out: Shipping can double the cost of your purchase. Also expect to pay U.S. duties when the goods get to you at home.

You may want to consider paying for excess baggage (rates vary with the airline), or else have your packages shipped independently. Independent operators are generally less expensive than the airlines. Try **London Baggage,** London Air Terminal, Victoria Place, SW1 (☎ **0171/828-2400;** tube: Victoria Station), or **Burns International Facilities,** at Heathrow Airport Terminal 1 (☎ **0181/745-5301**) and Terminal 4 (☎ **0181/745-7460**).

But remember, you can only avoid the VAT up front if you have the store ship directly for you. If you ship via excess baggage or London Baggage, you'll still have to pay the VAT up front, and apply for a refund.

1 London's Best Buys

Bargain hunters should zero in on goods that are manufactured in England and are liable to cost much more when exported. These are—above all— anything from **The Body Shop** and **Dr. Marten's;** many woolens and some cashmeres; most English brands of bone china; antiques, used silver, and rare books.

ANTIQUES Whether you're looking for museum-quality antiques or simply fun junk, London has the stores, the resources, the stalls, and the markets. While it might not be 1969 anymore (you can't get priceless majolica for £20 anymore), there's still plenty of great finds along Portobello Road and the myriad other markets.

AROMATHERAPY The British must have invented aromatherapy—just about every store sells gels, creams, lotions, and potions made with the right herbs and essential oils to cure whatever ails you, including jet lag. Whether it all works or not is secondary to the fact that most of the British brands are half the U.S. price when bought on home soil. **The Body Shop** becomes the best store in the world at prices like these. Check out drugstore brands as well, especially the Body Shop knock-offs that **Boots The Chemist** makes, as well as their own line (sold in another part of the store) of healing foot gels.

BONE CHINA Savings actually depend on the brand, but can be as much as 50% off U.S. prices. Shipping and U.S. duties may wipe out any savings, so know what you're doing before you buy.

DESIGNER WEAR Designer clothing from any of the international makers may be less in London than in the United States or Paris—but know your prices. Often, the only differential is the VAT refund, which at 15% to 17.5% is substantial. This game is also highly dependent on the value of the dollar.

While you won't get a VAT refund on used designer clothing, London has the best prices on used Chanel (and similar) clothing of any major shopping city.

TEEN FASHIONS   Street fashion, punk, grunge, whatever you want to call it—it's alive and well, with several areas in town, including Carnaby Street, Covent Garden, and Kensington High Street, catering to the young mod squad.

ALSO IN THE CHEAP THRILLS DEPARTMENT   Dime-store brands of makeup cost less than they do in the United States. The French line **Bourjois** (made in the same factories that make Chanel makeup) sells for less in London than in Paris and isn't sold in the United States; **Boots** makes its own Chanel knockoff line, No. 7.

2 The Top Shopping Streets & Neighborhoods

Thankfully for those with too little time to shop, there are several key streets that offer some of London's best retail stores—or simply one of everything—compactly located in a niche or neighborhood so you can just stroll and shop.

THE WEST END

As a neighborhood, the West End includes the tony Mayfair district and is home to the core of London's big-name shopping. Most of the department stores, designer shops, and multiples (chain stores) have their flagships in this area.

The key streets are **Oxford Street** for affordable shopping (start at Marble Arch tube station if you're ambitious, or Bond Street station if you just want to see some of it); and **Regent Street,** which intersects Oxford Street at Oxford Circus (tube: Oxford Circus). While there are several branches of the private-label department store **Marks & Spencer,** their Marble Arch store (on Oxford Street) is their flagship, and worth shopping for their high-quality goods. Regent Street has fancier shops—more upscale department stores (including the famed **Liberty of London**), multiples (**Laura Ashley**), and specialty dealers—and leads all the way to Piccadilly.

In between the two, parallel to Regent Street, is **Bond Street.** Divided into New and Old, Bond Street (tube: Bond Street) also connects Piccadilly with Oxford Street and is synonymous with the luxury trade. Bond Street has experienced a recent revival, and is the hot address for all the international designers; **Donna Karan** has not one but two shops here. A slew of international hotshots have their digs surrounding hers, from **Chanel** to **Ferragamo** to **Versace.**

Burlington Arcade (tube: Piccadilly Circus), the famous glass-roofed, Regency-style passage leading off Piccadilly, looks like a period exhibition and is lined with intriguing shops and boutiques. Lit by wrought-iron lamps and decorated with clusters of ferns and flowers, the small, smart stores specialize in fashion, jewelry, Irish linen, cashmere, and more.

If you linger in the arcade until 5:30pm, you can watch the beadles, those ever-present attendants in their black-and-yellow livery and top hats, ceremoniously put in place the iron grills that block off the arcade until 9am the next morning, at which time they just as ceremoniously remove them to mark the start of a new business day. (There are only three of these constables remaining; they're the last London representatives of Britain's oldest police force.) Also at 5:30pm, a hand bell called the Burlington Bell is sounded, signaling the end of trading.

Just off Regent Street (actually tucked right behind it) is **Carnaby Street** (tube: Oxford Circus), which is also having a comeback. While it no longer dominates the world of pacesetting fashion as it did in the 1960s, it's still fun to visit for cheap souvenirs, a purple wig, or a little something in leather. There's also a convenient branch of **Boots the Chemist** here.

For a total contrast, check out **Jermyn Street** (tube: Piccadilly Circus), on the far side of Piccadilly, a tiny 2-block-long street devoted to high-end men's haberdashers and toiletries shops; many have been doing business for centuries. Several hold royal warrants, including **Turnbull & Asser,** where His Royal Highness Prince Charles has his pj's made.

The West End leads to the theater district, so there are two more shopping areas: the still-not-ready-for-prime-time **Soho** (tube: Tottenham Court Road), where the sex shops are slowly being turned into cutting-edge designer shops; and **Covent Garden** (tube: Covent Garden), which is a masterpiece unto itself. The original marketplace has overflowed its boundaries and eaten up the surrounding neighborhood; it's fun to wander the narrow streets and shop. Covent Garden is especially mobbed on Sundays.

KNIGHTSBRIDGE & CHELSEA

Knightsbridge (tube: Knightsbridge) is the second-most famous of London's retail districts because it's the home of **Harrods.** A small street nearby, **Sloane Street,** is chock-a-block with designer shops; another street in the opposite direction, **Cheval Place,** is also lined with designer resale shops.

Walk toward Museum Row and you'll soon find **Beauchamp Place** (tube: Knightsbridge), pronounced "*bee*-cham." It's only 1 block long, but it's very "Sloane Ranger," featuring the kinds of shops where young British aristos buy their clothing for "The Season."

Head out at the **Harvey Nichols** end of Knightsbridge, away from Harrods, and shop your way through the designer stores on **Sloane Street** (**Hermès, Armani, Prada,** and the like), then walk past Sloane Square and you're in an altogether different neighborhood: King's Road.

King's Road (tube: Sloane Square), the main street of Chelsea, will forever remain a symbol of the Swinging '60s. Today, it's still popular with the young crowd, but there are fewer Mohawk haircuts, Bovver boots, and Edwardian ball gowns than before. More and more in the 1990s, King's Road is a lineup of markets and "multistores," large or small conglomerations of indoor stands, stalls, and booths within one building or enclosure. About a third of King's Road is devoted to these kinds of antiques markets; another third houses design-trade showrooms and stores of household wares for British Yuppies; and the remaining third is faithful to the area's teenybopper roots.

Chelsea doesn't begin and end with King's Road. If you walk in the other direction from Harrods you connect to a part of Chelsea called **Brompton Cross,** another hip area for designer shops made popular when Michelin House was rehabbed by Sir Terence Conran for **The Conran Shop.**

Also seek out **Walton Street,** a tiny little snake of a street running from Brompton Cross back toward to the museums. About 2 blocks of this 3-block street are devoted to fairy-tale shops for m'lady where you can buy aromatherapy from **Jo Malone,** needlepoint, or costume jewelry.

Finally, don't forget all those museums—they all have great gift shops.

KENSINGTON, NOTTING HILL & BAYSWATER

Kensington High Street (tube: High Street Kensington) is the hangout of the classier breed of teen, one who has graduated from Carnaby Street and is ready for street chic. While there are a few staples of basic British fashion on this strip, most of the stores feature items that stretch, are very, very short or very, very tight, and may be orange.

From Kensington High Street, you can walk up **Kensington Church Street,** which, like Portobello Road, is one of the city's main shopping avenues for antiques, selling everything from antique furniture to impressionist paintings.

Kensington Church Street dead-ends at the Notting Hill Gate tube station, which is where you arrive for shopping **Portobello Road;** the dealers and weekend market are 2 blocks beyond.

Not far from Notting Hill Gate is **Whiteleys of Bayswater,** Queensway, W2 (☎ **0171/229-8844;** tube: Bayswater or Queensway), an Edwardian mall whose chief tenant is Marks & Spencer. There are also 70 to 80 shops (the number varies from year to year), mostly specialty outlets, and an array of restaurants, cafes, and bars as well as an eight-screen movie theater.

3   Street & Flea Markets

If Mayfair stores are not your cup of tea, don't worry; you'll have more fun, and find a better bargain, at any of the city's street and flea markets.

THE WEST END

Covent Garden Market (☎ 0171/836-9136; tube: Covent Garden), the most famous market in all of England—possibly all of Europe—offers several different markets daily from 9am to 5pm (we think it's most fun to come on Sunday). It can be a little confusing until you are here, exploring it all. **Apple Market** is the fun, bustling market in the courtyard, where traders sell . . . well, everything. Many of the items are what the English call collectible nostalgia; they include a wide array of glassware and ceramics, leather goods, toys, clothes, hats, and jewelry. Some of the merchandise is truly unusual. Many items are handmade, with some of the craftspeople selling their own wares—except on Mondays, when the craftspeople are replaced by antiques dealers. Meanwhile, out back is **Jubilee Market** (☎ 0171/836-2139), which is also an antiques market on Mondays. Every other day of the week, it's sort of a fancy hippie-ish market with cheap clothes and books. Out front there are a few tents of cheap stuff, except again on Monday, when antiques dealers take over here, too.

The market itself (in the superbly restored hall) offers one of the best shopping opportunities in London. The specialty shops that fill the building sell fashions and herbs, gifts and toys, books and personalized dollhouses, hand-rolled cigars, automata, and much, much more. There are book shops and branches of famous stores (**Hamley's, The Body Shop**), and prices are kept moderate.

Chelsea Antiques Market, 245A–253 King's Rd., SW3 (☎ 0171/352-5686; tube: Sloane Square), sheltered in a rambling old building, offers endless browsing possibilities for the curio addict. About one-third of the market is given over to old or rare books. You're also likely to run across Staffordshire dogs, shaving mugs, Edwardian buckles and clasps, ivory-handled razors, old velours, lace gowns, wooden tea caddies, antique pocket watches, wormy Tudoresque chests, silver snuff boxes, grandfather clocks, and jewelry of all periods. Of note are the **Optical Department,** featuring surgeon's tools, microscopes, sextants, and compasses; and **Harrington Brothers'** selections of antiquarian children's and travel books. Closed Sunday.

On Sunday mornings along **Bayswater Road,** artists hang pictures, collages, and crafts on the railings along the edge of Hyde Park and Kensington Gardens for more than a mile. If the weather's right, start at Marble Arch and walk. You'll see much of the same thing by walking along the railings of **Green Park** along Piccadilly on Saturday afternoon.

NOTTING HILL

Portobello Market (tube: Notting Hill Gate) is a magnet for collectors of virtually anything. It's mainly a Saturday happening, from 6am to 5pm. You needn't be here at the crack of dawn like at Bermondsey (see below); 9am is fine. You just want to beat the motor-coach crowd. Once known mainly for fruit and vegetables (still sold here throughout the week), Portobello in the past 4 decades has become synonymous with antiques. But don't take the stallholder's word for it that the fiddle he's holding is a genuine Stradivarius left to him in the will of his Italian great-uncle; it might just as well have been "nicked" from an East End pawnshop.

The market is divided into three major sections. The most crowded is the antique section, running between Colville Road and Chepstow Villas to the south. *Warning:* There's a great concentration of pickpockets is in this area. The second section (and the oldest part) is the "fruit and veg" market, lying between Westway and Colville Road. In the third and final section there's a flea market, where Londoners sell bric-a-brac and lots of secondhand goods they didn't really want in the first place. But looking around still makes for interesting fun.

The serious collector can pick up a copy of a helpful official guide, *Saturday Antique Market: Portobello Road & Westbourne Grove,* published by the Portobello Antique Dealers Association. It lists where to find what, ranging from music boxes to militaria, lace to 19th-century photographs.

Note: Some 90 antiques and art shops along Portobello Road are open during the week when the street market is closed. This is actually a better time for the serious collector to shop, because you'll get more attention from dealers. And you won't be distracted by the organ grinder.

SOUTH BANK

New Caledonian Market is commonly known as the **Bermondsey Market,** because of its location on the corner of Long Lane and Bermondsey Street (tube: London Bridge, then bus 78 or walk down Bermondsey Street). The market is at the extreme east end, beginning at Tower Bridge Road. It's one of Europe's outstanding street markets in the number and quality of the antiques and other goods offered. The stalls are well known, and many dealers come into London from the country. Prices are generally lower here than at Portobello and the other markets. It gets underway on Fridays only at 5am and—with the bargains gone by 9am—closes at noon. Bring a "torch" (flashlight) if you go in the wee hours.

4 The Department Stores

DEPARTMENT STORES

Contrary to popular belief, Harrods is not the only department store in London. The British invented the department store, and they have lots of them—mostly in Mayfair, and each with its own customer profile.

Daks Simpson Piccadilly. 203 Piccadilly, W1. ☎ **0171/734-2002.** Tube: Piccadilly Circus.

Opened in 1936 as the home of DAKS clothing, Simpson's has been going strong ever since. It's known for menswear—its basement-level men's shoe department is a model of the way quality shoes should be fitted—as well as women's fashions, perfume, jewelry, and lingerie. Many of the clothes are lighthearted, carefully made, and well suited to casual elegance. Its Simpson Collection rubs shoulders with international designer names such as Armani and Yves Saint Laurent.

✪ **Fortnum & Mason, Ltd.** 181 Piccadilly, W1. ☎ **0171/734-8040.** Tube: Piccadilly Circus.

The world's most elegant grocery store is a British tradition dating back to 1707. Down the street from the Ritz, it draws the carriage trade, those from Mayfair to Belgravia who come seeking such tinned treasures as pâté de foie gras or a boar's head. This store exemplifies the elegance and style you would expect from an establishment with two royal warrants. Enter the doors and be transported to another world of deep-red carpets, crystal chandeliers, spiraling wooden staircases, and unobtrusive, tail-coated assistants.

The grocery department is renowned for its impressive selection of the finest foods from around the world—the best champagne, the most scrumptious Belgian chocolates, and succulent Scottish smoked salmon. You can wander through the four floors and inspect the bone china and crystal cut glass, perhaps find the perfect gift in the leather or stationery departments, or reflect on the changing history of furniture and ornaments in the antiques department. Dining choices include the Patio & Buttery, St. James Restaurant, and the Fountain Restaurant (for details on taking afternoon tea here, see "Teatime" in chapter 4).

✪ **Harrods.** 87–135 Brompton Rd., Knightsbridge, SW1. ☎ **0171/730-1234.** Tube: Knightsbridge.

Harrods is an institution. As firmly entrenched in English life as Buckingham Palace and the Ascot Races, it's an elaborate emporium, at times as fascinating as a museum. Some of the goods displayed for sale are works of art, and so are the 300 departments displaying them. The sheer range, variety, and quality of merchandise is dazzling. The motto remains, "If you can eat or drink it, you'll find it at Harrods."

The whole fifth floor is devoted to sports and leisure, with a wide range of equipment and attire. Toy Kingdom is on the fourth floor, along with children's wear. The Egyptian Hall, on the ground floor, sells crystal from Lalique and Baccarat, plus porcelain. There's also a men's grooming room, an enormous jewelry department, and a fashion-forward department for younger customers. Along with the beauty of the bounty, check out the tiles and architectural touches. When you're ready for a break, you have a choice of 18 restaurants and bars. Best of all are the Food Halls, stocked with a huge variety of foods and several cafes. Harrods began as a grocer in 1849, and that's still the heart of the business.

In the basement you'll find a bank, a theater-booking service, a travel bureau, and Harrods Shop for logo gifts.

Harvey Nichols. 109–125 Knightsbridge, SW1. ☎ **0171/235-5000.** Tube: Knightsbridge.

Locals call it Harvey Nicks. The store is large, but doesn't compete with Harrods because it has a much more upmarket, fashionable image (it was a favorite store of the late Princess Diana). Harvey Nicks has its own gourmet-food hall and fancy restaurant, The Fifth Floor, and a huge store crammed with the best designer home furnishings, gifts, and fashions for all, although women's clothing is the largest segment of its business. The store carries many American designer brands; avoid them, as they're more expensive in London.

Liberty of London. 214–220 Regent St., W1. ☎ **0171/734-1234.** Tube: Oxford Circus.

This major British department store is celebrated for its Liberty Prints—top-echelon, carriage-trade fabrics, often in floral patterns—that are prized by decorators for the way they add a sense of English tradition to a room. The front part of the store on Regent Street isn't particularly distinctive, but don't be fooled: Some parts of the place have been restored to Tudor-style splendor that includes half-timbering and lots of interior paneling. There are six floors of fashion, china, and home furnishings, as well as the famous Liberty Print fashion fabrics, upholstery fabrics, scarves, ties, luggage, and gifts.

Marks & Spencer. 458 Oxford St., W1. ☎ **0171/935-7954.** Tube: Marble Arch.

They call it M&S or sometimes Marks & Sparks; it's the most beloved of English institutions, ranking right up there with tea and scones and the Queen Mother. Their fortune has been made in selling high-quality, private-label clothing for all, plus home furnishings and groceries at slightly less-than-regular retail prices. For years, there were no discount stores in the United Kingdom, because everyone knew to shop here.

Despite the fact that the store offers value, it's not considered down-market—simply good, British common sense. Members of the aristocracy wouldn't shop anywhere else; many businessmen buy their business suits here. M&S is also famous for their cotton-knit underwear, which seven out of every ten women in London are wearing right now as you read this.

5 Goods A to Z

ANTIQUES

Alfie's Antique Market. 13–25 Church St., NW8. ☎ **0171/723-6066.** Tube: Marylebone or Edgware Road.

This is the biggest and one of the best-stocked conglomerates of antiques dealers in London, all crammed into the premises of what was built before 1880 as a department store. It has more than 370 stalls, showrooms, and workshops scattered over 35,000 square feet of floor space.

You'll find the biggest Susie Cooper collection in Europe here (Susie Cooper was a well-known designer of tableware and ceramics for Wedgwood). A whole antique district has grown up around Alfie's along Church Street.

Grays & Grays in the Mews. 58 Davies St., and 1–7 Davies Mews, W1. ☎ **0171/629-7034.** Tube: Bond Street.

These antiques markets have been converted into walk-in stands with independent dealers. The term "antique" here covers items from oil paintings to, say, the 1894 edition of the *Encyclopaedia Britannica*. Also sold here are exquisite antique jewelry; silver; gold; maps and prints; bronzes and ivories; arms and armor; Victorian and Edwardian toys; furniture; art nouveau and art deco items; antique lace; scientific instruments; craft tools; and Asian, Persian, and Islamic pottery, porcelain, miniatures, and antiquities. There's a cafe in each building.

ART & CRAFTS

Contemporary Applied Arts. 2 Percy St., W1. ☎ **0171/436-2344.** Tube: Goodge Street.

This association encourages both traditional and progressive contemporary artwork. Many of Britain's best-established craftspeople, as well as lesser-known but promising talents, are represented in galleries that house a diverse retail display of glass, ceramics, textiles, wood, furniture, jewelry, and metalwork—all by outstanding artisans currently producing in the country. A program of special exhibitions, including solo and small-group shows, focuses on innovations in craftwork.

Crafts Council Gallery. 44A Pentonville Rd., Islington, N1. ☎ **0171/278-7700.** Tube: Angel.

The largest crafts gallery is run by the Crafts Council, the national body for promoting contemporary crafts. You'll discover some of today's most creative work here. There's also a shop specializing in craft objects and publications, a picture library, a reference library, and a cafe.

England & Co. 216 Westbourne Grove, W11. ☎ **0171/221-0417.** Tube: Notting Hill Gate.

Under the guidance of the energetic Jane England, this gallery specializes in Outsider Art (by untrained artists) and Art in Boxes, which incorporates a box structure into the composition or frame of a three-dimensional work, while focusing attention on neglected postwar British artists such as Tony Stubbings and Ralph Romney. One-person and group shows are mounted frequently, and many young artists get early exposure here.

BATH & BODY

✪ **The Body Shop.** 375 Oxford St., W1. ☎ **0171/409-7868.** Tube: Bond Street. Other locations throughout London.

There's a branch of The Body Shop in every trading area and tourist zone in London. Some stores are bigger than others, but all are filled with politically and environmentally correct beauty, bath, and aromatherapy products. Prices are drastically lower in the United Kingdom than they are in the United States. There's an entire children's line, a men's line, and lots of travel sizes and travel products. You won't have as much fun in a candy store.

✪ **Boots The Chemist.** 72 Brompton Rd., SW3. ☎ **0171/589-6557.** Tube: Knightsbridge. Other locations throughout London.

This store has a million branches; we like the one across the street from Harrods for convenience and size. The house brands of beauty products are usually the best, be they Boots products (try the cucumber facial scrub), Boots's versions of The Body Shop (two lines, Global and Naturalistic), or Boots's versions of Chanel makeup (called No. 7). They also sell film, pantyhose (called tights), sandwiches, and all of life's little necessities.

✪ **Floris.** 89 Jermyn St., SW1. ☎ **0171/930-2885.** Tube: Piccadilly Circus.

A variety of toilet articles and fragrances fill Floris's floor-to-ceiling mahogany cabinets, which are architectural curiosities in their own right. They were installed relatively late in the establishment's history—that is, 1851—long after the shop had received its royal warrants as suppliers of toilet articles to the king and queen.

✪ **Penhaligon's.** 41 Wellington St., WC2. ☎ **0171/836-2150,** or 800/588-1992 in the U.S. for mail order. Tube: Covent Garden.

This Victorian perfumery, established in 1870, holds royal warrants to HRH Duke of Edinburgh and HRH Prince of Wales. All items sold are exclusive to Penhaligon's. It offers a large selection of perfumes, aftershaves, soaps, and bath oils for women and men. Gifts include antique-silver scent bottles, grooming accessories, and leather traveling requisites.

BOOKS, MAPS & ENGRAVINGS

In addition to the specialty bookstores listed below, you'll also find well-stocked branches of the **Dillon's** chain around town, including one at 82 Gower St. (tube: Euston Square).

Children's Book Centre. 237 Kensington High St., W8. ☎ **0171/937-7497.** Tube: High Street Kensington.

With thousands of titles, this is the best place to go for children's books. Fiction is arranged according to age, up to 16. There are also videos and toys for kids.

Hatchards. 187 Piccadilly, W1. ☎ **0171/439-9921.** Tube: Piccadilly Circus or Green Park.

On the south side of Piccadilly, Hatchards offers a wide range of books in all subjects and is particularly renowned in the areas of fiction, biography, travel, cookery, gardening, and art, plus history and finance. In addition, Hatchards is second to none in its range of books on royalty.

Stanfords. 12–14 Long Acre, WC2. ☎ **0171/836-1321.** Tube: Leicester Square or Covent Garden.

Established in 1852, Stanfords is the world's largest map shop. Many of its maps, which include worldwide touring and survey maps, are unavailable elsewhere. It's also London's best travel bookstore (with a complete selection of Frommer's guides!).

W & G Foyle, Ltd. 113–119 Charing Cross Rd., WC2. ☎ **0171/439-8501.** Tube: Tottenham Court Road.

Claiming to be the world's largest bookstore, W & G Foyle has an impressive array of hardcovers and paperbacks, as well as travel maps, records, videotapes, and sheet music.

CASHMERES & WOOLENS

British Designer Knitwear Group. 2–6 Quadrant Arcade, 80 Regent St., W1. ☎ **0171/734-5786.** Tube: Piccadilly Circus.

Here you'll find woolens from all over the British Islands, including the Scottish Shetlands. Some of the woolens are handmade; often, many of the designers are well known. Some have a tweedy English look, while others are more high-fashion.

Scotch House. 84–86 Regent St., W1. ☎ **0171/734-5966.** Tube: Piccadilly Circus.

For top-quality woolen fabrics and garments, go to Scotch House, renowned worldwide for its comprehensive selection of cashmere and wool knitwear for men, women, and children. Also available is a wide range of tartan garments and accessories, as well as Scottish tweed classics.

FASHION
THE TRUE BRIT

Austin Reed. 103–113 Regent St., W1. ☎ **0171/734-6789.** Tube: Piccadilly Circus.

Austin Reed has long stood for superior-quality clothing and excellent tailoring. The suits of Chester Barrie, for example, are said to fit like bespoke (custom-made) clothing. The polite employees are unusually honest about telling you what looks good. The store always has a wide variety of top-notch jackets and suits, and men can outfit themselves from dressing gowns to overcoats. For women, there are carefully selected suits, separates, coats, shirts, knitwear, and accessories.

✪ **Burberry.** 18–22 Haymarket, SW1. ☎ **0171/930-3343.** Tube: Piccadilly Circus.

The name has been synonymous with raincoats ever since Edward VII publicly ordered his valet to "bring my Burberry" when the skies threatened. An impeccably trained staff sells the famous raincoats, plus excellent men's shirts, sportswear, knitwear, and accessories. Raincoats are available in women's sizes and styles as well. Prices are high, but you get quality and prestige.

Dr. Marten's Department Store. 1–4 King St., WC2. ☎ **0171/497-1460.** Tube: Covent Garden.

Dr. Marten (called Doc Marten) makes a brand of shoe that has become so popular—internationally—that now there's an entire department store selling them in a huge variety of styles, plus accessories, gifts, and even clothes. Teens come to worship here because ugly is beautiful, and because the prices are far better than they are in the United States or elsewhere in Europe.

Gieves & Hawkes. 1 Savile Row, W1. ☎ **0171/434-2001.** Tube: Piccadilly Circus or Green Park.

This place has a prestigious address and a list of clients that includes the Prince of Wales; yet its prices aren't as lethal as others on this street. They're high, but you get good quality. Cotton shirts, silk ties, Shetland sweaters, and exceptional ready-to-wear and bespoke suits are sold.

Laura Ashley. 256–258 Regent St., W1. ☎ **0171/437-9760.** Tube: Oxford Circus. Other locations around London.

This is the flagship store of the company whose design ethos embodies the English country look. The store carries a wide choice of women's clothing and home furnishings. Prices are lower than in the United States.

✪ **Thomas Pink.** 85 Jermyn St., SW1. ☎ **0171/930-6364.** Tube: Green Park.

This Jermyn Street shirtmaker, named after an 18th-century Mayfair tailor, gave the world the phrases "hunting pink" and "in the pink." It has a prestigious reputation for well-made cotton shirts, for both men and women, made from Egyptian and Sea Island cotton. The shirts are created from the finest two-fold pure-cotton poplin, coming in a wide range of patterns, stripes, and checks, as well as in plain colors. Some patterns are classic, others new and unusual. All are generously cut, with extra-long tails and finished with a choice of double cuffs or single-button cuffs. A small pink square in the tail tells all.

Turnbull & Asser. 71–72 Jermyn St., SW1. ☎ **0171/930-0502.** Tube: Piccadilly Circus.

Over the years, everyone from David Bowie to Ronald Reagan has been seen in a custom-made shirt from Turnbull & Asser. Excellent craftspersonship and simple lines—even bold colors—distinguish these shirts. The outlet also sells shirts and blouses to women, a clientele that has ranged from Jacqueline Bisset to Candice Bergen. Note that T&A shirts come in only one sleeve length and are then altered to fit. The sales department will inform you that its made-to-measure service takes 10 to 12 weeks, and you must order at least a half-dozen. Of course, the monograms are included.

THE CUTTING EDGE

Anya Hindmarch. 91 Walton St., SW3. ☎ **0171/584-7644.** Tube: South Kensington.

Although her fashionable bags are sold at Harvey Nichols, Liberty, Harrods, and in the United States and Europe, this is the only place to see the complete range of Anya Hindmarch's designs. Featuring handbags, wash bags, wallets, purses, and key holders, smaller items range in price from £38 ($60.80) whereas handbag prices stretch from £150 ($240.00) and up, with alligator being the most expensive. There's a limited bespoke service, and you may bring in your fabric to be matched.

✪ **Browns.** 23–27 S. Molton St., W1. ☎ **0171/491-7833.** Tube: Bond Street.

This is the only place in London to find the designs of Alexander McQueen, now head of the House of Givenchy in Paris, and one of the fashion industry's rising stars. Producing his own cottons, silks, and plastics, McQueen creates revealing and feminine women's couture and ready-to-wear, and has recently started marketing a well-received menswear line. McQueen made his reputation creating shock-value apparel more eagerly photographed by the media than worn. But recently his outfits have been called more "consumer friendly" by fashion critics.

Egg. 36 Kinnerton St., SW1. ☎ **0171/235-9315.** Tube: Hyde Park Corner or Knightsbridge.

This shop is hot, hot, hot with fashionistas. It features imaginatively designed, contemporary clothing by Indian textile designer Asha Sarabhai and knitwear by Eskandar. Designs created from handmade textiles from a workshop in India range from everyday dresses and coats to hand-embroidered silk coats. Prices begin at £60 ($96). Crafts and ceramics are also available.

Joseph. 23 Old Bond St., W1. ☎ **0171/629-3713.** Tube: Green Park. Also at 16 Sloane St., SW1 (☎ 0171/235-1991; tube: Sloane Square); 26 Sloane St., SW1 (☎ 0171/235-5470; tube: Sloane Square); and 77 Fulham Rd., SW3 (☎ 0171/823-9500; tube: South Kensington). Joseph's Own APC, Inc. is at 124 Draycott Ave., SW3 (☎ 0171/225-0364; tube: South Kensington).

Joseph Ettedgui, a fashion retailer born in Casablanca, is considered a maverick in the fashion world—he's known for his daring designs and his ability to attract some of the most talented designers in the business to work with him. This is the flagship store among five London branches, and it carries the Ettedgui collection of suits, knitwear, suede, and leather clothing for men and women. The stretch jeans with flair ankles are the label's best-selling items.

Katharine Hamnett. 20 Sloane St., SW1. ☎ **0171/823-1002.** Tube: Knightsbridge.

One of Britain's big-name designers—her so-called "slut dresses" earned her the title of the bad girl of Brit fashion—Katharine Hamnett is best known for her slogan T-shirts. Her recent collections, although greeted with a media feeding frenzy, got mixed reviews. You can judge for yourself while browsing through her complete line of men's and women's day and evening wear. She's also a strong environmental activist and is known for using "nature friendly" fabrics.

✪ **Vivienne Westwood.** 6 Davies St., W1. ☎ **0171/629-3757.** Tube: Bond Street. Branches: World's End, 430 King's Rd., SW3 (☎ 0171/352-6551; tube: Sloane Square); and Vivienne Westwood, 43 Conduit St., W1 (☎ 0171/439-1109; tube: Oxford Circus).

No one in British fashion is hotter than the unstoppable Vivienne Westwood. While it's possible to purchase select Westwood pieces around the world, her U.K. shops are the best places to find her full range of fashion designs. The flagship location concentrates on her couture line, or The Gold Label, as it's known. Using a wide range of uniquely British resources, Westwood creates jackets, skirts, trousers, blouses, dresses, and evening dresses. Her latest line features taffeta ball gowns, made-to-measure tailored shirts, and even some Highland plaids. If all this weren't enough, she came out with her own perfume in 1997 (who hasn't?).

The World's End branch carries casual designs, including T-shirts, jeans, and other sportswear; the sale shop on Conduit Street has a bit of everything: The Gold Label; her second women's line, The Red Label; and The Man Label, her menswear collection. Accessories available include women's and men's shoes, belts, and jewelry.

VINTAGE & SECONDHAND

Note that there's no VAT refund on used clothing.

Old Hat. 62 and 66 Fulham High St., SW6. ☎ **0171/736-5446.** Tube: Putney Bridge.

This large dealer of secondhand menswear is the place to find Savile Row suits, Jermyn Street silk ties, Burberry raincoats, and Turnbull & Asser shirts for a fraction of their original cost. There's a variety of styles from the last 80 years on hand, and everything's in good condition. Prices range from £40 to £90 ($64–$144); tailoring is available for about £30 ($48). Be sure to check out the window displays, which regularly feature such incongruities as a pair of BSA Bantam motorcycles (also available for purchase).

Pandora. 16–22 Cheval Place, SW7. ☎ **0171/589-5289.** Tube: Knightsbridge.

A London institution since the 1940s, Pandora stands in fashionable Knightsbridge, a stone's throw from Harrods. Several times a week, chauffeurs will drive up with bundles packed anonymously by England's gentry. One woman voted best dressed at Ascot several years ago was wearing a secondhand dress acquired here. Prices are generally one-third to one-half the retail value. Chanel and Anne Klein are among the designers represented. Outfits are usually no more than two seasons old.

FOOD

English food has come a long way lately; it's worth enjoying and bringing home. Don't pass up the Food Halls in Harrods; consider the Fifth Floor at Harvey Nicks if Harrods is crammed with too many tourists—it isn't the same, but it'll do. Also, Fortnum & Mason is internationally famous as a food emporium. See "The Department Stores," above.

Charbonnel et Walker. 1 The Royal Arcade, 28 Old Bond St., W1. ☎ **0171/491-0939.** Tube: Green Park.

Charbonnel et Walker is famous for its hot chocolate in winter (buy it by the tin) and their strawberries-and-cream chocolates during "The Season." The firm will send messages of thanks or love spelled out on the chocolates themselves. Ready-made presentation boxes are also available.

MUSIC

Collectors should browse Notting Hill; there's a handful of good shops near the Notting Hill Gate tube stop. Also browse Soho in the Wardour Street area, near the Tottenham Court Road tube stop. Sometimes dealers show up at Covent Garden on the weekends.

In addition to the two listed below, also worth checking out is the ubiquitous **Our Price** chain, which offers only the current chart-toppers, but usually at great prices.

Americans should beware of buying videotapes in the United Kingdom; the British standard is PAL, which is incompatible with the U.S. standard, NTSC. Even if a tape says VHS, it probably won't play in your machine at home.

Tower Records. 1 Piccadilly Circus, W1. ☎ **0171/439-2500.** Tube: Piccadilly Circus. Other locations throughout London.

Attracting the throngs from a neighborhood whose pedestrian traffic is almost overwhelming, this is one of the largest record and CD stores in Europe. Sprawling over four floors, it's practically a tourist attraction in its own right. In addition to a huge selection of most of the musical styles ever recorded, there's everything on the cutting edge of technology, including interactive hardware and software, CD-ROMs, and laser discs.

Virgin Megastore. 14–16 Oxford St., W1. ☎ **0171/631-1234.** Tube: Tottenham Court Road. Also at 527 Oxford St., W1 (☎ 0171/491-8582; tube: Oxford Circus).

If a record has just been released—and if it's worth hearing in the first place—chances are this store carries it. It's like a giant musical grocery store, and you get to hear the release on headphones at listening stations before making a purchase. Even visiting rock stars come here to pick up new releases. A large selection of classical and jazz recordings is sold, as are computer software and video games. In between selecting your favorites, you can enjoy a coffee at the cafe, or purchase an airline ticket from the Virgin Atlantic office.

MUSEUM SHOPS

London Transport Museum Shop. Covent Garden, WC2. ☎ **0171/379-6344.** Tube: Covent Garden.

This museum shop carries a wide range of reasonably priced repro and antique travel posters as well as tons of fun gifts and souvenirs. Those great London Underground maps that you see at every tube station can be purchased here.

Victoria & Albert Gift Shop. Cromwell Rd., SW7. ☎ **0171/938-8500.** Tube: South Kensington.

Run by the Craft Council, this is the best museum shop in London—indeed, one of the best in the world. It sells cards, a fabulous selection of art books, and the usual items, along with reproductions from the museum archives.

SHOES

One of London's most famous shoe stores, Dr. Marten's Department Store, is listed above in "The Department Stores."

Church's. 13 New Bond St., W1. ☎ **0171/493-1474.** Tube: Bond Street.

Well-made shoes, the status symbol of well-heeled executives in financial districts around the world, have been turned out by these famous shoemakers since 1873. Today, well-outfitted English gents usually prefer to stamp around London in their Church's shoes. These are said to be recognizable to all the maîtres d'hôtel in London, who have always been suspected of appraising the wealth of their clients by their footwear.

Lilley & Skinners. 360 Oxford St., W1. ☎ **0171/629-6381.** Tube: Bond Street.

This is the largest shoe store in Europe, displaying many different brands over three floors staffed by an army of salespeople. It specializes in not particularly glamorous names, but offers good value and a wide selection of difficult-to-find sizes.

TEAS

Of course, don't forget to visit Fortnum & Mason as well (see "The Department Stores," above).

The Tea House. 15A Neal St., WC2. ☎ **0171/240-7539.** Tube: Covent Garden.

This shop sells everything associated with tea, tea drinking, and tea-time. It boasts more than 70 quality teas and tisanes, including whole-fruit blends, the best tea of China (Gunpowder, jasmine with flowers), India (Assam leaf, choice Darjeeling), Japan (Genmaicha green), and Sri Lanka (pure Ceylon), plus such longtime favorite English blended teas as Earl Grey. The shop also offers novelty tea-pots and mugs, among other items.

TOYS

✪ **Hamleys.** 188–196 Regent St., W1. ☎ **0171/734-3161.** Tube: Oxford Circus. Also at Covent Garden and Heathrow Airport.

This flagship is the finest toy shop in the world—more than 35,000 toys and games on seven floors of fun and magic. The huge selection includes soft, cuddly stuffed animals as well as dolls, radio-controlled cars, train sets, model kits, board games, outdoor toys, and computer games.

7

London After Dark

*L*ondon's pulsating scene is the most vibrant in Europe. Although pubs still close at 11pm, the city is staying up later. More and more clubs extend partying into the wee hours.

London is on a real high right now, especially in terms of music and dance; much of the current techno and electronica (including the trip-hop, jungle, and drum-and-bass styles being appropriated by aging rockers like Bowie and U2) originated in London clubs. Sounds made hip by Tricky and Aphex Twin reverberate not only throughout the city, but across the continent and the Atlantic as well. Youth culture prevails; downtown denizens flock to the latest clubs where pop-culture superstars are routinely spotted, such as Liam Gallagher (of Oasis fame) and actress Patsy Kensit, or Keith Allen (cult-figure actor) and Damien Hirst (known for suspending dead animals in formaldehyde and calling it Art).

London nightlife is notorious for being in a state of constant flux. What is hot today probably just opened; some clubs no doubt will have the life span of fruitflies. **Groucho,** at 44 Dean St., W1 (☎ **0171/439-4685**), remains for the moment the *in* club, though it is still members-only. The Marquee, the legendary live-music venue where the Rolling Stones played when they were still bad boys, has regrettably shut its doors. But a few perennials, like Ronnie Scott's, are still around.

London nightlife, however, is not just music and dance clubs. The city abounds with what's probably the world's best live-theater scene, pubs oozing historic charm, and many more options for a night out on the town.

HOW TO FIND OUT WHAT'S GOING ON

Weekly publications such as *Time Out* and *Where* provide the most complete, up-to-the-minute entertainment listings. They contain information on the live-music and dance clubs of the moment as well as London's diverse theater scene, which includes everything from big-budget West End shows to fringe productions. Daily newspapers, notably *The Times* and *The Telegraph,* also provide listings. The arts section of the weekend *Independent* is also a good reference.

If you really want to take full advantage of London's arts scene, your best bet might be to do a bit of research before you leave home—even a few months in advance. To get a good idea of what's going on, check out *Time Out*'s **World Wide Web page** on the Internet at http://www.timeout.co.uk. If you're not on-line, *Time Out* is available at many international newsstands in the United States and Canada. In London it can be picked up almost anywhere.

1   The Play's the Thing: The London Theater Scene

Perhaps even more so than New York, London is the theater capital of the world; the number and variety of productions, as well as high standards of acting and directing, are practically unrivaled. London stage offers both the traditional and the avant-garde and is uniquely accessible and affordable.

After its Elizabethan heyday, England's dramatic glory suffered periodic declines that nearly brought it to extinction; the first was an outgrowth of Cromwell's official Puritanism, which banned *all* stage performances (along with the celebration of Christmas) as "heathenish and un-Godly."

The Great Thaw in London theater occurred sometime during the mid-1950s. In truth, the theater's recovery was more like a volcanic eruption. The pressures of repressed talent, creativity, and artistic expression—which had been building since World War II—broke loose in a steady stream of stage and film productions that swept away London's dusty theatrical mores and swung open the gates of a second Elizabethan dramatic era.

Britain hasn't looked back since, and London theater is still a wellspring of originality. The greatest theatrical excitement in the city today is being stirred up by the new Globe Theatre. Since this is also a sightseeing attraction, it's previewed in chapter 5 (see "Shakespeare's Globe Theatre & Exhibition").

Few things in London are as entertaining and rewarding as the theater. A trip to London could be nothing more than a splendid orgy of drama and musicals.

GETTING TICKETS

Prices for London shows vary widely—usually from £15 to £52 ($24–$83.20), depending on the theater and, logically, the seat.

Matinees, performed Tuesday to Saturday, are cheaper than evening performances. Evening performances begin between 7:30 and 8:30pm, midweek matinees at 2:30 or 3pm, and Saturday matinee at 5:45pm. West End theaters are closed Sundays. Many theaters offer the bonus of licensed bars on the premises and coffee at intermissions (which Londoners call "intervals").

Many theaters accept telephone bookings at regular prices with a credit card. They'll hold your tickets for you at the box office, where you'll pick them up at show time with a credit card.

TICKET AGENCIES   If you've got your heart set on seeing a specific show, particularly one of the big hits, you'll have to reserve in advance through one of the many London ticket agencies. For tickets and information before you go, on just about any show and entertainment option in London, **Edwards & Edwards** has a New York office at 1270 Ave. of the Americas, Suite 2414, New York, NY 10029 (☎ **800/223-6108** or 914/328-2150; fax 914/328-2752). They also have offices in London: **Edwards & Edwards** at the Palace Theatre, Shaftesbury Avenue, W1 8AY (☎ **0171/734-4555**), or at **Harrods** ticket desk (☎ **0171/225-6666**). A personal visit isn't necessary; they'll mail tickets to your home, fax you a confirmation or leave your tickets at the box office. Instant confirmations are available with special "overseas" rates for most shows. A booking and handling fee of up to 20% is added to the ticket price.

You might also try calling **Keith Prowse/First Call** (☎ **0171/836-9001**). This agency also has an office in the United States, which allows you to reserve weeks or even months in advance for hit shows: 234 W. 44th St., Suite 1000, New York, NY 10036 (☎ **800/669-8687** or 212/398-1430). Various locations exist in London. The fee for booking a ticket is 25% in London and 35% in the United States.

Another option is **Theatre Direct International (TDI)** (☎ **800/334-8457**). TDI specializes in providing London theater and fringe production tickets, but also has tickets to most London productions, including the Royal National Theatre and Barbican. The service allows you to arrive in London with your tickets or have them held for you at the box office.

GALLERY & DISCOUNT TICKETS   London theater tickets are quite reasonable compared to those in the United States. Sometimes gallery seats (the cheapest) are sold only on the day of the performance; you'll need to head to the box office early in the day and, since these are not reserved seats, return an hour before the performance to queue up.

Many major theaters offer reduced-price tickets to *students* on a standby basis. When available, these tickets are sold 30 minutes prior to curtain. Line up early for popular shows, as standby tickets get snapped up. Of course, you'll need a valid student ID.

The **Society of London Theatre** (☎ **0171/836-0971**) operates a **discount ticket booth** in Leicester Square, where tickets for many shows are available at half price, plus a £2 ($3.20) service charge. Tickets (limited to four per person) are sold only on the day of performance. You cannot return tickets, and credit cards are not accepted. Hours are daily from 12:30 to 6:30pm, except on days with scheduled matinees, when the booth opens from noon to 6:30pm. Many less-that-scrupulous agents near Leicester Square offer "discounted" tickets that are nothing of the kind. Out-of-towners could pay $30 to $35 for a "discount" ticket only to find them available at the box office for $25. If you believe you've been ripped off, you can complain directly to the theater or call ☎ **0171/798-1111.**

MAJOR THEATERS & COMPANIES

Barbican Theatre—Royal Shakespeare Company. In the Barbican Centre, Silk St., Barbican, EC2. ☎ **0171/638-8891.** Barbican Theatre £6–£26.50 ($9.60–$42.40); The Pit £10–£17 ($16–$27.20) matinees and evening performances. Box office daily 9am–8pm. Tube: Barbican or Moorgate.

The Barbican is the London home of the Royal Shakespeare Company, one of the world's finest theater companies. The core of its repertoire remains, of course, the plays of William Shakespeare. It also presents a wide-ranging program of three different productions each week in the Barbican Theatre—a 2,000-seat main auditorium with excellent sightlines throughout, thanks to a raked orchestra—and in The Pit, a small studio space where much of the company's new writing is presented. The Royal Shakespeare Company is in residence in London during the winter months; it spends the summer touring in England and abroad.

Open-Air Theatre. Inner Circle, Regent's Park, NW1. ☎ **0171/486-2431.** Tickets £8–£20 ($12.80–$32). Tube: Baker Street.

This outdoor theater is in Regent's Park; the setting is idyllic, and both seating and acoustics are excellent. Presentations are mainly Shakespeare, usually in period costume. Its theater bar, the longest in London, serves both drink and food. In the case of a rained-out performance, tickets are given for another date. The season runs from the end of May to mid-September, Monday to Saturday at 8pm, plus Wednesday, Thursday, and Saturday matinees at 2:30pm.

✪ **Royal National Theatre.** South Bank, SE1. ☎ **0171/928-2252.** Tickets £8–24 ($12.80–$38.40); midweek matinees, Sat matinees, and previews cost less. Tube: Waterloo, Embankment, or Charing Cross.

Home to one of the world's greatest stage companies, the Royal National Theatre is not one but three theaters—the Olivier, reminiscent of a Greek amphitheater with its open stage; the more traditional Lyttelton; and the Cottesloe, with its flexible stage and seating. The National presents the finest in world theater, from classic drama to award-winning new plays, including comedy, musicals, and shows for young people. The theater offers a choice of at least six plays at any one time. It's also a full-time theater center, featuring an amazing selection of bars, cafes, restaurants, free foyer music and exhibitions, short early-evening performances, book shops, backstage tours, riverside walks, and terraces. Options abound: You can have a three-course meal in Mezzanine, the National's restaurant; enjoy a light meal in the brasserie-style Terrace Café; or have a snack in one of the coffee bars.

2 The Rest of the Performing Arts Scene

Currently, London supports five major orchestras—the **London Symphony,** the **Royal Philharmonic,** the **Philharmonia Orchestra,** the **BBC Symphony,** and the **BBC Philharmonic**—several choirs, and many smaller chamber groups and historic instrument ensembles. Look for the **London Sinfonietta,** the **English Chamber Orchestra,** and of course the **Academy of St. Martin-in-the-Fields.** Performances are in the South Banks Arts Centre and the Barbican. For smaller recitals, there's Wigmore Hall and St. John's Smith Square.

The **British Music Information Centre,** 10 Stratford Place, W1 (☎ **0171/499-8567**), is the city's clearinghouse and resource center for "serious" music. The center is open Monday to Friday, noon to 5pm, and provides free telephone and walk-in information on current and upcoming events. Recitals featuring 20th-century British classical compositions cost up to £5 ($8) and are offered here weekly, usually on Tuesday and Thursday at 7:30pm; call ahead for day and time. You may want to check early, as capacity is limited to 40. Take the tube to Bond Street.

English National Opera. Performing in the London Coliseum, St. Martin's Lane, WC2. ☎ **0171/632-8300.** Tickets £6.50–£8 ($10.40–$12.80) balcony,

£12–£55 ($19.20–$88) Upper Dress Circle or stalls; about 100 discount balcony tickets sold on the day of performance from 10am during the season. Tube: Charing Cross or Leicester Square.

Built in 1904 as a variety theater and converted into an opera house in 1968, the London Coliseum is the city's largest theater. One of two national opera companies, the English National Opera performs a wide range of works, from classics to Gilbert and Sullivan to new and experimental works, each staged with flair and imagination. All performances are in English. A repertory of 18 to 20 productions is presented 5 or 6 nights a week for 11 months of the year (dark in July). Although the balcony seats are cheaper, many visitors seem to prefer the Upper Circle or Dress Circle.

✪ **The Royal Opera House—The Royal Ballet & The Royal Opera.** Bow St., Covent Garden, WC2. Box office ☎ **0171/304-4000.** Opera tickets £4–£147.50 ($6.40–$236); ballet tickets £2–£62 ($3.20–$99.20). Tube: Covent Garden.

England's most elite opera company and leading ballet company both perform at one of the capital's most glamorous theaters, the Royal Opera House. Restoration has temporarily dislodged the companies from their home stage, but they should be returning here in autumn 1999. In the meantime, they will be appearing at a number of places in London and abroad. Temporary locales include the Barbican, Royal Albert Hall, and a West End theater, while ballet seasons will be held at the Labatts Apollo in Hammersmith, the Royal Festival Hall, and the London Coliseum. Check local listings for complete details. If you'd like to find out about these fabled troupes, you can call ☎ **0171/240-1200.**

Note that the Royal Opera performs an international repertoire, and performances are usually sung in the original language with projected supertitles that translate the libretto for the audience. Currently under the direction of Sir Anthony Dowell, the Royal Ballet performs a varied ballet repertory with a nod toward the classics and works by its earlier choreographer-directors Sir Frederick Ashton and Sir Kenneth MacMillan.

✪ **Barbican Centre—London Symphony Orchestra (& more).** Silk St., the City, EC2. ☎ **0171/638-8891.** Tickets £6–£30 ($9.60–$48). Tube: Barbican or Moorgate.

The largest art and exhibition center in Western Europe, the roomy and comfortable Barbican is a perfect setting for enjoying music and theater. *Barbican Theatre* is the London home of the **Royal Shakespeare Company** (see above), while *Barbican Hall* is the permanent home address of the **London Symphony Orchestra** and host to visiting orchestras and performers, from classical to jazz, folk, and world music.

In addition to the hall and theater, the Barbican Centre includes: The Pit, a studio theater; the Barbican Art Gallery, a showcase for visual arts; the Concourse Gallery and foyer exhibition spaces; Cinemas One and Two, which show recently released mainstream films and film series; the Barbican Library, a general lending library that places a strong emphasis on the arts; the Conservatory, one of London's largest plant houses; and three restaurants, cafes, and bars. The box office is open daily from 9am to 8pm.

London Palladium. Argyll St. (corner of Oxford St.), W1. ☎ **0171/ 494-5020.** Tickets £10–£32.50 ($16–$52), depending on the show. Show times vary. Tube: Oxford Circus.

This legendary theater has figured into the dreams of every up-and-coming star in the British stage. (Alfred Hitchcock once used it to stage scenes in some of his thrillers.) In days of yore, the Palladium hosted such stars as Judy Garland, Tom Jones, Perry Como, and Sammy Davis, Jr. In recent years, it was the setting for gangbuster musicals including revivals of *Oliver!, Fiddler on the Roof,* and *Joseph and the Amazing Technicolor Dreamcoat.*

✪ **Royal Festival Hall.** On the South Bank, SE1. ☎ **0171/960-4242.** Tickets £5–£35 ($8–$56). Box office daily 10am–9pm. Tube: Waterloo or Embankment Station.

In the aftermath of World War II, the principal site of London's music scene shifted to a specialized complex of buildings erected between 1951 and 1964 on the site of a bombed-out 18th-century brewery. In the midst of industrial wastelands on the rarely visited south side of the Thames arose three of the most comfortable and acoustically perfect concert halls in the world. They include Royal Festival Hall, Queen Elizabeth Hall, and the Purcell Room. Together they hold more than 1,200 performances a year, including classical music, ballet, jazz, popular music, and contemporary dance. Also here is the internationally renowned Hayward Gallery, showcasing both contemporary and historical art. Recent exhibitions have included works by Andy Warhol, Pierre-Auguste Renoir, Jasper Johns, Leonardo da Vinci, Le Corbusier, and Salvador Dalí.

Royal Festival Hall, which opens at 10am every day, offers an extensive array of things to see and do, including free exhibitions in the foyers and free lunchtime music at 12:30pm. The Poetry Library is open from 11am to 8pm, and shops offer a wide selection of books, records, and crafts. The Festival Buffet has a wide variety of food at reasonable prices, and bars dot the foyers. The **People's Palace** offers lunch and dinner with a panoramic view of the River Thames. Reservations are recommended by calling ☎ **0171/ 921-0800.**

Dance Umbrella. 20 Chancellor's St., W6. ☎ **0181/741-4040.** Tickets £10– £15 ($16–$24).

This company's fall-season showcase became *the* contemporary dance event in London. During its 6-week season, new works by up-and-coming choreographers are featured. Performances are held at a variety of theaters.

Sadler's Wells Theater. Rosebery Ave., EC1. ☎ **0171/312-1996.** Tickets £7.50–£32 ($12–$51.20). Performances usually at 8pm; box office Mon–Sat 10am–8pm. Tube: Angel.

Set in the north London neighborhood of Islington, this theater is London's premier venue for the presentation of both traditional and experimental dance theater at reasonable prices. In the early 1990s, the turn-of-the-century theater that had evolved from an original 17th-century core was demolished, and construction began on an innovative new design that's scheduled for completion sometime during the life of this edition. In the interim, performances are being staged at the **Peacock Theater** on Portugal Street, WC2 (same phone; tube: Holburn). Once the new theater is completed, performances will be held at both venues.

3   The Club & Music Scene

It's the nature of live music and dance clubs to come and go with sometimes alarming speed, or to embody a violent shift from one trend to another. *Time Out* is your best resource for staying current on the club scene.

LIVE MUSIC
ROCK
The Rock Garden. 6–7 The Piazza, Covent Garden, WC2. ☎ **0171/836-4052.** Cover £5 ($8), diners enter free. Mon–Thurs 5pm–3am, Fri 5pm–6am, Sat 4pm–4am, Sun 7:30–11pm. Tube: Covent Garden. Bus: Any of the night buses that depart from Trafalgar Square.

A long-established performance site for a wide array of bands, The Rock Garden maintains a bar and a stage in the cellar, and a restaurant on the street level. The cellar, known as The Venue, has hosted such acts as Dire Straits, the Police, and U2 before their rises to stardom. Today bands vary widely, from promising up-and-comers to some who'll never be heard from again. Simple American-style fare is served in the restaurant.

The VorteX Ltd. 79 Oxford St. ☎ **0171/439-7250.** Cover £8–£16 ($12.80–$25.60) varies. Sun–Thurs 9pm–3am, Fri 9pm–4am, Sat 9pm–6am. Tube: Tottenham Court Road.

Loud, unconventional, and catering to the punk crowd, this brash cellar bar welcomes music lovers and late-night revelers. It's become very touristy, however. The heavily-promoted year-old incarnation of a club opened in the 1970s, The VorteX is set in the basement of an Oxford Street building below, of all things, a Pizza Hut. Entertainment, which includes both recorded and live performers, varies nightly. Thursday's soul and R&B segues into Friday's rock and heavy metal. Saturday is for house and garage jams, while on Sunday, white-suited disco fever returns. Snack items and munchies, and of course beer, are available in quantities.

Wag Club. 35 Wardour St., W1. ☎ **071/437-5534.** Cover £5–£10 ($8–$16). Tues–Fri 10pm–4am, Sat 10pm–5am, Sun 10pm–3am. No credit cards. Tube: Leicester Square or Piccadilly Circus.

The split-level Wag Club is one of the more stylish live-music places in town. The downstairs stage usually attracts newly signed, cutting-edge rock bands, while a DJ spins dance records upstairs. Door policy can be selective.

JAZZ & BLUES

Ain't Nothing But Blues Bar. 20 Kingly St., W1. ☎ **0171/287-0514.** Cover Fri–Sat £5 ($8). Mon–Thurs 5:30pm–1am, Fri–Sat 6pm–3am, Sun 7:30pm–midnight. Tube: Oxford Circus.

The club, which bills itself as the only true blues venue in town, features mostly local acts and occasional touring American bands. On weekends prepare to queue. From the Oxford Circus tube, walk south on Regent Street, turn left on Great Marlborough Street, and then make a quick right on Kingly Street.

✪ **Pizza Express.** 10 Dean St., W1. ☎ **0171/439-8722.** Cover £10–£25 ($16–$40). Mon–Fri 7:45pm–midnight, Sat–Sun 9pm–12:30am. Tube: Tottenham Court Road.

Don't let the name fool you: This restaurant-bar serves up some of the best jazz in London by mainstream artists. While enjoying a thin-crust Italian pizza, you can check out a local band or a visiting group, often from the United States. Although the club has been enlarged, it's important to reserve, as it fills up quickly.

✪ **Ronnie Scott's Club.** 47 Frith St., W1. ☎ **0171/439-0747.** Cover Mon–Thurs £12 ($19.20), Fri–Sat £15 ($24); with student ID, £8 ($12.80) Mon–Thurs only. Mon–Sat 8:30pm–3am. Tube: Leicester Square or Piccadilly Circus.

Inquire about jazz in London and people immediately think of Ronnie Scott's, long the European forerunner of modern jazz. Only the best English and American combos, often fronted by a top-notch vocalist, are booked here. The programs inevitably make for an entire evening of cool jazz. In the heart of Soho, Ronnie Scott's is a 10-minute walk from Piccadilly Circus along Shaftesbury Avenue. You don't have to be a member, although you can join if you wish. In the Main Room you can either stand at the bar to watch the show or sit at a table, from which you can order dinner. The Downstairs Bar is more intimate; among the regulars at your elbow may be some of the world's most talented musicians. On weekends, the separate Upstairs Room has a disco called Club Latino.

DANCE, DISCO & ECLECTIC

Bar Rumba. 26 Shaftesbury Ave., W1. ☎ **0171/287-2715.** Cover £2–£10 ($3.20–$16). Mon–Thurs 5pm–3:30am, Fri 5pm–4:30am, Sat 6pm–6am, and Sun 8pm–1:30am. Tube: Piccadilly Circus.

Despite its location on Shaftesbury Avenue, this Latin bar and club could be featured in a book of "Underground London." A hush-hush address among Latin types, it leans toward radical jazz fusion on some nights, phat funk on other occasions. Boasting two full bars and a different musical theme every night, Tuesday and Wednesday are the only nights you probably won't have to queue at the door. Monday's "That's How It Is" showcase features jazz, hip-hop, and drum and bass; Friday's "KAT Klub" grooves with soul, R&B, and swing; and Saturday's "Garage City" buzzes with house and garage. On weeknights you have to be 18 and up; the age limit is 21 on Saturday and Sunday.

Equinox. Leicester Sq., WC2. ☎ **0171/437-1446.** Cover £5–£12 ($8–$19.20), depending on the night of the week. Mon–Thurs 9pm–3am, Fri–Sat 9pm–4am. Tube: Leicester Square.

Built in 1992 on the site of the London Empire, a dance emporium that witnessed the changing styles of social dancing since the 1700s, the Equinox has established itself as a perennial favorite among Londoners. It contains nine bars, the largest dance floor in London, and a restaurant modeled after a 1950s American diner. With the exception of rave, virtually every kind of dance music is featured here, including dance hall, pop, rock, and Latin. The setting is lavishly illuminated with one of Europe's largest lighting rigs, and the crowd is as varied as London itself.

Hanover Grand. 6 Hanover St., W1. ☎ **0171/499-7977.** Cover £8–£16 ($12.80–$25.60). Thurs–Sat 10pm–4am. Tube: Oxford Circus.

Thursdays are funky and down and dirty. Fridays and Saturdays the crowd dresses up in their disco finery, clingy and form-fitting or politicized and punk. Dance floors are always crowded, and masses seem to surge back and forth between the two levels. Age and gender is sometimes hard to make out at this cutting-edge club of the minute.

Iceni. 11 White Horse St., W1. ☎ **0171/495-5333.** Cover Fri £12 ($19.20), Sat £10 ($16). Fri 11pm–3am, Sat 10pm–3am. Tube: Queen's Park.

Attracting an older twenty-something crowd on Fridays, and 18 to 25ers on Saturdays, this funky three-story nightclub features films, board games, tarot readings, and dancing to swing, soul, hip-hop, and R&B. You can even get a manicure. Leave your name at the door and make a love connection courtesy of Flipside Dating Service.

Limelight. 136 Shaftesbury Ave., WC2. ☎ **0171/434-0572.** Cover £2 ($3.20) before 10pm, £12 ($19.20) thereafter. Mon–Sat 9pm–3am, Sat 10pm–3am, Sun 6–11pm. Tube: Leicester Square.

Although opened in 1985, this large dance club—located inside a former Welsh chapel that dates to 1754—has only recently come into its own. The dance floors and bars share space with plenty of cool Gothic nooks and crannies. DJs spin the latest house music.

✪ **Ministry of Sound.** 103 Gaunt St., SE1. ☎ **0171/378-6528.** Cover £12–£20 ($19.20–$32). Fri–Sat midnight–9am. Tube: Elephant and Castle.

Removed from the city center, this club-of-the-hour is relatively devoid of tourists. With a large bar and an even bigger sound system, it blasts garage and house music to energetic crowds that pack the two dance floors. If the stimulants in the rest of the club have gone to your head, you can chill in the cinema room. Note that the club's cover charge is stiff, and bouncers will definitely decide who is cool enough to enter.

✪ **Venom Club/The Zoo Bar.** 13–18 Bear St., WC2. ☎ **0171/839-4188.** Zoo Bar, daily 4pm–2am; Venom Club, daily 9:30pm–3am. Entrance to both venues free before 10pm, cover charge £5 ($8) after that. Tube: Leicester Square.

Its owners spent millions of pounds outfitting this club with the slickest, flashiest, and most psychedelic decor in London. If you're looking for a true Euro nightlife experience replete with gorgeous *au pairs* and trendy Europeans, this is it. Zoo Bar upstairs is a menagerie of mosaic animals beneath a glassed-in ceiling dome. Downstairs, the music is so intrusive that conversation is futile. Clients are over 18 but younger and hipper than 35. Androgyny is the look of choice. The first Wednesday of every month is devoted to the sugar pop of Boy George, whose groupies cavort here in hopes of glimpsing the campy star.

4 Cocktail Bars

For a complete selection of Pubs & Wine Bars, see chapter 4.

American Bar. In The Savoy, The Strand, WC2. ☎ **0171/836-4343.** Jacket and tie required for men. Tube: Charing Cross, Convent Garden, or Embankment.

This is still one of the most sophisticated gathering places in London. The bartender is known for his special concoctions, "Savoy Affair" and "Prince of Wales," as well as what is reputedly the best martini in town. Monday to Saturday evenings, jazz piano is featured from 7 to 11pm. The location—near many West End theaters—is ideal for a pre- or posttheater drink.

Cocktail Bar. In the Café Royal, 68 Regent St., W1. ☎ **0171/437-9090.** Tube: Piccadilly Circus.

In business since 1865, this bar was once patronized by Oscar Wilde, James McNeill Whistler, and Aubrey Beardsley. Its 19th-century rococo decor, which includes one of the most beautiful frescoed ceilings in London, exudes glamour. The bartender's specialties are the Café Royal cocktails, which include the Golden Cadillac and the Prince William (would you drink a Prince William?).

The Dorchester Bar. In the Dorchester, Park Lane. ☎ **0171/629-8888.** Tube: Hyde Park Corner or Marble Arch.

This sophisticated and modern bar is on the lobby level of one of the most lavishly decorated hotels in the world. You'll find an international clientele confident of its good taste and privilege. The bartender knows his stuff. The bar serves Italian snacks, lunch, and dinner. A pianist performs every evening after 7pm; he is joined by a jazz trio Wednesday to Saturday.

5 The Gay & Lesbian Scene

The most reliable source of information on gay clubs and activities is the **Lesbian and Gay Switchboard** (☎ **0171/837-7324**). The staff runs a 24-hour service for information on places and activities catering to homosexual men and women. *Time Out* also carries listings on such clubs.

The Box. 32–34 Monmouth St. (at Seven Dials), WC2. ☎ **0171/240-5828.** Mon–Sat 11:30am–11:30pm, Sun noon–6pm. Tube: Covent Garden.

Adjacent to one of Convent Garden's best-known junctions, Seven Dials, this sophisticated Mediterranean-style bar attracts more lesbians than many of its competitors. This is especially the case on women-only Sunday nights, cutely labeled "Girl Bar at the Box." The rest of the week, men slightly outnumber women. From noon to 5:30pm, this is primarily a restaurant, serving meal-sized salads, club sandwiches, and soups. Food service ends abruptly at 5:30pm, after which the place reveals its core: a cheerful, popular place of rendezvous for London's gay and countercultural crowds. The Box considers itself a "summer bar," throwing open its doors and windows to a cluster of outdoor tables that attracts a crowd at the slightest hint of sunshine.

The Edge. 11 Soho Sq., W1. ☎ **0171/497-3154.** Mon–Sat noon–1am, Sun noon–10:30pm. No cover. Tube: Tottenham Court Road.

Few bars in London can rival the tolerance, humor, and sexual sophistication found here. The first two floors are done up with accessories that, like an English garden, change with the seasons. Dance music can be found on the high-energy and crowded lower floors, while the upper floors are best if you're looking for intimate conversation. Three menus are featured: a funky daytime menu, a cafe menu, and a late-night menu. Dancers hit the floors starting around 7:30pm. Clientele ranges from the flamboyantly gay to hetero pub crawlers out for a night of slumming.

Madame Jo Jo's. 8 Brewer St., W1. ☎ **0171/734-2473.** Cover £12.50–£22.50 ($20–$36). Mon–Sat 10pm–3:30am. Tube: Piccadilly Circus.

Tucked alongside Soho's most explicit girlie shows, Madame Jo Jo's also presents "girls"—more accurately described as drag queens. London's most popular transvestite showplace—an eye-popper with decadent art nouveau interior—has attracted film directors such as Stanley Kubrick, who filmed scenes from *Eyes Wide Shut,* starring Tom Cruise, here. Other celebrities, including Hugh Grant and Mick Jagger, have dropped in to check out Jo Jo's drag cabaret. Drag shows are Thursday to Saturday nights, with outside promoters organizing entertainment on other nights.

Index

See also separate Accommodations and Restaurant indexes, below.